# Reporting and Producing for Digital Media

# Reporting and Producing for Digital Media

Vivek Sehgal

CYBER TECH PUBLICATIONS
4264/3, Ansari Road, Daryaganj, New Delhi-110002 (India)
Ph.: 011-23244078. Fax: 011-23280028
E-Mail: cyberpublicationsdelhi@yahoo.com

# REPORTING AND PRODUCING FOR DIGITAL MEDIA

**Vivek Sehgal**



First Edition 2009

**Reprint 2024**



*Published by :*

G.S. Rawat for Cyber Tech Publications
4264/3, Ansari Road, Daryaganj, New Delhi-110002 (India)
Ph.: 011-23244078. Fax: 011-23280028
E-Mail: cyberpublicationsdelhi@yahoo.com

*Printed at :* Amit Enterprises, Maujpur, Delhi, (9810878184)

# Preface

During the recent years mass media has invaded the life of a common man in a big way. Upto seventies, mass media mainly remained confined to cinema, newspaper and radio. It was in the early eighties that audio-visual electronic medium in the form of television invaded the Indian scenario in a big way. The Government created huge infrastructure for spread of television network in the country. During this decade itself, advent of computers and Video Cassette Recorders (VCR) also supplemented the audio-visual media, putting well established medium of cinema to shade.

During the early nineties, satellite television revolutionised the audio-visual media by reaching most of the households in the urban areas. The latest invasion of audio-visual electronic media has suddenly increased the demand for professionals in journalism, technicians and other service individuals. These careers not only offer excellent opportunities, salaries, challenge and satisfaction of work, but also provide an opportunity for self-employment in various fields.

—*Author*

# CONTENTS

**1**

# Press and its Freedom

Freedom of the press (or press freedom) is the guarantee by a government of free public press for its citizens and their associations, organizations, and their published reporting. It also extends to news gathering, and processes involved in obtaining information for public distribution.

In the U.S. this right is guaranteed by the First Amendment to the United States Constitution. Not all countries are protected by a bill of rights, or the constitutional provision pertaining to Freedom of the Press. For example, Australia's constitution makes no mention of Freedom of the Press.

With respect to governmental information, a government distinguishes which materials are public or protected from disclosure to the public based on classification of information as sensitive, classified or secret and being otherwise protected from disclosure due to relevance of the information to protecting the national interest. Many governments are also subject to sunshine laws or freedom of information legislation that are used to define the ambit of national interest.

## BASIC PRINCIPLES

In developed countries, freedom of the press implies that all people should have the right to express themselves in writing or in any other way of expression of personal opinion or creativity. The Universal Declaration of Human Rights indicates: "Everyone has the right to freedom of opinion and expression; this right includes freedom to hold opinions without interference and to seek, receive, and impart information and ideas through any media regardless of frontiers"

This philosophy is usually accompanied by legislation ensuring various degrees of freedom of scientific research (known as scientific freedom), publishing, press and printing the depth to which these laws are entrenched in a country's legal system can go as far down as its constitution. The concept of freedom of speech is often covered by the same laws as freedom of the press, thereby giving equal treatment to media and individuals.

Besides said legal environment, some non-governmental organizations use more criteria to judge the level of press freedom around the world. Reporters Without Borders considers the number of journalists murdered, expelled or harassed, and the existence of a state monopoly on TV and radio, as well as the existence of censorship and self-censorship in the media, and the overall independence of media as well as the difficulties that foreign reporters may face. Freedom House likewise studies the more general political and economic environments of each nation in order to determine whether relationships of dependence exist that limit in practice the level of press freedom that might exist in theory. So the concept of independence of the press is one closely linked with the concept of press freedom.

## Media and Government

The notion of the press as the fourth branch of government is sometimes used to compare the press (or media) with Montesquieu's three branches of government, namely an addition to the legislative, the executive and the judiciary branches. Edmund Burke is quoted to have said: "Three Estates in Parliament; but in the Reporters' Gallery yonder, there sat a Fourth estate more important far than they all."

The development of the Western media tradition is rather parallel to the development of democracy in Europe and the United States. On the ideological level, the first advocates of freedom of the press were the liberal thinkers of the 18th and 19th centuries. They developed their ideas in opposition to the monarchist tradition in general and the divine right of kings in particular. These liberal theorists argued that freedom of press was a right claimed by the individual and grounded in natural law. Thus, freedom of the press was an integral part of the individual rights promoted by liberal ideology.

Freedom of the press was (and still is) assumed by many to be a necessity to any democratic society. Other lines of thought later argued in favor of freedom of the press without relying on the controversial issue of natural law; for instance, freedom of expression began to be regarded as an essential component of the social contract (the agreement between a state and its people regarding the rights and duties that each should have to the other).

## WORLDWIDE FREEDOM

Every year, the Reporters Without Borders organization establishes a ranking of countries in terms of their freedom of the press. The list is based on responses to surveys sent to journalists that are members of partner organisations of the RWB, as well as related specialists such as researchers, jurists and human rights activists. The survey asks questions about direct attacks on journalists and the media as well as other indirect sources of pressure against the free press, such as pressure on journalists by non-governmental groups. RWB is careful to note that the index only deals with press freedom, and does not measure the quality of journalism.

In 2003, the countries where press was the most free were Finland, Iceland, the Netherlands and Norway.

In 2004, Denmark, Ireland, Slovakia, and Switzerland were tied at the top of the list, followed by New Zealand and Latvia. The countries with the least degree of press freedom were ranked with North Korea having the worst, followed by Burma, Turkmenistan, Eritrea, People's Republic of China (mainland only), Vietnam, Nepal, Saudi Arabia, and Iran.

### Non-democratic States

According to Reporters Without Borders, more than a third of the world's people live in countries where there is no press freedom. Overwhelmingly, these people live in countries where there is no system of democracy or where there are serious deficiencies in the democratic process.

Freedom of the press is an extremely problematic concept for most non-democratic systems of government since, in the modern age, strict control of access to information is critical to the existence of most non-democratic governments and their associated control systems and security apparatus. To this end, most non-democratic societies employ state-run news organisations to promote the propaganda critical to maintaining an existing political power base and suppress (often very brutally, through the use of police, military, or intelligence agencies) any significant attempts by the media or individual journalists to challenge the approved "government line" on contentious issues.

In such countries, journalists operating on the fringes of what is deemed to be acceptable will very often find themselves the subject of considerable intimidation by agents of the state. This can range from simple threats to their professional careers (firing, professional blacklisting) to death threats, kidnapping, torture, and assassination.

Reporters Without Borders reports that, in 2003, 42 journalists lost their lives pursuing their profession and that, in the same year, at least 130 journalists were in prison as a result of their occupational activities.

In 2005, 63 journalists and 5 media assistants were killed worldwide.

- The Lira Baysetova case in Kazakhstan.
- In Nepal, Eritrea and China (mainland only), journalists may spend years in jail simply for using the "wrong" word or photo.
- The Georgiy R. Gongadze case in Ukraine.

## History

### *England*

The English revolution of 1688 resulted in the supremacy of Parliament over the Crown and, the right of revolution. The main theoretical inspirator of Western liberalism was John Locke. Having decided to grant some of his basic freedoms in the state of nature (natural rights) to the common good, the individual placed some of his rights in trusteeship with the government. A social contract was entered into by the people, and the Sovereign (*i.e.* government) was instructed to protect these individual rights on behalf of the people, argues John Locke in his book Two Treatises of Government.

Until 1694,-England had an elaborate system of licensing. No publication was allowed without the accompaniment of a government-granted license. Fifty years earlier, at a time of civil war, John Milton wrote his pamphlet Areopagitica. In this work Milton argued forcefully against this form of government censorship and parodied the idea, writing "when as debtors and delinquents may walk abroad without a keeper, but unoffensive books must not stir forth without a visible jailer in their title." Although at the time it did little to halt the practice of licensing it would be viewed later a significant milestone in press freedom.

Milton's central argument was that the individual is capable of using reason and distinguishing right from wrong, good from bad. In order to be able to exercise this ration right, the individual must have unlimited access to the ideas of his fellow men in "a free and open encounter". From Milton's writings developed the concept of "the open market place of ideas": When people argue against each other, the good arguments will prevail. One form of speech that was widely restricted in England was the law of seditious libel that made criticizing of the government a crime. The King was above public criticism and that statements critical of the government were forbidden, according to the English Court of the Star Chamber. Truth was not a defense to seditious libel because the goal was to prevent and punish all condemnation of the government.

John Stuart Mill approached the problem of authority versus liberty from the viewpoint of a 19th century utilitarian: The individual has the right of expressing himself so long as he does not harm other individuals. The good society is one in which the greatest number of persons enjoy the greatest possible amount of happiness. Applying these general principles of liberty to freedom of expression, Mill states that if we silence an opinion, we may silence the truth. The individual freedom of expression is therefore essential to the well-being of society.

Mill's application of the general principles of liberty is expressed in his book On Liberty: "If all mankind minus one, were of one opinion, and one, and only one person were of the contrary opinion, mankind would be no more justified in silencing that one person, than he, if he had the power, would be justified in silencing mankind".

### *Germany*

The dictatorship of Adolf Hitler largely suppressed freedom of the press through Joseph Goebbels' Propaganda Ministry. As the Ministry's name implies, propaganda did not carry the negative connotations that it does today (or did in the Allied countries); how-to manuals were openly distributed by that same ministry explaining the craft of effective propaganda. The Ministry also acted as a central control-point for all media, issuing orders as to what stories could be run and what stories would be suppressed. Anyone involved in the film industry--from directors to the lowliest assistant--had to sign an oath of loyalty to the Nazi Party, due to opinion-changing power Goebbels perceived movies to have. (Goebbels himself maintained some personal control over every single film made in Nazi Europe.) Journalists who crossed the Propaganda Ministry were routinely imprisoned or shot as traitors.

### *India*

The Indian Constitution, while not mentioning the word "press", provides for "the right to freedom of speech and expression" (Article 19(1)a). However this right is subject to restrictions under subclause (2), whereby this freedom can be restricted for reasons of "sovereignty and integrity of India, the security of the State, friendly relations with foreign States, public order, preserving decency, preserving morality, in relation to contempt of court, defamation, or incitement to an offence". Laws such as the Official Secrets Act and Prevention of Terrorism Act (PoTA) have been used to limit press freedom. Under PoTA, person could be detained for up to six months for being in contact with a terrorist or terrorist group. PoTA was repealed in 2006, but the Official Secrets Act 1923 continues.

For the first half-century of independence, media control by the state was the major constraint on press freedom. Indira Gandhi famously stated in 1975 that All India Radio is "a Government organ, it is going to remain a Government organ..." With the liberalization starting in the 1990s, private control of media has burgeoned, leading to increasing independence and greater scrutiny of government. Organizations like Tehelka and NDTV have been particularly influential, e.g. in bringing about the resignation of powerful Haryana minister Vinod Sharma.

### *United States*

John Hancock was the first person to write newspapers in the British colonies in North America were published "by authority," that is, under license from and as the mouthpiece of the colonial governors. The first regularly published newspaper was the Boston News-Letter of John Campbell, published weekly beginning in 1704. The early colonial publishers were either postmasters or government printers, and therefore unlikely to challenge government policies.

The first independent newspaper in the colonies was the New-England Courant, published in Boston by James Franklin beginning in 1721. A few years later, Franklin's younger brother, Benjamin, purchased the Pennsylvania Gazette of Philadelphia, which became the leading newspaper of the colonial era.

During this period, newspapers were unlicensed, and able freely to publish dissenting views, but were subject to prosecution for libel or even sedition if their opinions threatened the government. The notion of "freedom of the press" that later was enshrined in the United States Constitution is generally traced to the seditious libel prosecution of John Peter Zenger by the colonial governor of New York in 1735. In this instance of jury nullification, Zenger was acquitted after his lawyer, Andrew Hamilton, argued to the jury (contrary to established English law) that there was no libel in publishing the truth. Yet even after this celebrated case, colonial governors and assemblies asserted the power to prosecute and even imprison printers for publishing unapproved views.

During the American Revolution, a free press was identified by Revolutionary leaders as one of the elements of liberty that they sought to preserve. The Virginia Declaration of Rights (1776) proclaimed that "the freedom of the press is one of the greatest bulwarks of liberty and can never be restrained but by despotic governments." Similarly, the Constitution of

Massachusetts (1780) declared, "The liberty of the press is essential to the security of freedom in a state: it ought not, therefore, to be restrained in this commonwealth." Following these examples, the First Amendment to the United States Constitution restricted Congress from abridging the freedom of the press and the closely associated freedom of speech.

John Locke's ideas had inspired both the French and American revolutions. Thomas Jefferson wanted to unite the two streams of liberalism, the English and the French schools of thought. His goal was to create a government that would provide both security and opportunity for the individual. An active press was essential as a way of educating the population. In order to be able to work freely, the press must be free from control by the state. Jefferson was a person who himself suffered great calumnies of the press. Despite this, in his second inaugural address, he proclaimed that a government that could not stand up under criticism deserved to fall.

Jefferson said: "No experiment can be more interesting than that we are now trying, and which we trust will end in establishing the fact, that man may be governed by reason and truth. Our first object should therefore be, to leave open to him all avenues of the truth".

In 1931, the U.S. Supreme Court decision in Near v. Minnesota used the 14th Amendment to apply the freedom of the press to the States. Other notable cases regarding free press are:

- *New York Times Co. v. United States:* The Supreme Court upheld the publication of the Pentagon Papers.
- *New York Times Co. v. Sullivan:* The Court decided that in order for written words to be libel, it must be, first of all, false. It must also be published with the deliberate intent to ruin someone's reputation.

In Branzburg v. Hayes (1972), the Court placed limits on the ability of the Press to refuse a subpoena from a Grand Jury by claiming Freedom of the Press. The issue decided in the case was whether a reporter could refuse to "appear and testify before state and Federal grand juries" by claiming such appearance and testimony "abridges the freedom of speech and press guaranteed by the First Amendment." The 5-4 decision was that such a protection was not provided by the First Amendment.

## NOTABLE EXCEPTIONS

In 1798, not long after the adoption of the Constitution, the governing Federalist Party attempted to stifle criticism by means of the Alien and Sedition Acts. (It was notable that the Sedition Act made criticism of Congress, and of the President, a crime, but not criticism of the Vice-President. Jefferson, a non-Federalist, was Vice-President at the time the Act was passed.) These restrictions on freedom of the press proved very unpopular and worked against the Federalists. Thomas Jefferson was among those who opposed the Acts, and he was elected President in the election of 1800. Jefferson then pardoned all those convicted under the Acts. He made it a principle not to ask what they had done, but only whether they had been charged under the Acts.

In his first Inaugural Address in 1801 he reiterated his longstanding commitment to freedom of speech and of the press: "If there be any among us who would wish to dissolve this Union or to change its republican form, let them stand undisturbed as monuments of the safety with which error of opinion may be tolerated where reason is left free to combat it."

- The Espionage Act of 1917 and the Sedition Act of 1918, which amended it, imposed restrictions on the free press during wartime. It carried fines of $10,000 and up to 20 years imprisonment for people publishing "... disloyal, profane, scurrilous, or abusive language about the form of government of the United States or the Constitution of the United States, or the military or naval forces of the United States..." In Schenck v. United States (1919), the Supreme Court upheld the laws, setting the "Clear and present danger" standard. Congress repealed both laws in 1921, and Brandenburg v. Ohio (1969) revised the "Clear and present danger" test to the "Imminent lawless action" test, which is less restrictive.

- 1988: Hazelwood School District vs. Kuhlmeier: The Supreme Court upheld that the principal of a school has the right to review and block controversial articles of a school paper funded by the school and published in the school's name.
- In the United States in 2005, interpretation of the Bipartisan Campaign Reform Act may consider political statements as being the equivalent of campaign donations. Because access to Internet statements are weakly controlled, the campaign value of statements is not known in advance and a high ultimate value may trigger large fines for violations. This particularly threatens Internet statements by individuals, and ambiguous definitions of membership in the press make the possible effects ambiguous.

## IMPLICATIONS OF NEW TECHNOLOGIES

Many of the traditional means of delivering information are being slowly superseded by the increasing pace of modern technological advance. Almost every conventional mode of media and information dissemination has a modern counterpart that offers significant potential advantages to journalists seeking to maintain and enhance their 'freedom of speech'. A few simple examples of such phenomena include:

- Terrestrial television versus satellite television: Whilst terrestrial television is relatively easy to manage and manipulate, satellite television is much more difficult to control as journalistic content can easily be broadcast from other jurisdictions beyond the control of individual governments. An example of this in the Middle East is the satellite broadcaster Al Jazeera. This Arabic language media channel operates out of the 'relatively liberal' state of Qatar, and often presents views and content that are problematic to a number of governments in the region and beyond. However, because of the increased affordability and miniaturisation of satellite technology (e.g. dishes and receivers) it is simply not practicable for most states to control popular access to the channel.

- Web-based publishing (e.g., blogging) vs. traditional publishing: Traditional magazines and newspapers rely on physical resources (e.g. offices, printing presses) that can easily be targeted and forced to close down. Web-based publishing systems can be run using ubiquitous and inexpensive equipment and can operate from any global jurisdiction. To get control over web publications, nations and organisations are using Geolocation and Geolocation software.
- Voice over Internet protocol (VOIP) vs. conventional telephony: Although conventional telephony systems are easily tapped and recorded, modern VOIP technology can employ sophisticated encryption systems to evade central monitoring systems. As VOIP and similar technologies become more widespread they are likely to make the effective monitoring of journalists (and their contacts and activities) a very difficult task for governments.

Naturally, governments are responding to the challenges posed by new media technologies by deploying increasingly sophisticated technology of their own (a notable example being China's attempts to impose control of through a state run internet service provider that controls access to the Internet) but it seems that this will becomes an ever increasingly difficult task as nimble, highly motivated journalists continue to find ingenious novel ways to exploit technology and stay one step ahead of the generally slower moving government institutions that they necessarily do battle with.

## GENERAL CHARACTERISTICS

India is the world's largest democracy. Its mass media culture, a system that has evolved over centuries, is comprised of a complex framework. Modernization has transformed this into a communications network that sustains the pulse of a democracy of about 1.1 billion people. India's newspaper evolution is nearly unmatched in world press history. India's newspaper industry and its Westernization-or mondialisation as French would call it-go hand in hand. India's press is a metaphor for its advancement in the globalized world.

The printing press preceded the advent of printed news in India by about 100 years. It was in 1674 that the first printing apparatus was established in Bombay followed by Madras in 1772. India's first newspaper, Calcutta General Advertise, also known as the Hicky's Bengal Gazette was established in January 1780, and the first Hindi daily, Samachar Sudha Varshan, began in 1854. The evolution of the Indian media since has been fraught with developmental difficulties; illiteracy, colonial constraints and repression, poverty, and apathy thwart interest in news and media. Within this framework, it is instructive to examine India's press in two broad analytical sections: pre-colonial times and the colonial, independent press (which may, again be classified into two: preceding and following the Emergency rule imposed by Indira Gandhi's government in 1975). The post-Emergency phase, which continues at the present, may be the third independent phase of India's newspaper revolution (Jeffrey).

## THE NATURE OF THE AUDIENCE

While a majority of the poor working people in rural and urban areas still remain oppressed and even illiterate, a significant proportion of people-roughly about 52 percent of the population over 15 years of age were recorded as being able to read and write. That breaks down to 65.5 percent of males and an estimate of 37.7 percent of females. After the liberalization of the economy, the growth of industry, and a rise in literacy, the post-Emergency boom rekindled the world's largest middle class in news, politics, and consumerism. Since private enterprise began to sustain and pay off, mass communications picked up as a growth industry.

In 1976, the Registrar of Newspapers for India had recorded 875 papers; in 1995 there were 4,453. Robin Jeffrey comments:

"Newspapers did not expand simply because the technology was available to make Indian scripts live as they had not been able to live before. Nor did newspaper grow simply because more people knew how to read and write. They grew because entrepreneurs detected a growing hunger for information among ever-widening sections of India's people, who were potential consumers as well as newspaper readers. A race began to reach this audience advertising avenues were the prizes and these would come largely to newspapers that could convince advertisers that they had more readers than their rivals. Readers, meanwhile, were saying implicitly: 'We will read newspapers that tell us about ourselves and reflect our concerns."

Common contenders for readership and advertising are: the National Herald, the Hindustan Times, Time, Illustrated Weekly, e Pioneer, and Filmfare.

## HISTORICAL TRADITIONS

"Newspaper history in India is inextricably tangled with political history," wrote A. E. Charlton (Wolseley 3). James Augustus Hicky was the founder of India's first newspaper, the Calcutta General Advertiser also known as Hicky's Bengal Gazette, in 1780. Soon other newspapers came into existence in Calcutta and Madras: the Calcutta Gazette, the Bengal Journal, the Oriental Magazine, the Madras Courier and the Indian Gazette. While the India Gazette enjoyed governmental patronage including free postal circulation and advertisements, Hicky's Bengal Gazette earned the rulers' wrath due to its criticism of the government. In November 1780 its circulation was halted by government decree. Hicky protested against this arbitrary harassment without avail, and was imprisoned. The Bengal Gazette and the India Gazette were followed by the Calcutta Gazette which subsequently became the government's "medium for making its general orders" (Sankhdher 24-32).

The Bombay Herald, The Statesmen in Calcutta and the Madras Mail and The Hindu, along with many other rivals in Madras represented the metropolitan voice of India and its people. While Statesman voiced the English rulers' voice, The Hindu became the beacon of patriotism in the South. The Hindu was founded in Madras as a counter to the Madras Mail.

Patriotic movements grew in proportion with the colonial ruthlessness, and a vehicle of information dissemination became a tool for freedom struggle. In the struggle for freedom, journalists in the twentieth century performed a dual role as professionals and nationalists. Indeed many national leaders, from Gandhi to Vajpayee, were journalists as well. Calcutta,

Madras, Bombay and Delhi were four main centers of urban renaissance which nourished news in India. It was only during and after the seventies, especially after Indira Gandhi's defeat in 1977, that regional language newspapers became prevalent.

There were nationalist echoes from other linguistic regional provinces. Bengal, Gujarat, Tamil, Kerala, Punjab and Uttar Pradesh produced dailies in regional languages. Hindi and Urdu were largely instrumental in voicing the viewpoints and aspirations of both Hindus and Muslims of the Northern provinces. As communalism and religious intolerance increased before and after partition, Urdu remained primarily the language of Muslims, as Pakistan chose this language as its lingua franca. After partition, the cause of Urdu and its newspapers, suffered a setback as Hindu reactionaries began to recognize the association of Urdu with Islam and Pakistan.

## DIVERSITY AND THE LANGUAGE PRESS

Naresh Khanna summarizes the trends in circulatory growth and decline varied in regional language papers during 1998-2000: In the three-year period from 1998-2000, circulation of dailies in the country increased marginally from 58.37 to 59.13 million copies. This represents a growth of 1.3 percent on the basis of data published by the Registrar of Newspapers for India in its annual reports. In this time, two distinct groups of newspapers emerge-the first including five languages that have collectively grown in circulation by a healthy 5.65 percent and representing a combined circulation of 43.35 million copies. Amongst these newspapers, those in Malayalam and Bengali grew fastest at 12.9 percent and 12.8 percent respectively, while Hindi dailies grew by 5 percent and English dailies by 4.7 percent over the three-year period. Although Marathi newspapers increased circulation by 2.75 percent over the three years it would seem that they are in danger of falling out of this group and perhaps entering the phase of stagnation and circulation decline (Khanna 2002).

The second group of stagnating and declining circulations includes newspapers in seven languages with a combined circulation of 14.8 million copies in 2000. These dailies lost almost 1.8 million copies (10.62 percent) of their combined circulation in the last three years. Daily newspaper circulation plummeted most dramatically in Telugu, which fell from 2.28 million to 1.68 million copies, a fall of more than 26 percent. Urdu newspaper circulation fell by more than 12 percent and Tamil dailies' circulation declined by 10.8 percent with circulation of Gujarati dailies falling by 10.5 percent. Over the same period circulations of Oriya dailies declined by 2.8 percent and that of Punjabi dailies by 3.2 percent. Although over the three years Kannada newspapers show an insignificant fall in circulation they seem to have entered a period of stagnation and decline of their own. It would seem that in spite of new editions being added by Hindi, English, Malayalam and Bengali dailies, the print media is losing its dominance of advertising market share to television, radio and outdoor media (Khanna 2002).

## ECONOMIC FRAMEWORK

India's language newspapers enjoy a relatively new entrepreneurial prowess. A mutually convenient relationship between the owners and capitalists keeps a financial balance between local/regional and national spheres in both private and public sectors. "Like coral in a reef, newspapers grew and died in a process inseparable from the creation of a 'public sphere' in the classical liberal sense. Individual proprietors sometimes brought to their newspapers a crusader's zeal for a particular cause or a diehard's loathing for a rival" (Jeffrey 105). The Second Press Commission in 1982 tried to liberate the press from the monopoly houses. In 1995 the Audit Bureau of circulations had 165 newspapers as members, with a combined circulation of about 16 million copies a day. The top ten newspapers control roughly 50 percent of daily circulations in all languages. Bennett Coleman and the Indian Express own roughly 20 percent of daily circulations (Jeffrey 108).

While capitalists sustained national newspapers, the big houses, Dalmias, Jains, Goenka et al., monopolized and corrupted free journalism. The family and caste controlled small newspapers regionally maintain their freedom from big monopolies, thriving on their loyal supporters in north and south India. Diversity of ownership is reflective of cultural variation in India's multilingual landscape. Twenty-one newspapers control two-thirds of all circulations.

## PRESS LAWS

Much of India's legal framework is built upon its colonial legacy. Legal statutes and regulations have been undergoing certain changes as India's democracy grows. India's freedom came at a high cost. The country was divided. India's border conflicts with two hostile neighbors, which forced at least three large scale wars, eclipsed other political issues. The democratic process, corrupted by criminals, unscrupulous bureaucrats and politicians, created a social climate that widened social and economic inequality.

Freedom of speech and expression is a constitutionally guaranteed fundamental right of the Indian people. Article 19 (1; a) ensures the implicit freedom but Article 19 (2) qualifies this in explicit terms. The Parliamentary Proceedings (protection of Publication) Act of 1977 and the Prevention of Publication of Objectionable Matter (Repeal Act) of 1977 further reinforce and restrict these freedoms. While constitutional guarantees ensure freedom of the press and expression, press and media are obligated by a self-regulatory system of ethics that protect individuals and organizations from libelous behavior. "Freedom of the press is an institutional freedom," wrote Sachin Sen (19). The Press Council Bill of 1956, introduced in the Indian parliament, stipulated the establishment of the Press Council of India representing working journalists, the newspaper management, literary bodies and the Parliament. The Indian Press commission accepted the following postulate: "Democratic society lives and grows by accepting ideas, by experimenting with them, and where necessary, rejecting them...The Press is a responsible part of a democratic society" (quoted by Sen 42).

While The Central Press Accreditation Committee seeks to ensure quality and self-renewal, The Press Council of India was established in 1966 to uphold editorial autonomy. Restrictions on free speech were imposed after Indira Gandhi's infamous Emergency rule. The Press Council of India was abolished after editor George Verghese's criticisms of the Indira government. The Ministry of Information and Broadcasting carefully regulates the press and its liberties. The Maintenance of Internal Security Act (MISA) was enforced to intimidate reputedly autonomous newspapers in the seventies. The Press Council, resurrected in 1979, has no legal standing to impose penalties. The Indian press, generally believed as "managed," is a self-restrained institution generally reluctant to take on the governmental policies. All India Radio (AIR) and its management exemplify this "man-aged" system.

## THE REGISTRAR OF NEWSPAPERS

The Registrar of Indian newspapers, among these official and professional agencies, regulates and records the status of newspapers. Electronic news, Web sites, magazines and house publications, and a number of professional organizations (like Editors Guild of India, Indian Language Newspapers' Association, and All India Newspapers Editors' Conference etc.) enrich the self-renewal process of the news enterprise. Educational and training programs are gaining importance as professionalization of specialized fields is a prioritized activity under the privatization process.

### The Office of the Registrar

The Office of the Registrar of Newspapers for India, popularly known as RNI came into being on July 1, 1956, on the recommendation of the First Press Commission in 1953 and by amending the Press and Registration of Books Act (PRB Act) 1867. The functions of RNI involve both statutory and non-statutory functions.

Statutory Functions The RNI compiles and maintains a register of newspapers containing particulars about all the newspapers published in the country; it issues certificates of registration to the newspapers published under valid declaration. It scrutinizes and analyzes annual statements sent by the publishers of newspapers every year under Section 19-D of the Press and Registration of Books Act containing information on circulation, ownership, etc. The RNI informs the District Magistrates about availability of titles to intending publishers for filing declaration and ensures that newspapers are published in accordance with the provisions of the Press and Registration of Books Acts. It verifies under Section 19-F of the PRB Act of circulation claims, furnished by the publishers in their Annual Statements and Preparation and submission to the Government on or before September 30 each year, a report containing all available information and statistics about the press in India with particular reference to the emerging trends in circulation and in the direction of common ownership units. Non-Statutory Functions Non-statutory functions of the RNI include the formulation of a Newsprint Allocation Policy-guidelines and the ability to issue Eligibility Certificates to the newspapers to enable them to import newsprint and to procure indigenous newsprint. The RNI assesses and certifies the essential needs and requirements of newspaper establishments to import printing and composing machinery and allied materials.

From April 1998 to February 1999, RNI scrutinized 18,459 applications for availability of titles, of which 7,738 titles were found available for verification, while in the remaining applications, titles were not found available. During the same period, 2,693 newspapers/periodicals were issued Certificates of Registration (2,145 fresh CRs and 548 revised CRs) and circulation claims of 1536 newspapers/periodicals were assessed.

## Newsprint

Until 1994-95, newsprint allocation was regulated by the Newsprint Control Order (1962) and the Newsprint Import Policy announced by the government every year. Newspapers were issued Entitlement Certificates for importation and purchase from the scheduled indigenous newsprint mills. However, Newsprint Policy is modified every year depending upon the import policy of the government. Newsprint has been placed under 'Open General License' with effect from May 1, 1995, and all types of newsprint became importable by all persons without any restriction. Under the latest newsprint policy/guidelines for the import of newsprint issued by the Ministry of Information and Broadcasting, authentication of certificate of registration is done by the Registrar of Newspapers for India for import of newsprint, on submission of a formal application and necessary documentary evidence.

### De-Blocking of Titles

For the first time in the history of RNI, a massive work of de-blocking 200,000 titles was undertaken. As per the decision, all such titles of newspapers were certified till December 31, 1995, and those publications which had not registered with RNI have been de-blocked.

The work of entering registered titles has been completed and the lists have been dispatched to state governments. Nearly 150,000 of unused titles have become available for allocation to other newspapers from January 1, 1999.

### Printing Machinery

The RNI is the sponsoring authority for the import of printing machinery and allied materials at the concessional rate of custom duty available to the newspapers. During April 1998-February 1999, applications of four newspaper establishments were recommended for import of printing machinery and allied equipment.

### Censorship

Even though India is committed to the freedom of the press, censorship is not unknown to the media. With increased privatization and entrepreneurial advancements, colonial and bureaucratic censorship no longer exists. However, the nexus of criminal politics and unethical monopolies continue to threaten the freedom of press.

Nehru famously said: "I would rather have a completely free press with all the dangers involved in the wrong use of that freedom than a suppressed or regulated press" (quoted by Kamath 272). After 1977 people's interest and involvement in regional and national affairs increased dramatically. This development helped promote the dualism of India's patriotic passions marked by linguistic chauvinism and national unity.

## STATE-PRESS RELATIONS

### Public Grievances

A Public Grievances Cell is functioning in the Main Secretariat of the Ministry headed by the Joint Secretary (Policy). In order to tone up the Grievance Redressal System of the Ministry, its time limits have been fixed for completion of various activities coming under the purview of the grievance redressal mechanism. Grievance Officers have been appointed in all the subordinate organizations of the Ministry who have been made responsible for timely redress of grievances. Keeping in view the need for effective monitoring of the progress in the grievance redressal, the Ministry has developed a computerized Grievance Monitoring System. The grievances received in the Ministry are sent to the concerned Grievance Officer in the attached subordinate offices of the Ministry. Periodical review meetings are held in the Ministry to ensure that the grievances are processed within a stipulated time limit.

## ATTITUDE TOWARD FOREIGN MEDIA

India is a founding member of the United Nations Educational, Scientific, and Cultural Organization (UNESCO). UNESCO's main goal is to promote international cooperation in the field of education, science and technology, social sciences, culture and mass communication. In order to promote the communication capabilities of developing countries. The 21st Session of the General Conference of UNESCO in 1981 approved the establishment of an International Program for the Development of Communication (IPDC). India played a significant role in its inception and has been a member of the Inter-governmental Council (IGC) and also of the IPDC Bureau. India has played a leading role in its activitics over the years. Being one of the founding members of IPDC, this Ministry has been a representative at the meetings of the General Conference of UNESCO and Bureau Session of IPDC.

India participated in the First South Asian Association for Regional Cooperation (SAARC) Information Ministers Meeting held in Dhaka (Bangladesh) in 1998. The Meeting discussed the need for greater cooperation among media personnel, cooperation among news agencies, improving the programs under SAARC Audio Visual Exchange, and taking steps to project SAARC outside the region.

More indications of India's support of international cooperation is its participation in the meeting of Asia-Pacific Regional Experts on the Legal Framework for Cyberspace from

8 to 10 September 1998 and the Third Regulatory Round Table for the Asia and the Pacific at Seoul from 14 to 16 September 1998 for finalizing the report on Trans-border Satellite Broadcasting.

## NEWS AGENCIES

News agencies provide regularity and authenticity to news. K.C. Roy is credited with establishing the first Indian news agency, which became The Associated Press of India (API). However, it soon became a British-controlled agency unwilling to report about the national freedom movement. The Free Press of India News Agency came into existence under the management of S. Sadanand who had served Reuters. The United Press of India, The Orient Press, The Globe News Agency, The NAFEN News Agency, The United News of India and a number of syndicates later came to serve the news business.

The Non-aligned News Agencies Pool (NANAP), formally constituted in 1976 for the purpose of correcting imbalances in the global flow of information, is an arrangement for exchange of news and information among the national news agencies of non-aligned countries, including Asia, Africa, Europe and Latin America. Its affairs are managed by a coordinating committee elected for a term of three years. India is at present a member of the coordinating committee. The cost of running the pool is met by the participating members. The Press Trust (PTI) continued to operate the India News Pool Desk (INDP) of the NANAP on behalf of the government of India. India continued to contribute substantially to the daily news file of the Pool Network. The reception of news into the Pool Desk during the year 1998-99 has been in the range of 20,000 words per day. INDP's own contribution to the Pool partners during the year has averaged 7,000 words per day.

The organization and structure of Indian news agencies has been undergoing a controversial transformation for quite sometime. This represents a mutual mistrust between privately owned news agencies and governmental structures. Their autonomy, believed to be crucial for objectivity and fairness, is based on their role as cooperatives and non-profit groups. News agencies in general are discouraged from taking any governmental favors. There is nothing in the Indian constitution, however, that can prevent government to nationalize its news agencies. There are four dominant news agencies in India: The Press Trust of India (PTI); the United News of India (UNI); the Hindustan Samachar (HS); and Samachar Bhatia (SB).

## BROADCAST MEDIA

The Ministry of Information & Broadcasting, through the mass communication media of radio, television, films, the press, publications, advertising and traditional modes of dance and drama, plays a significant part in helping the people to have access to information. It fosters the dissemination of knowledge and entertainment in all sectors of society, striking a careful balance between public interest and commercial needs in its delivery of services. The Ministry of Information & Broadcasting is the highest body for formulation and administration of the rules, regulations and laws relating to information, broadcasting, the press and films.

The ministry is responsible for international cooperation in the field of mass media, films and broadcasting, and interacts with its foreign counterparts on behalf of Government of India. The mandate of the Ministry of Information & Broadcasting is to provide:

- News Services through All India Radio (AIR) and Doordarshan (DD) for the people
- Development of broadcasting and television
- Import and export of films
- Development and promotion of film industry
- Organization of film festivals and cultural exchanges
- Advertisement and visual publicity on behalf of the Government of India
- Handling of press relations to present the policies of Government of India and to seek feedback on government policies
- Administration of the Press and Registration of Books Act of 1867 in respect of newspapers

- Dissemination of information about India within and outside the country through publications on matters of national importance
- Research, reference, and training to assist the media units of the Ministry to meet their responsibilities
- Use of interpersonal communication and traditional folk art forms for information/publicity campaigns on public interest issues
- International co-operation in the field of information and mass media

The main Secretariat of the Ministry is divided into three wings: the information wing, the broadcasting wing, and the film wing. The media units engaged in press and publicity activities include:

- Press: (1) Press Information Bureau; (2) Photo Division; (3) Research Reference & Training Division; (4) Publications Division.
- Publicity: (5) Directorate of Advertising and Visual Publicity; (6) Directorate of Field Publicity; (7) Song and Drama Division
- Regulation of the Press: (8) Registrar of Newspapers for India; (9) Press Council of India
- Training: (10) Indian Institute of Mass Communication (Government of India, 2002)

## ELECTRONIC NEWS MEDIA

Most Indian newspapers, magazines, and media outlets are easily accessible through the Internet. Internet Public Library (IPL) is a concise Internet source for information on Indian newspapers. The Onlinenewspapers.com Web site lists about 120 online newspapers for India with access to each of those papers for reading.

The official Web site for the Library of Congress in New Delhi is also accessible on the Internet, where e-mail contact information is provided. This directory is published biennially. The directory includes newspapers published in India, the name and language of the newspapers, circulation, frequency of publication, and names and addresses for the publishers of each paper. Paper status is also included.

Internet Public Library's list of India's contemporary newspapers exists to enable instant access to existing information resources. Among them in 2002 were 62 Indian newspapers that were available online.

## EDUCATION AND TRAINING

The first diploma in Journalism was offered at Aligarh Muslim University in 1938 by the late Sir shah Muhammad Sulaiman, a Judge in India (Wolseley 224). Later on, after partition, universities in Punjab, Madras, Delhi, Calcutta, Mysore, Nagpur, and Osmania offered courses at undergraduate levels. Professional education in India is largely a need-based enterprise. Journalists and other mass communicators can perform without specialized training and skills, and can succeed without advanced degrees.

## Summary

The media in India represents a confluence of paradoxes: tradition and modernity; anarchy and order; diversity and unity; conflict and cooperation; news and views; feudalism and democracy; the free market and monopoly. Economic realities and relationships between press, television and those who own these engines of control and change will eventually determine the future of India's communication culture.

India's complex cultural mosaic, especially linguistic and communal, strengthens its diversity. The media and press continue to play a dominant role in deconstructing the diversity discourse that sometimes flares up in explosive situations.

Capitalism, the press, and public hunger for news promote a culture of media that is fast replacing the legacy of a feudal/ colonial system.

While corporatization and state regulations can muffle free expression, the force of public interest and the market economy strive for greater freedom and openness. Both politics and capitalism thrive on the liberties of a democratic system that continues to evolve into a functional hybrid of chaos and order.

## SIGNIFICANT DATES

- 1990: Nikhil Wagle publishes a Mumbai evening tabloid Hamara Mahanagar, 'Our great city' (January).
- 1991: Mahanagar is vandalized by a Shiva Sena gang
- 1995: The politician-proprietor of a Telgu daily embroiled in controversy was murdered, allegedly by the People's War Group (December)
- 1997: Dainik Bhaskar, the Bhopal-based Hindi daily opened a Jaipur edition, self-acclaimed its status as "India's Fastest Growing Newspaper"

## News Media

Compared with many other developing countries, the Indian press has flourished since independence and exercises a large degree of independence. British colonialism allowed for the development of a tradition of freedom of the press, and many of India's great English-language newspapers and some of its Indian-language press were begun during the nineteenth century. As India became independent, ownership of India's leading English-language newspapers was transferred from British to Indian business groups, and the fact that most English-language newspapers have the backing of large business houses has contributed to their independence from the government. The Indian press has experienced impressive growth since independence. In 1950 there were 214 daily newspapers, with forty-four in English and the rest in Indian languages. By 1990 the number of daily newspapers had grown to 2,856, with 209 in English and 2,647 in indigenous languages. The expansion of literacy and the spread of consumerism during the 1980s fueled the rapid growth of news weeklies and other periodicals. By 1993 India had 35,595 newspapers--of which 3,805 were dailies--and other periodicals. Although the majority of publications are in indigenous languages, the English-language press, which has widespread appeal to the expanding middle class, has a wide multicity circulation throughout India.

There are four major publishing groups in India, each of which controls national and regional English-language and vernacular publications. They are the Times of India Group, the Indian Express Group, the Hindustan Times Group, and the Anandabazar Patrika Group. The Times of India is India's largest English-language daily, with a circulation of 656,000 published in six cities.

The Indian Express, with a daily circulation of 519,000, is published in seventeen cities. There also are seven other daily newspapers with circulations of between 134,000 and 477,000, all in English and all competitive with one another. Indian-language newspapers also enjoy large circulations but usually on a statewide or citywide basis. For example, the Malayalam-language daily Malayala Manorama circulates 673,000 copies in Kerala; the Hindi-language Dainik Jagran circulates widely in Uttar Pradesh and New Delhi, with 580,000 copies per day; Punjab Kesari, also published in Hindi and available throughout Punjab and New Delhi, has a daily circulation of 562,000; and the Anandabazar Patrika, published in Calcutta in Bengali, has a daily circulation of 435,000. There are also numerous smaller publications throughout the nation. The combined circulation of India's newspapers and periodicals is in the order of 60 million, published daily in more than ninety languages.

India has more than forty domestic news agencies. The Express News Service, the Press Trust of India, and the United News of India are among the major news agencies. They are headquartered in Delhi, Bombay, and New Delhi, respectively, and employ foreign correspondents.

Although freedom of the press in India is the legal norm--it is constitutionally guaranteed--the scope of this freedom has often been contested by the government. Rigid press censorship was imposed during the Emergency starting in 1975 but quickly retracted in 1977. The government has continued, however, to exercise more indirect controls. Government advertising accounts for as much as 50 percent of all advertisements in Indian newspapers, providing a monetary incentive to limit harsh criticism of the administration.

Until 1992, when government regulation of access to newsprint was liberalized, controls on the distribution of newsprint could also be used to reward favored publications and threaten those that fell into disfavor. In 1988, at a time when the Indian press was publishing investigative reports about corruption and abuse of power in government, Parliament passed a tough defamation bill that mandated prison sentences for offending journalists. Vociferous protests from journalists and opposition party leaders ultimately forced the government to withdraw the bill. Since the late 1980s, the independence of India's press has been bolstered by the liberalization of government economic policy and the increase of private-sector advertising provided by the growth of India's private sector and the spread of consumerism.

## EMERGING PERSPECTIVE

In spite of a number of efforts for developing science journalism in India, there are certain challenges before us, to be met. Some of them are listed below:

(a) As an average, the science coverage in India is around 3%, which we intend to enhance up to 15%, as per a resolution of Indian Science Writers' Association.

(b) The number of capable science journalists/writers and popular science magazines is alarmingly low and hardly sufficient to cater to the large target audience.

(c) The science has still not succeeded in attracting the media to the extent that it could appear on the front page or become a lead story, like the politics, films or sports. Mass media has its commercial compulsions, which superimpose all the science communication efforts and leave a negative impact in the minds of the audiences. Instead of including scientific information, they prefer to generate more revenue by including non-scientific, meta-scientific or occult information, etc.

(d) It is rather disappointing to note that leading science magazines have ceased their publication, like Science Today, Science Age, Bulletin of Sciences, Research and Industry, etc. and Indian editions of foreign science magazines, like Vigyan (Scientific American), World Scientist (La Recherche), etc. could not survive, however, recently Indian edition of Popular Science has been started from New Delhi.

(e) India has 18 recognized regional languages. Science writing in many languages is yet another great challenge, as scientific information is generally available in English. The quality of scientific translation could not achieve the level of excellence.

(f) The science writing is still dry and boring, and interesting styles of writing, like fiction, poetry, satires, skits, discussions, etc. have not found adequate space and time in the media. Even most of the science writers could not contribute sufficiently such an interesting science material. Merely occasional appearance of something in the name of science fiction cannot serve the purpose.

(g) Misleading scientific information, a continuous decay of creativity in presentation, distortion in translation, inconsistency in organizing the contents, lapses in the use of language, and many more deviations can be seen on media frequently.

(h) There has been emerging conflict between scientists and journalists, which is a great impediment towards the progress of science journalism in India. This can be resolved by way of organizing scientists-journalists meets on regular basis.

(i) As far as science writing and science journalism are concerned, there is ample scope for furthering such efforts in developing countries, especially in South Asian Region. A common science and technology news and features pool can be formed to facilitate writers/ journalists to get/ exchange information on scientific research.

(j) There is a great shortage of properly trained science writers, journalists, communicators, illustrators in various parts of the world, though, a number of training programmes are conducted at various places. Therefore, more training programmes are needed, which may preferably be conducted to give more opportunity to developing countries.

(k) Popular science writing in India is still shackled by complacency and over dependence on foreign sources. It is very difficult to get information from a scientific laboratory. The scientists in some organizations are not allowed to talk to the media about the research being carried out by them or in their laboratory. This requires a science media centre, including a centralized website to facilitate media persons to get research reports well in time.

(l) All India Radio has started science news based on the research papers appearing in Indian research journals. Print media can follow similar practice as well.

(m) Following the industrial revolution in the western countries, the level of science coverage in mass media was exponentially increased. As such, India is passing through the same stage, in the present time. As the technology advances, the need of scientific information would also increase. Accordingly, the industrial India would soon witness the high time of science journalism, but the scientific community, media persons and public have to be vigilant enough to harness this opportunity.

(n) Generally, science journalism is misunderstood merely as communication of data; it must go beyond data. The logical and rational interpretation must come up to the fore, enabling the target audiences to shape their lives, ideas and thinking, as well.

(o) There is a need of debates in mass media on emerging issues of science and technology which are relevant to the people and are of their immediate concern to enable them to take informed decisions to lead their life in a democratic society.

Though, challenges are many, we could see some rays of hope, as India has been able to take initiatives in a number of newer programmes in the area of science communication, such as, Vigyan Jatha, Children's Science Congress, and Scientific Explanation of So-called miracles, etc., which were not tried out elsewhere and can take lead in these innovative areas of science communication to better serve the mankind.

## CONCLUSION

In order to identify and evaluate the present status of science journalism in India, various parameters were used. On the basis of a survey conducted, some interesting inferences were drawn. Near about 12.66% respondents were interested in science and technology coverage. This inference seems to be exactly in conformity with the desired level (10-15%) of science coverage in the country. While looking at the demand and supply analysis, the demand seems to be very less in some cases. This however, is a false situation limited by the necessary expansion, which may leap many times in near future.

Science certainly does not fare well when we talk of readers' interest but it is also true that we need to work in the direction of making science interesting.

A lot more creativity is required in the field of science writing and journalism; perhaps this is what we lack at the moment. Science fiction has achieved the status of best sellers in the west, whereas we hardly have anything significant of this type of science writing. Low interest in sciences can be traced to another reason that we are not prioritising two important segments of our readers, the students and the farmers, in the manner that is of interest to them. There is reasonable interest in the folk media, especially in the rural areas and this media does not find enough attention vis-à-vis science journalism.

It is time to recognize the shift in target population's interest, i.e. towards television, and science programmes should be created in enough number through formats, which are most attractive to them. It may not be incorrect to say that docu-drama would be the most sought after format of science communication through television.

When, India is passing through a crucial turning point of its development, we must take emerging trends into our stride and redraw our policies and plans, to be a nation of scientifically thinking and scientifically informed people. Hence, the efforts directed towards enhancing science coverage in mass media through effective and creative science journalism need to be given more priority. This is an issue, which scientists, media persons and the public have to take seriously and other side of the coin needs to be focussed now.

## List of Organisations Working in the Field of Promotion and Development of Languages

### *Central Hindi Directorate*

The Central Hindi Directorate was established on 1st March, 1960 by Government of India to promote and propagate Hindi and to develop it as a link language throughout India in pursuance of Article 351 of the Constitution of India.

The Directorate has been implementing a number of schemes to achieve the objective as enshrined in the Constitution. The Headquarter of the Central Hindi Directorate is located in New Delhi with four Regional Offices situated in Chennai, Kolkata, Hyderabad and Guwahati.

### *Scheme of Preparation and Publication of Dictionaries*

For developing and strengthening Hindi language the Directorate has been developing and publishing bilingual, trilingual, multilingual dictionaries from Hindi language to other languages and vice versa. Besides this the Directorate prepares conversational guides and self-teaching course material for beginners of Hindi learners.

### *Scheme of Teaching Hindi Through Correspondence*

Correspondence Courses Department has been functioning since 1968 for teaching Hindi to the Non-Hindi speaking Indians and foreigners stationed in India and abroad as second and foreign language through the medium of English, Tamil, Malayalam and Bangla languages. The on-going courses of the Directorate, viz., Certificate Course in Hindi and Diploma Course in Hindi are aimed at imparting basic knowledge of Hindi language and skill in day-to-day communication.

### Extension Programmes

The Extension Programme aim at promotion and propagations of Hindi in non-Hindi-speaking states by bringing together non-Hindi speaking lovers of Hindi, scholars, authors, researchers, students and professors, and providing a common forum. This not only imparts latest information about the Indian languages and their literature through Hindi medium but also helps in developing understanding through mutual discussions and dialogues by appreciating each other's traditions. In fact, these schemes encourage lingual unity by displaying common features programme that provides practical information about the all-India character of Hindi. Under this programme the Directorate conducts workshops for Neo-Hindi Writers of Non-Hindi-Speaking States, National Symposia, travel grants to Hindi research scholars, Study tours and lecture series.

### Scheme of Financial Assistance for the Promotion of Hindi

Under this scheme, financial assistance may be given to the Organizations/Educational Institutions to continue and/or to expand their activities or tread fresh ground in the propagation and development of Hindi. Activities such as organizing Hindi classes, Hindi Shorthand and typing classes and for running Hindi Libraries/Reading Rooms, and supporting the efforts of Hindi organizations in general for promotion of Hindi language are covered under the scheme.

### Free Distribution of Hindi Books and Exhibition of Hindi Books

Under the scheme of Free distribution of Hindi books about 800 institutions have been supplied Hindi books during the current financial year. Under the scheme of Exhibition of the Publications of the Central Hindi Directorate 11 exhibitions have been organized.

### Awards Scheme

The Directorate is also giving awards to Hindi Writers of non-Hindi-speaking states and 'Shiksha Puraskar'. The Award scheme provides for a total of 24 awards of the value of Rupees One lakh each under these schemes. 19 awards and 5 awards are given under the first and second category respectively. writers/authors.

# 2

# Today's Media

During the recent years mass media has invaded the life of a common man in a big way. Upto seventies, mass media mainly remained confined to cinema, newspaper and radio. It was in the early eighties that audio-visual electronic medium in the form of television invaded the Indian scenario in a big way. The Government created huge infrastructure for spread of television network in the country. During this decade itself, advent of computers and Video Cassette Recorders (VCR) also supplemented the audio-visual media, putting well established medium of cinema to shade.

During the early nineties, satellite television revolutionised the audio-visual media by reaching most of the households in the urban areas. The latest invasion of audio-visual electronic media has suddenly increased the demand for professionals in journalism, technicians and other service individuals. These careers not only offer excellent opportunities, salaries, challenge and satisfaction of work, but also provide an opportunity for self-employment in various fields.

## PRINT MEDIA

An old saying goes "pen is mightier than sword". The saying is not just a rhetoric. It reflects the power of print media. Being the most important media, print media pertains to broad activity of publication of newspapers, magazines and books and all persons connected with this activity have their contribution in successful running of this medium. While writing of books and contributing to magazines is largely a self-employment occupation, publication of newspapers and magazines involves a huge work force such as editors, technicians, printing technicians, composers, etc. In all these jobs the options of either working on desk or working in the field are available to the candidates. Reporters and correspondents generally operate in the field and submit their reports or stories on local, national or international issues pertaining to politics, trade, commerce, defence, sports, etc. One special category of reporters and correspondents operates in the field of investigative journalism.

This category of reporting pertains to investigation on the issues of public importance. This type of journalism and reporting attracts public attention instantaneously. Special attention in such reporting is required in the authenticity of information, selection of issues of public interest and succinct reporting in interesting and convincing language. In case of magazine reporting, many a times the reports, stories and features are contributed by free-lance reporters and part-time amateur writers. To pursue the career as a reporter one may attain bachelor's degree or post-graduate diploma in journalism. Some of the universities offer post graduate diplomas of 9-month duration while others offer post-graduate one-year diploma in Public Relations or post graduate degree in mass-communication.

Latest trend in this regard is that big groups of newspapers advertise the posts of trainees in any of the above categories for which all graduates are eligible. After conducting the entrance examination, suitable graduate trainees, with flair for writing are selected and employed. In other words, now the formal academic qualification for being a reporter, copy writer or correspondent is not an essential qualification. Similarly, for writing features or analytical articles in magazines, one need not have any formal and professional academic qualification.

What is required is in-depth knowledge, command over the language concerned and outstanding analytical capability. Broadly speaking, anyone keen to pursue this career in any capacity must have outstanding general awareness, good perception, an eye for details and very keen observation. In turn, the career offers challenge, immense job satisfaction and fairly good compensation. For acquiring general awareness regular reading of newspapers, magazines and books on variety of topics is a must. Discussions on current topics also go a long way in widening the horizons of knowledge. For the beginners, it is better to consult a good book on the background to current affairs so that further knowledge is strengthened after acquiring fundamental knowledge. Latest edition of "Current Affairs and Backgrounders" published by M/s Khanna Brothers (Publishers) Pvt Ltd is an ideal book for this purpose. Command over the concerned language is not a capability which can be acquired overnight. Regular and intensive reading as well as regular writing practice not only improves the command over the language, but also improves the flair for writing.

Candidates seriously pursuing this career should also go in for academic degree/diploma in Journalism/Public Relations/ Mass Communication from a good university or institute to have an edge over others.

## AUDIO-VISUAL MEDIA

The requirement of personnel for the audio and audio-visual media is a little different than that for the print media. Traditionally, Radio has been the audio media having farthest reach. It was only with effect from the early eighties that Radio started getting replaced by Television. In most of the cases TV just supplemented the Radio. Despite the recent invasion by Doordarshan channels and Satellite and Cable TV, importance of Radio has not been undermined. The percentage of population covered by Radio is much more than the TV, mainly due to better technical infrastructure, longer range of short wave radio and cheaper cost and running cost of radio and transistors. Hence, Radio still remains very important medium.

Radio needs various types of personnel which includes announcers, news-readers, news-composers, writers, producers, commentators, and various categories of radio artists like singers, musicians, drama artists, narrators, etc. There is also a growing demand for good programmes and producers of such programmes. Audio-visual media is the strongest form of medium, but has limited reach. The earliest form of audio-visual medium was cinema which had very limited reach and people had to spend some money to have an access to it.

Cinema, however, still enjoys the most glamorous place in the entire media. In this feature, Cinema as career in audio-visual media has been left out and will be covered later in a separate feature on careers.

Television, satellite and cable TV offer varied opportunities for career seekers. This medium offers excellent opportunities for newsreaders, composers, announcers, technicians, commentators, producers, models, actors, cameramen, script writers, etc. In addition to the Government-run Doordarshan, all other companies in the field of television, be it in production, direction, acting, cable operation and satellite TV operation, are handled by the individuals or private companies. The choice of career is available in a variety of fields, not only with Doordarshan but with commercially-run media companies also. Candidates seeking any type of career in audio-visual electronic media must have characteristics like artistic inclination, expertise in own field of activity, pleasing personality, adaptability, general awareness, quick reflexes, flexibility and imagination. All these qualities must be coupled with the required technical and academic qualifications and professional competence. In case of announcers and newsreaders the qualities of good voice and presentable and photogenic face are additional requirements.

Good flow of spoken language and command over the language concerned are also pre-requisites in these cases. Capabilities to compare and compose become added qualifications. In addition to programmes and news, three other aspects of advertisement, engineering and management are also of paramount importance in TV and other electronic media. Technical and professional staff provide engineering services and act from behind the screen. These personnel are responsible for providing support services so essential for good quality of transmission, colour combinations, creation of support infrastructure for transmission, day-to-day management of video recording, time-management and other related aspects.

## HOW TO JOIN

Career in News-reading and announcing does not require any professional or technical qualifications. Any simple graduate with good command over the language, with pleasing face and personality, accurate pronunciation and a good voice can hope to enter this career. Experience of stage and theatre also helps a candidate. Most important of all these qualities is the aptitude for a particular job and keen interest in it. To provide technical support service, trainee Transmission Executives are recruited. The recruitment for trainee Transmission Executives is made by the Staff Selection Commission (SSC).

SSC holds a selection test and all candidates who are between 18 to 25 years of age and have diploma from National School of Drama (NSD) and Film and Television Institute of India (FTII), Pune are eligible to take test. After selection, trainee Transmission Executives are made responsible for making timely transmission of scheduled programmes. They are also expected to ensure proper quality of transmission. This is achieved by properly conceptualising the programme, their timings and ensuring technical precision. Transmission Executives may rise to the levels of Programme Executive, Assistant Station Director or even Station Directors.

The higher level managerial posts are held by the officers of Central Information Service (Group-A). Recruitment to this service is made by the combined Civil Services Examination which is held by the Union Public Service Commission every year. It is one of the allied services in this examination and recruitment for this service takes place every year. Officers from this service also hold senior level posts in All India Radio and in the Department of Information and Broadcasting. In addition, technical positions like cameramen, make-up-men, video technicians, editors, etc need specific technical qualifications and specific experience in the related fields.

## JOURNALISM

Journalism fascinates many young people who have a keen desire of seeing their name in print. Anyone who has written something for the college paper believes a career in journalism can be pursued. This feature points out that a career in journalism means more than merely writing well. As we receive a number of queries from our readers who want to become famous journalists and editors, we decided to describe in detail the requirements of newspapers and television channels today. This feature describes the skills required, as also the upside and the downside of the field. It also gives information about how one can become a journalist, the qualities that are required to be a successful one and addresses of some of the well known institutes.

To an outsider, journalism is an exciting field in which fame and fortune can be achieved if one is able to write well. The names of some famous journalists come easily to mind. Khushwant Singh, who writes columns in several newspapers; M.J. Akbar, the editor of The Asian Age; and Shobha De, former editor of Stardust and now a celebrated writer. Opportunities in the field have also multiplied with the boom in magazines and television channels.

Each of these requires people who can report and interpret events in a coherent and interesting manner. To assess whether you can be a famous journalist, you have to first know the skills that are required. The first is a good command over language. You must be able to express yourself well. A course in journalism will help sharpen these skills. But this is not all. What is required is the ability to collect information and report events quickly. If you are in a television channel, it may mean going on camera as the event is happening, often a difficult task. In newspapers one has to write out the story before the deadline and it must contain all the correct information and the drama. Even a small error can destroy the credibility of the journalist. So journalism is just not about being able to write well alone.

The nature of a journalist's job is also changing. With news becoming competitive and personality-oriented, the job of a TV journalist often means waiting outside the offices or homes of politicians for hours and trying to catch a "sound byte" as the leader comes out. The pursuit of truth does not extend beyond getting a small segment in the news programme. In this race, there is no room for being creative or following stories that one may like to. Threats of law-suits have made news channels and newspapers increasingly wary about publishing scoops and many of the investigative stories are just killed. There is little room for creativity in today's news organisations.

## INCREASING SCOPE

Once you accept these limitations, a career in journalism may be a good option. Some years back there was a boom in television channels which led to an increase in opportunities for aspiring journalists. Many print journalists shifted to television. Salaries had jumped. Today, there is a shakeout among the channels, which has led to the opportunities being reduced drastically. Newspapers and magazines continue to employ journalists, but with circulations and profitability under stress, three has been a decrease in opportunities somewhat. However, this situation may be linked to the economic slowdown and things may become better once the economy picks up. It may be mentioned that there are over 4,000 newspapers in 100 languages registered in India and the scope for employment will always exist, despite difficulties.

Avenues in journalism have multiplied because of unexpected growth in two new areas: (a) Niche publications; and (b) Web editing. We explain these below: Niche Publications: This means special purpose publications catering to particular industries, for example, travel and tourism, hotels, textiles or computers. Many such publications have been started in the past few years. These "niche" publications may not have the mass circulations of newspapers but are highly profitable. However, to work in them one needs to have journalistic skills as well as industry knowledge. Hence, MBAs are employed in business publications while computer experts find jobs in information technology magazines. The idea is to develop a specialisation and build on it. In the future, journalists with specialised skills in an industry may be more in demand than those with mere writing skills.

## WEB EDITING

Another avenue has opened up in recent times and that is because of the Internet. Many newspapers and magazines have web editions and require skilled people to maintain their sites. Web newspapers have also started, which do not have print editions. This has opened up a great opportunity but here those journalists would be required who have knowledge of websites and how to make them attractive. The work involves content creation, layout, graphics and text on the Web newspage. The scope of journalists is, therefore, increasing by the day, though the role has changed a great deal. Earlier, journalists collected their daily quota of news at the Press Club and this was rehashed for publication the next day. Today, however, a journalist must be a professional like any other and must have technical skills as well.

## DEVELOP THE NECESSARY SKILLS

One major shortcoming of the Indian press has been its failure to follow up stories. Scandals are reported but soon forgotten because the press finds something else to report. This has led to the unfortunate situation where newspapers are not taken seriously any more. If this continues, the privileges enjoyed by journalists may well become a thing of the past. The day of famous editors is also over. Today, different editors are employed for different sections and there is no one person who is all powerful in a newspaper organisation, except perhaps the owner. Do not thus think of a career in journalism because of privileges that you might get. Instead, get a specialisation and try to make a name in your chosen field. The modern journalist should have skills of expression as well as technical skills. Even if you are a reporter, you will have to type in your stories on a page-making and publishing software. Nor is it necessary to have a journalism degree. One can belong to any discipline and hope to join journalism if one has demonstrated qualities of writing and reporting. Niche magazines, in any case, want specialists and not mere journalists. On the other hand, a journalism degree will help you acquire skills and also enable you an entry into a newspaper or television organisation. The ideal thing might be to zero-in on your area of specialisation, acquire a degree, and then do journalism.

This may be a better career option than doing just a journalism course. To acquire fame, of course, one has to be a good journalist. Merely getting a journalism degree does not make you good at your job. First, one must have the capability of getting information. This means that you must have a "head for the news". Then, you must have the perseverance and grit to obtain the information, considering the fact that most people do not like to part with information. Finally, you must have the ability to transform the information into an interesting story.

## FUTURE PROSPECTS

After your basic training, you are ready to enter the world of journalism. Whether you wish to join TV journalism or a newspaper, you can expect to be a reporter at a starting salary of Rs 5,000 per month. Growth is fast, especially if you show an aptitude for the job. After a few years you can expect to be a senior reporter and move in the salary of around Rs 10,000 and thereafter it all depends on how famous and good you become. A sub-editor's job consists of editing what others have written and prepare the pages that will be printed. The schedule is usually unearthly, with shifts ending at 2 or 3 am, which means that social life has to be discarded. Once you get used to it, however, it becomes enjoyable. In TV journalism one can start as a reporter or do some research work and later become a correspondent and anchor. There are thousands of people who want to become newsreaders and anchors but they lack training. There are few institutes available which can train you to become a newsreader. Even if you have training, it is a tough field, since newsreaders are employed on contract. Presenters are given the boot for minor mistakes. In Doordarshan the situation is worse and requires political patronage. Think of this option only as part-time work or look for employment in organisations like NDTV or Sun TV. Another option could be to start out on your own and become a private producer. If you have an idea about a programme that can click, approach a company which supplies programmes to channels.

## BRIDGING ACADEMIA AND JOURNALISM

For much of the last century, journalism has been a major influence on the way we perceive the world. Whether we live in a democratic society with a central tenet of press freedom, in an environment where state-controlled media direct our thinking, or somewhere between the two, the information we gather through newsprint, television and radio broadcasting is enormously influential. Political life today is conducted largely through the media, which increasingly sets the agenda and judges success and failure, truth and lies, within some framework of undeclared criteria. Recent years have seen the growth of global media corporations and, in counterpoint, the rise of the 'citizen reporter' publishing first-hand information on the Internet. Increasingly, as allegations of 'spin' abound, it can be hard to know which media sources to trust-and how far.

Closely scrutinising those with power and calling them to account is one of the core principles of journalism, yet journalism itself is not often on the receiving end of such inspection. Against this backdrop, in September 2006 Oxford launched the Reuters Institute for the Study of Journalism, based in the Department of Politics and International Relations. This ground-breaking research institute, which has been established with £1.75 million funding from the Reuters Foundation, will provide high-calibre analysis of the practice of journalism in all media forms, examining both its ethical framework and evolution and the realities of journalistic practice.

By bringing together academic rigour and the expertise of working journalists, the Reuters Institute will strive to further our understanding of journalism and the challenges it faces as the digital age dissolves our local and national boundaries.

The Director of the Institute is Dr Sarmila Bose, whose respected academic career at universities in the UK, USA and India has been complemented by her work as a broadcast and print journalist, particularly in the area of electoral politics and public policy issues for the Indian press. The Director of Journalism is John Lloyd, contributing editor of the Financial Times. The Institute's Advisory Committee is chaired by the Chancellor, Lord Patten, and its Steering Committee by Tim Gardam, Principal of St Anne's College and former Director of Television at Channel 4. Other Steering Committee members include Geert Linnebank, Editor-in-Chief of Reuters, and Professor Timothy Garton Ash, a regular contributor to the Guardian and the New York Times.

The establishment of the Reuters Institute boosts a growing engagement on the part of the University with the media. For almost 25 years, Reuters Fellowships have allowed distinguished mid-career journalists from around the world to take time out from the daily tyranny of deadlines and spend study breaks of one to three terms using the University's facilities, whilst being welcomed as Visiting Scholars at Green College. Since 1996, the Centre for Socio-Legal Studies has been home to the Programme in Comparative Media Law and Policy, which examines issues such as media regulation and the legal and social implications of new media technologies.

The more recently established Oxford Internet Institute is examining the ways in which the Internet is pushing the borders of what we mean by journalism and how it should be controlled, and within the Saïd Business School, the study of media management and media strategy is creating real excitement. Through a combination of innovative research and seminars around the world with high-profile participants, the University is taking a genuinely international approach.

The Reuters Institute will reinforce this global perspective, whilst being firmly anchored within the University's academic programme. 'Our task will be to bring together scholars and practitioners from the world of journalism to study the content of news media and the issues it raises', says Dr Bose. 'We are an institute for the study of journalism, not a school of journalism, and that, together with our global outlook, probably makes us unique. We hope to draw in scholars from all parts of the University, including areas like medicine, science and philosophy, and we are also keen to extend the links we are already forging with a number of colleges and centres.'

'We have five core areas where we will initially focus our research', she adds.

'First, the challenge of freedom and responsibility in journalism. We want to look at established open societies, such as Western Europe, the USA and India, where freedom of the media is constitutionally guaranteed and is part of democratic society, but examine the ways in which, in practice, there may not be complete freedom.

Secondly, we want to compare the situation in emerging societies that were formerly closed, for example Russia.

Thirdly, we want to look at journalistic coverage of scientific and medical issues, building on work already ongoing at Green College; and fourthly, we want to study business and economics journalism, working with our legal and business school colleagues to create an international dimension. Finally, we will examine the representation of religion in media, starting with the representation of Islam.' A three-year research project that compares journalism across Europe has just begun, funded by the Swedish Ax:son Johnson Foundation.

As befits an organisation working on issues of relevance to the world of practice, the Reuters Institute is keen to ensure that its findings are aired and debated in the media-and fed back to its practitioners. As well as academic publications, books, seminars and articles, the Institute website will host a running commentary on the media itself and include space for blogging. 'We've had great interest from both academics and journalists who are keen to share their experiences and ideas', says Dr Bose. 'By creating a real partnership between these worlds, we intend to study the content of journalism in global comparison, combining the analytic rigour of Oxford and policy relevance to the world of practice.'

# 3

# The Principles and Ethics

In 1997, an organization then administered by PEJ, the Committee of Concerned Journalists, began a national conversation among citizens and news people to identify and clarify the principles that underlie journalism. After four years of research, including 20 public forums around the country, a reading of journalism history, a national survey of journalists, and more, the group released a Statement of Shared Purpose that identified nine principles. These became the basis for The Elements of Journalism, the book by PEJ Director Tom Rosenstiel and CCJ Chairman and PEJ Senior Counselor Bill Kovach. Here are those principles, as outlined in the original Statement of Shared Purpose.

## A STATEMENT OF PURPOSE

After extended examination by journalists themselves of the character of journalism at the end of the twentieth century, we offer this common understanding of what defines our work. The central purpose of journalism is to provide citizens with accurate and reliable information they need to function in a free society. This encompasses myriad roles--helping define community, creating common language and common knowledge, identifying a community's goals, heros and villains, and pushing people beyond complacency. This purpose also involves other requirements, such as being entertaining, serving as watchdog and offering voice to the voiceless.

Over time journalists have developed nine core principles to meet the task. They comprise what might be described as the theory of journalism:

### Journalism's First Obligation is to the Truth

Democracy depends on citizens having reliable, accurate facts put in a meaningful context. Journalism does not pursue truth in an absolute or philosophical sense, but it can--and must--pursue it in a practical sense. This "journalistic truth" is a process that begins with the professional discipline of assembling and verifying facts. Then journalists try to convey a fair and reliable account of their meaning, valid for now, subject to further investigation. Journalists should be as transparent as possible about sources and methods so audiences can make their own assessment of the information. Even in a world of expanding voices, accuracy is the foundation upon which everything else is built--context, interpretation, comment, criticism, analysis and debate. The truth, over time, emerges from this forum. As citizens encounter an ever greater flow of data, they have more need--not less--for identifiable sources dedicated to verifying that information and putting it in context.

### Its First Loyalty is to Citizens

While news organizations answer to many constituencies, including advertisers and shareholders, the journalists in those organizations must maintain allegiance to citizens and the larger public interest above any other if they are to provide the news without fear or favor. This commitment to citizens first is the basis of a news organization's credibility, the implied covenant that tells the audience the coverage is not slanted for friends or advertisers. Commitment to citizens also means journalism should present a representative picture of all constituent groups in society. Ignoring certain citizens has the effect of disenfranchising them. The theory underlying the modern news industry has been the belief that credibility builds a broad and loyal audience, and that economic success follows in turn. In that regard, the business people in a news organization also must nurture--not exploit--their allegiance to the audience ahead of other considerations.

### Its Essence is a Discipline of Verification

Journalists rely on a professional discipline for verifying information. When the concept of objectivity originally evolved, it did not imply that journalists are free of bias. It called, rather, for a consistent method of testing information--a transparent approach to evidence--precisely so that personal and cultural biases would not undermine the accuracy of their work. The method is objective, not the journalist. Seeking out multiple witnesses, disclosing as much as possible about sources, or asking various sides for comment, all signal such standards. This discipline of verification is what separates journalism from other modes of communication, such as propaganda, fiction or entertainment. But the need for professional method is not always fully recognized or refined. While journalism has developed various techniques for determining facts, for instance, it has done less to develop a system for testing the reliability of journalistic interpretation.

### Its Practitioners must Maintain an Independence from those they Cover

Independence is an underlying requirement of journalism, a cornerstone of its reliability. Independence of spirit and mind, rather than neutrality, is the principle journalists must keep in focus. While editorialists and commentators are not neutral, the source of their credibility is still their accuracy, intellectual fairness and ability to inform--not their devotion to a certain group or outcome. In our independence, however, we must avoid any tendency to stray into arrogance, elitism, isolation or nihilism.

### It must Serve as an Independent Monitor of Power

Journalism has an unusual capacity to serve as watchdog over those whose power and position most affect citizens. The Founders recognized this to be a rampart against despotism when they ensured an independent press; courts have affirmed it; citizens rely on it. As journalists, we have an obligation to protect this watchdog freedom by not demeaning it in frivolous use or exploiting it for commercial gain.

### It must Provide a Forum for Public Criticism and Compromise

The news media are the common carriers of public discussion, and this responsibility forms a basis for our special privileges. This discussion serves society best when it is informed by facts rather than prejudice and supposition. It also should strive to fairly represent the varied viewpoints and interests in society, and to place them in context rather than highlight only the conflicting fringes of debate. Accuracy and truthfulness require that as framers of the public discussion we not neglect the points of common ground where problem solving occurs.

### It must Strive to Make the Significant Interesting and Relevant

Journalism is story-telling with a purpose. It should do more than gather an audience or catalogue the important. For its own survival, it must balance what readers know they want with what they cannot anticipate but need. In short, it must strive to make the significant interesting and relevant. The effectiveness of a piece of journalism is measured both by how much a work engages its audience and enlightens it. This means journalists must continually ask what information has most value to citizens and in what form. While journalism should reach beyond such topics as government and public safety, a journalism overwhelmed by trivia and false significance ultimately engenders a trivial society.

### It must keep the News Comprehensive and Proportional

Keeping news in proportion and not leaving important things out are also cornerstones of truthfulness. Journalism is a form of cartography: it creates a map for citizens to navigate society. Inflating events for sensation, neglecting others, stereotyping or being disproportionately negative all make a less reliable map. The map also should include news of all our communities, not just those with attractive demographics. This is best achieved by newsrooms with a diversity of backgrounds and perspectives. The map is only an analogy; proportion and comprehensiveness are subjective, yet their elusiveness does not lessen their significance.

### Its Practitioners must be Allowed to Exercise their Personal Conscience

Every journalist must have a personal sense of ethics and responsibility--a moral compass. Each of us must be willing, if fairness and accuracy require, to voice differences with our colleagues, whether in the newsroom or the executive suite. News organizations do well to nurture this independence by encouraging individuals to speak their minds. This stimulates the intellectual diversity necessary to understand and accurately cover an increasingly diverse society. It is this diversity of minds and voices, not just numbers, that matters.

## ETHICS OF JOURNALISM

The Assembly affirms the following ethical principles for journalism and believes that they should be applied by the profession throughout Europe.

### News and Opinions

1. In addition to the legal rights and obligations set forth in the relevant legal norms, the media have an ethical responsibility towards citizens and society which must be underlined at the present time, when information and communication play a very important role in the formation of citizens' personal attitudes and the development of society and democratic life.
2. The journalist's profession comprises rights and obligations, freedoms and responsibilities.
3. The basic principle of any ethical consideration of journalism is that a clear distinction must be drawn between news and opinions, making it impossible to confuse them. News is information about facts and data, while opinions convey thoughts, ideas, beliefs or value judgments on the part of media companies, publishers or journalists.
4. News broadcasting should be based on truthfulness, ensured by the appropriate means of verification and proof, and impartiality in presentation, description and narration. Rumour must not be confused with news. News headlines and summaries must reflect as closely as possible the substance of the facts and data presented.
5. Expression of opinions may entail thoughts or comments on general ideas or remarks on news relating to actual events. Although opinions are necessarily subjective

and therefore cannot and should not be made subject to the criterion of truthfulness, we must ensure that opinions are expressed honestly and ethically.

6. Opinions taking the form of comments on events or actions relating to individuals or institutions should not attempt to deny or conceal the reality of the facts or data.

The right to information as a fundamental human right- Publishers, proprietors and journalists

7. The media's work is one of "mediation", providing an information service, and the rights which they own in connection with freedom of information depends on its addressees, that is the citizens.
8. Information is a fundamental right which has been highlighted by the case-law of the European Commission and Court of Human Rights relating to Article 10 of the European Convention on Human Rights and recognised under Article 9 of the European Convention on Transfrontier Television, as well as in all democratic constitutions. The owner of the right is the citizen, who also has the related right to demand that the information supplied by journalists be conveyed truthfully, in the case of news, and honestly, in the case of opinions, without outside interference by either the public authorities or the private sector.
9. The public authorities must not consider that they own information. The representativeness of such authorities provides the legal basis for efforts to guarantee and extend pluralism in the media and to ensure that the necessary conditions are created for exercising freedom of expression and the right to information and precluding censorship. Moreover, the Committee of Ministers is aware of this fact, as demonstrated by its Declaration on the Freedom of Expression and Information adopted on 29 April 1982.
10. When dealing with journalism it must be borne in mind that it relies on the media, which are part of a corporate structure within which a distinction must be made

between publishers, proprietors and journalists. To that end, in addition to safeguarding the freedom of the media, freedom within the media must also be protected and internal pressures guarded against.

11. News organisations must consider themselves as special socio-economic agencies whose entrepreneurial objectives have to be limited by the conditions for providing access to a fundamental right.
12. News organisations must show transparency in matters of media ownership and management, enabling citizens to ascertain clearly the identity of proprietors and the extent of their economic interest in the media.
13. Inside the news organisation, publishers and journalists must co-exist, bearing in mind that the legitimate respect for publishers' and owners' ideological orientations is limited by the absolute requirements on truthful news reporting and ethical opinions. This is essential if we are to respect the citizens' fundamental right to information.
14. These requirements are such that we must reinforce the safeguards of the journalist's freedom of expression, for they must in the last instance operate as the ultimate sources of information. In this connection we must legally expand and clarify the nature of the conscience clause and professional secrecy vis-à-vis confidential sources, harmonising national provisions on this matter so that they can be implemented in the wider context of democratic Europe.
15. Neither publishers and proprietors nor journalists should consider that they own the news. News organisations must treat information not as a commodity but as a fundamental right of the citizen. To that end, the media should exploit neither the quality nor the substance of the news or opinions for purposes of boosting readership or audience figures in order to increase advertising revenue.
16. If we are to ensure that information is treated ethically, its target audience must be considered as individuals and not as a mass.

17. Information and communication as conveyed by journalism through the media, with powerful support from the new technologies, has decisive importance for the development of the individual and society. It is indispensable for democratic life, since if democracy is to develop fully it must guarantee citizens participation in public affairs. Suffice it to say that such participation would be impossible if the citizens were not in receipt of the information on public affairs which they need and which must be provided by the media.
18. The importance of information, especially radio and television news, for culture and education was highlighted in Assembly Recommendation 1067. Its effects on public opinion are obvious.
19. It would be wrong to infer from the importance of this role that the media actually represent public opinion or that they should replace the specific functions of the public authorities or institutions of an educational or cultural character such as schools.
20. This would amount to transforming the media and journalism into authorities or counter-authorities ("mediocracy"), even though they would not be representative of the citizens or subject to the same democratic controls as the public authorities, and would not possess the specialist knowledge of the corresponding cultural or educational institutions.
21. Therefore journalism should not alter truthful, impartial information or honest opinions, or exploit them for media purposes, in an attempt to create or shape public opinion, since its legitimacy rests on effective respect for the citizen's fundamental right to information as part of respect for democratic values. To that end, legitimate investigative journalism is limited by the veracity and honesty of information and opinions and is incompatible with journalistic campaigns conducted on the basis of previously adopted positions and special interests.
22. In journalism, information and opinions must respect the presumption of innocence, in particular in cases

which are still sub judice, and must refrain from making judgments.

23. The right of individuals to privacy must be respected. Persons holding office in public life are entitled to protection for their privacy except in those cases where their private life may have an effect on their public life. The fact that a person holds a public post does not deprive him of the right to respect for his privacy.

24. The attempt to strike a balance between the right to respect for private life, enshrined in Article 8 of the European Convention on Human Rights, and the freedom of expression set forth in Article 10, is well documented in the recent case-law of the European Commission and Court of Human Rights.

25. In the journalist's profession the end does not justify the means; therefore information must be obtained by legal and ethical means.

26. At the request of the persons concerned, the news media must correct, automatically and speedily, and with all relevant information provided, any news item or opinion conveyed by them which is false or erroneous. National legislation should provide for appropriate sanctions and, where applicable, compensation.

27. In order to harmonise the application and exercise of this right in the member states of the Council of Europe, we must implement Resolution (74) 26 on the right of reply _ Position of the individual in relation to the press, adopted by the Committee of Ministers on 2 July 1974, and also the relevant provisions of the European Convention on Transfrontier Television.

28. In order to ensure high-quality work and independence on the part of journalists, they must be guaranteed decent pay and proper working conditions and facilities.

29. In the relations which the journalist must maintain in the course of his duties with the public authorities or the various economic sectors, care should be taken to avoid any kind of connivance liable to affect the independence and impartiality of journalism.

30. In journalism, controversial or sensational items must not be confused with subjects on which it is important to provide information. The journalist must not exploit his duties for the principal purpose of acquiring prestige or personal influence.

31. In view of the complexity of the process of providing information, which is increasingly based on the use of new technologies, speed and conciseness, journalists must be required to have appropriate professional training.

32. Within the newspaper business, publishers, proprietors and journalists must live side by side. To that end, rules must be drawn up for editorial staff in order to regulate professional relations between the journalists and the publishers and proprietors within the media, separately from the normal requirements of labour relations. Such rules might provide for the setting up of editorial boards.

33. In society, situations of tension and conflict sometimes arise under the pressure of factors such as terrorism, discrimination against minorities, xenophobia or war. In such circumstances the media have a moral obligation to defend democratic values: respect for human dignity, solving problems by peaceful, tolerant means, and consequently to oppose violence and the language of hatred and confrontation and to reject all discrimination based on culture, sex or religion.

34. No-one should remain neutral vis-à-vis the defence of democratic values. To that end the media must play a major role in preventing tension and must encourage mutual understanding, tolerance and trust between the various communities in regions where conflict prevails, as the Secretary General of the Council of Europe has set out to do with her confidence-building measures in the former Yugoslavia.

35. Having regard to the very specific influence of the media, notably television, on the attitudes of children and young people, care must be taken not to broadcast programmes, messages or images glorifying violence, exploiting sex

and consumerism or using deliberately unsuitable language.

36. Having regard to the requisite conditions and basic principles enumerated above, the media must undertake to submit to firm ethical principles guaranteeing freedom of expression and the fundamental right of citizens to receive truthful information and honest opinions.

37. In order to supervise the implementation of these principles, self-regulatory bodies or mechanisms must be set up comprising publishers, journalists, media users' associations, experts from the academic world and judges; they will be responsible for issuing resolutions on respect for ethical precepts in journalism, with prior commitment on the part of the media to publish the relevant resolutions. This will help the citizen, who has the right to information, to pass either positive or negative judgment on the journalist's work and credibility.

38. The self-regulatory bodies or mechanisms, the media users' associations and the relevant university departments could publish each year the research done a posteriori on the truthfulness of the information broadcast by the media, comparing the news with the actual facts. This would serve as a barometer of credibility which citizens could use as a guide to the ethical standard achieved by each medium or each section of the media, or even each individual journalist. The relevant corrective mechanisms might simultaneously help improve the manner in which the profession of media journalism is pursued.

## PUBLIC SERVICE BROADCASTING

While all countries of the region have legislative frameworks governing the freedom of speech, expression, information and publication, the effect of such laws is to indicate the limits of expression negatively so as to protect the rights of individuals, the interests of the state, law and order and public security. The specific statutes pertaining to radio and television also relate to the content of programmes and the obligation not to condone or incite crime, not to blaspheme or offend religious beliefs and susceptibilities and not to offend good taste or decency. Regulations may also be framed to ensure that these standards are observed.

But state ownership of most radio and television stations puts the onus of monitoring programmes and ensuring the observance of standards on the government itself. There is now in India an attempt to create an independent monitoring body and forum for redressing complaints under the provisions of the Prasar Bharati Act. In Sri Lanka a Media Council Act has been advocated to carry out similar functions.

The structural constraint of state ownership of the electronic media also engenders functional constraints. There is an absence of editorial autonomy for the broadcaster, who is ultimately responsible to the political authorities. Although the five countries under study claim to be democracies, a culture of dialogue that also respects the opinions of dissenters is lacking. For the most part the state in the respective countries uses the public-funded electronic media in a politically partisan manner. The state's justification for such use is that the government of the day needs to project its development activities to the public as an expression of accountability.

In doing so the state overlooks the requirement of the media to inform the public on matters of public interest and to act as a watchdog of governance. This is difficult to realise in a culture of compliance, the absence of authentic professionalism and observance of a concomitant ethic.

The state's attitude to the information process has traditionally been to disclose as little as possible to the media, secrecy being the norm. Where it chooses the path of disclosure it is usually to further the interest of the regime or to embarrass its political opponents. The manipulation of the electronic media that function under government auspices leads to officialisation of the information process. Thereby broadcasters are denied their editorial independence and the professional obligation to observe ethical norms of communication such as accuracy, fairness, objectivity, right of reply and of dissent, and responsiveness to social need.

The absence of a clearly articulated media policy in respect of public-funded media organisations in pluralist societies such as the South Asian often results in propagandist and partisan use of such media, resort to self-censorship and cronyism among communicators.

## HUMAN RIGHTS AND JOURNALISTIC ETHICS

The foregoing critique of state-run and public-funded electronic media institutions is also valid for newspapers that function under state auspices. Some such criticism is also valid for newspapers that are privately owned and deny editorial autonomy to journalists. Nor do such newspapers foster the observance of journalistic ethics in day-to-day functioning by providing for professional training and observance of ethical norms.

Although the newspaper enterprise in most South Asian countries is over 150 years old (except explicitly in Bangladesh and Pakistan for reasons of their recent creation as separate nations) there has been no formal code until recently. However, there are laws pertaining to newspapers and printing presses and the general law, several provisions of which are incorporated in the Penal Code.

It was noted earlier in this essay that private newspapers that were supportive of the ruling power in the respective countries experienced a sense of political, social and economic power. Consequently, they could hire and fire journalists at will and felt that their newspapers had no moral obligation to serve the public interest or to accommodate news and views favourable to those with whom they disagreed or whom they disliked.

It was the intensely partial, divisive and restrictive stance of some newspapers, albeit influential with the ruling elites, which led to public clamour for press commissions in some countries of South Asia. Partly, they were inspired by the initiatives taken in Britain (Royal Commission on the Press, 1947-1949) and in the United States with the publication in 1947 of "A Free and Responsible Press." An independent Commission on the Freedom of the Press issued it. Its report deals with the responsibilities of the owners and managers of the press to their consciences and the common good for the formation of public opinion. The Commission comprised persons of standing drawn from civil society.

The special significance of the US commission is that it predates the Universal Declaration of Human Rights of 1948 and the International Covenant on Civil and Political Rights in 1976, in particular Articles 14, 17 and 19. The Commission focused on the moral aspect of freedom of expression, the right being based on the duty of a person to the common good and to his own thought. "In the absence of moral duties, there are no moral rights," the report states.

The jurisprudence derived from the recognition of human rights and duties, the inspirational religious and cultural values of the South Asian civilisations and a shared public repugnance at the abuse of power by some newspapers and journalists supportive of regimes that were authoritarian led to the appointment of press commissions.

In India the first press commission was set up in 1952 and reported on the status of the press. Its unique feature is that it is multi-lingual, publishing in as many as 90 languages. The ownership pattern of some 25,000 newspapers and journals is varied, the largest number (nearly two thirds) being published by individuals. Their combined share of circulation is about equal to that of newspapers published by joint stock companies. The number of company newspapers is only about one eighteenth of the number published by private individuals. Societies and associations, firms and partnerships, trusts, cooperative societies and educational institutions are among the other publishers of newspapers. This varied pattern of ownership, the multi-lingual character of the press, the diversity of the readership and the absence of an ethic shared by journalists and the public compound the issue of a common code of communication ethics.

The Press Council of India, set up by an Act of Parliament in 1965, was empowered to draft a code of conduct for newspapers, news agencies and journalists in accordance with high professional standards. But it refrained from doing so, hoping that a code would evolve from its own deliberations.

In 1984 the Press Council published an 11-point set of guidelines, which could serve as norms in the event of editors and journalists themselves deciding to draft a code. They were as follows.

- Accuracy and fairness
- Verification before publication
- Respect for privacy
- Recognition of the right of reply
- Restraint in the coverage of communal disputes/clashes
- Avoidance of plagiarism
- Principles regarding recording interviews and phone conversations
- Avoidance of vulgarity and obscenity
- Caution in criticising judicial actions
- Restraint in the use of photographs of bodies of victims of crime/accidents
- Avoidance of crass commercialism

It has been observed that there is a low degree of voluntary compliance with the code. Nevertheless, public faith in the Press Council as a forum for redressing complaints against newspapers is borne out by the number of complaints it receives and investigates. The Council has on occasion deplored conflict between owners and editors that tends to affect editorial freedom as well as the proper functional relationship between the proprietors and the staff engaged in the production of the paper.

A cause of conflict between owners and editors is the interlocking of the press with industry. Consequently, owners warn editors not to be too critical of the government, fearing reprisals that may affect their business interests.

Another ethical issue arises from the attitude to the newspaper as a saleable commodity, expressed by the Managing Director of Benett Coleman and Company, publishers of "The Times of India."

Such an attitude negates the human rights basis of media ethics. It is refreshing therefore to find a Code of Ethics of the All-India Newspapers Editors Conference. In several respects it is similar to the Guidelines of the Indian Press Council.

Significant departures from the Council principles are that journalists are enjoined to promote the unity of the country and to be circumspect in dealing with movements and ideas which promote regionalism at the cost of national unity; the integrity of the country is to be regarded as sacrosanct; confidentiality and professional secrecy; obligations of propriety to fellow journalists, and personal integrity of conduct.

The Code of Conduct 1993 for Newspapers, News Agencies and Journalists of Bangladesh framed under the Press Council Act of 1974 introduces the expression "moral duty" in several of its provisions. Among such moral duties is that the editor must accept full and sole responsibility for all that is published in his newspaper; that journalists should highlight degeneration of moral values in Bangladesh society; and exercise caution in publishing news of man-woman relationships or any report relating to women.

In Nepal the preamble to the Code of Conduct for Journalists (1992) states that the country's new Constitution (1990) has established democratic principles and values, and by enhancing the dignity of the press has placed a greater responsibility on its practitioners to fulfil the professional duty entrusted to them by making it responsible to society.

The Code, issued by the Press Council (initially set up in 1970 and reconstituted in 1992) requires journalists to "always remain dedicated to human values, democratic behaviour, national interest and public welfare."

Another article of the Code states that "news and views leading to communal fighting, terrorism and differences between different races, religious groups and communities should not be entertained."

Another provision states that resort to blackmail through journalism for economic or other benefit "is a serious moral crime." In other respects the Code is comparable with codes elsewhere.

In 1993 the Nepal Journalists Association adopted a Code of Conduct for Journalists, also called the Birgunj Declaration 1993 after the venue of the meeting. While it is similar to other codes for journalists, it is significant in that it requires journalists to be dedicated to ensuring that the people's right to be informed is secured. They are also required to "remain dedicated to human values, democratic culture, the country's well-being and for the public well-being."

The relaxation of restrictions on the Nepalese press owes a great deal to a 1981 Royal Commission on the Press that led to the enactment of the Press and Publications Act of 1982, a measure of reform. The Constitution of 1990 reinforced the liberalisation. Of special interest is Article 16, which states, "Every person shall have the right to demand and receive information on any matter of public importance." The Press and Publications Act of February 1992 further consolidated the earlier gains. Pakistan's articulation of media ethics is unique in that it illustrates how Islam tends to reshape the values and ethics of Pakistan's society.

The authoritarian regime of Field Marshal Ayub Khan had in 1963 promulgated the restrictive Press and Publications Ordinance. It was replaced by a mild regulatory law, the Registration of Press and Publications Ordinance of 1988, as a result of the Federal Shariat Court judgement on a petition which entailed examination of the 1963 Ordinance.

In its judgment the Shariat Court relied heavily on the Islamic Declaration for the mass media prepared and published by the Islamic Press Union. According to the Islamic Declaration, Islam lays great emphasis on freedom of expression and human dignity. It not only gives people the right of dissent but also makes it obligatory on them to protest against tyranny, injustice and oppression.

The Declaration adds, "Islam aims at creating a disciplined society where the rights and obligations of the individuals are in harmony with the broader interests of the community.

"These rights and obligations must not be curtailed, abrogated, suspended or transgressed by individuals, governments, parliaments or other institutions."

The Declaration articulates in some detail the rights of freedom of expression, or protest against injustice and evil and the individual's right to privacy. It goes on to spell out the concept of authenticity, which the media are required to uphold in practice.

Article 19 of the Constitution of the Islamic Republic of Pakistan, besides guaranteeing to citizens freedom of speech and expression, also guarantees freedom of the press, subject, however, to reasonable restrictions imposed by law "in the interest of the glory of Islam, of the integrity, security or defence of Pakistan or any part thereof, friendly relations with foreign states, public order, decency or morality, or in relation to contempt of court, defamation or incitement to any offence."

The Sri Lanka Press Council Code of Ethics for journalists was drawn up in consultation with a group of editors and approved by parliament in October 1981. The Press Council was established in 1973 by an act of parliament. Its institution was recommended by the Press Commission of 1963, which recommended the broadbasing of the ownership of the press besides other matters.

The Code of Ethics is comparable with codes in most Western countries, but many journalists are not aware of its existence nor does it form part of whatever training is provided in newspaper establishments. Even some legislators are unaware that the Code has been there since 1981. The principles enshrined in the Code derive from the human rights jurisprudence, which draws attention to both rights and duties.

## OBSERVANCE OF MEDIA ETHICS

The South Asian experience points to a gulf between the values and norms enshrined in the respective codes and the actual practice of journalism. It derives partly from a mistaken notion that the press is in a privileged position and that journalists are entitled to greater freedom of expression than ordinary citizens. Further, breach of the code of ethics is not punishable by courts except where the infringement is also an offence against some statutory provision.

While freedom of expression is exercised, at times to the point of license, there is insufficient evidence of the duty of care and respect for the rights of others. That the right of expression and publication has to be exercised with responsibility for accuracy, objectivity, fairness and balance appears not to be part of a professional code.

It requires an activist Press Council and a self-regulatory professional body of journalists to ensure high standards of journalism and promotion of the ethical values that the codes seek to uphold. Nevertheless, the interventionist role of the Press Council is minimal. It often acts only on complaints by aggrieved readers. It does not in addition perform a monitoring role. In any case, after inquiry all that the Press Council can do is to order the newspaper to publish a correction; an apology where it is required; and it could reprimand the offending newspaper. It has no penal power. So it tends to be regarded as toothless.

The situation is further compounded by the absence of a public ethic based on a concept of morality and respect for human rights. At times readers tend to consider public curiosity about the private lives of politicians and celebrities a matter of public interest although the private conduct of such persons does not always impinge on the performance of their public duty.

The fact that newspapers are in a competitive industry is another functional constraint on the observance of media ethics. Papers not only strive to be first with the news, but also tend to sensationalise it to get the edge on competitors.

The link between newspaper circulation and advertising also tends to blur the ethical dimension. Dramatisation of news promotes sales and circulation and helps increase advertising revenue. Note the cynical attitude of the proprietors of The Times of India who regard the newspaper primarily as a saleable commodity.

Journalism schools endeavour to instil an awareness of the ethics of principle. But only a very small proportion of South Asian journalists have had pre-entry training in such schools of journalism. In-plant training is mainly craft-oriented. Even if media ethics is part of the curriculum of such training, the practice of journalism leaves much to be desired.

The absence of professional bodies of journalists comparable with bodies for such professions as law, medicine, engineering and accountancy is a drawback to the self-regulation of the profession.

While there are many associations of journalists in the respective countries they function more like trade unions and are concerned mainly with working conditions, salaries, pensions, ancillary facilities and security of service.

The need for codes of media ethics is unquestionable. But codes alone have not been effective in raising ethical standards in the media. This was the consensus of a three-day seminar on "Communication Ethics from a

South Asian Perspective," held in Colombo, Sri Lanka, in November 1993.

The participants included 20 senior journalists and communication scholars from the South Asian region. The seminar was organised by the Asian Media Information and Communication Centre (AMIC) Singapore, the World Association of Christian Communication, UK, and the International Centre for Ethnic Studies, Colombo, with support from the Friedrich Ebert Foundation, Colombo.

The seminar recommended replacement of press councils by media councils, which, unlike the former, should not be perceived as an extension of the state but as genuinely independent bodies. They should comprise respected media practitioners and eminent persons from public life chosen through a mechanism ensured by appropriate legislation.

The seminar also commented on the paucity of professional bodies of media practitioners in the region and called for the status of such bodies to be recognised by both the state and the social community.

It would be the responsibility of such bodies to promote observance of ethical standards among media practitioners and a greater sense of social responsibility among media institutions. While there is a growing degree of awareness among senior media practitioners of the need for adherence to media ethics there is little evidence of discussion of media ethics at the level of media owners. However, there is discussion by media owners on what they perceive as the intrusive role of the state in introducing new regulatory measures especially in relation to electronic media.

Perhaps the weakest aspect of media ethics in South Asia is the absence of an articulate public ethic that could act as a countervailing force to both the state and media institutions.

The restraint on such a cohesive public ethic emerging is media audiences being heterogeneous in composition and values, levels of appreciation of media content, diverse in taste and apparently shunning an activist role in safeguarding cultural values and promoting high standards of media performance.

## JOURNALISM CODES OF ETHICS NOW FOCUSED MORE ON FINANCIAL SUCCESS

What a beautiful idea! Bonnie Brennen and Lee Wilkins, researchers at the Missouri School of Journalism recently analyzed and compared two early codes, the 1923 American Society of Newspaper Editors (ASNE) code and the 1934 American Newspaper Guild (ANG) code, with the 2003 New York Times code of ethics.

They found that changes to the journalism code of ethics have played a significant part in the negative perception of today's media.

**The whole Article:** For the past 15 years, the public's perception of the news media has been becoming more negative, causing historic professional stress for journalists. The industry has moved from privately owned to publicly traded and toward conglomeration of ownership in order to maximize profits. Readership of newspapers and viewership of broadcast news have fallen. A new study by researchers at the University of Missouri-Columbia found that changes to the journalism code of ethics have played a significant part in the negative perception of today's media.

Two journalism professors at MU's School of Journalism, Bonnie Brennen and Lee Wilkins, recently analyzed and compared two early codes, the 1923 American Society of Newspaper Editors (ASNE) code and the 1934 American Newspaper Guild (ANG) code, with the 2003 New York Times code of ethics and found several significant changes and shifts in professional thinking.

"The ASNE code set out to maintain the rights and dignity of the profession and tried to establish ethical standards for journalistic conduct," said Brennen. "For example, the ASNE code says that invasions of privacy should be avoided unless the public warrants such intrusion, and editors are asked to not publish unofficial charges without giving the people the opportunity to defend themselves."

The ANG code, Brennen and Wilkins found, insists that reporters respect the rights of individuals by crafting factual and fair news reports that accurately represent an unbiased account of the news. It gives reporters little room for exceptions or extenuating conditions.

When the researchers looked at the Times code, they found striking differences from the ASNE and ANG code. The Times code focuses mainly on conflicts of interest, economic health and financial success. For example, staff members are prohibited from free-lance work that competes with the Times while noting that the Times sphere of influence is larger than ever. Also, according to the code: "Staff members may not appear on broadcasts that directly compete with the Times' own offerings on television or the Internet...As the paper moves further into these new fields, its direct competitors, clients or potential clients will undoubtedly grow in number."

In terms of conflicts of interest, the code, Brennen and Wilkins said, interprets the subject broadly, linking conflict of interest to perception of the newspaper's impartiality, neutrality and the integrity of news reports. Other elements that influence the integrity of the news reports, such as accuracy and tough-minded evaluation of both sources and the information they provide, are not mentioned in the Times code.

Brennen and Wilkins found that the sections in the code based on economic and financial success of the Times are one of the main fault lines in the profession: the tension between economic goals and the traditional view of journalism as a public service, something emphasized in the earlier codes. The Times, they believe, has placed its economic health on an equal footing with the public trust.

"If the recent Jayson Blair incident is any indication, management's financial concerns as articulated in the ethics code ? Have their parallels in real life," Brennen and Wilkins said. "The emphasis reveals something central about the profession: concerns about financial profitability do remain on an equal footing with journalistic duty and service."

# 4

# Mass Media: Theory and Practices

"Cultivation analysis concentrates on the enduring and common consequences of growing up and living with television. Theories of the cultivation process attempt to understand and explain the dynamics of television as the distinctive and dominant cultural force of our age. Cultivation analysis uses a survey instrument, administered to representative samples of respondents. The responses are analyzed by a number of demographic variables including gender, age, race, education, income, and political self-designation (liberal, moderate, conservative). Where applicable, other controls, such as urban-rural residence, newspaper reading, and party affiliation are also used.

Cultivation analysis is a part of the Cultural Indicators (CI) research project. CI is a data base and a series of reports relating recurrent features of the world of television to viewer conceptions of reality. Its cumulative content data archive contains observations on over 4,500 programmes and 40,000 characters coded according to many thematic, demographic and action categories."

"...specifies that repeated, intense exposure to deviant definitions of 'reality' in the mass media leads to perception of the 'reality' as normal. The result is a social legitimisation of the 'reality' depicted in the mass media, which can influence behavior. (Gerbner, 1973 & 1977; Gerbner et al., 1980.)"

Gerbner first introduced cultivation theory in 1969 with his work Toward "Cultural Indicators": The Analysis of Mass Mediated Public Message Systems. Gerbner begins developing cultivation as a structural piece for the long-term examination of public messages in media influence and understanding. He notes in the introduction that "the approach is based on conception of these message systems as the common culture through which communities cultivate shared and public notions about facts, values, and contingencies of human existence". Gerbner clarifies that his objectives are not with "information, education, persuasion, and the like, or with any kind of direct communication 'effects.'" More accurately, his concern remains with "the collective context within which, and in response to which, different individual and group selections and interpretations of messages take place". Nonetheless, Gerbner's works present a social psychology theory on communication effects, and consequently, on persuasion as related to mass media.

Gerbner speaks of the "cultivation of collective conscious" in relation to the rapid growth of media outlets (in particular, television) and the capacity of mass media to transcend traditional "barriers of time, space, and social grouping". Cultivation then describes the process in which entire publics are affected by content on television. Potter (1993) notes Gerbner's intentions for using "cultivation" as an academic term to define his interest in "the more diffuse effects on perceptions that are shaped over a long period of exposure to media messages". "Cultivation," rather than "long-term effects" indicates the emphasis on the constant nurturing, exposure, and consistent incorporation the viewing public experiences through mass media channels.

## COMMUNICATION

Humans communicate with each other across time, space, and contexts. Those contexts are often thought of as the particular combinations of people comprising a communication situation. For example, theories of interpersonal communication address the communication between dyads (two people). Group communication deals with groups, organizational communication addresses organizations, mass communication encompasses messages broadcast, usually electronically, to mass audiences, intercultural communication looks at communication among people of different cultures, and gender communication focuses on communication issues of women and between the sexes. Newer contexts include health communication and computer-mediated communication.

Contexts of communication are best thought of as a way to focus on certain communication processes and effects. Communication context boundaries are fluid. Thus, we can see interpersonal and group communication in organizations. Gender communication occurs whenever people of different sexes communicate. We can have mass communications to individuals, group, and organizations. Using communication contexts as a means to help us study communication helps us out of problems some people associate with the intrapersonal context (some say the "so-called" intrapersonal context). Some people facetiously say intrapersonal communication exists when someone talks to themselves. It's more accurate to define intrapersonal communication as thinking. While thinking normally falls within the purview of psychology we can recognize that we often think, plan, contemplate, and strategize about communication past, present, and future. It is legitimate to study the cognitive aspects of communication processes. So, even if some people call those cognitive aspects of communication thinking, it can be helpful to allow the context of intrapersonal communication to exist, thereby legitimating an avenue of communication research.

## COORDINATED MANAGEMENT OF MEANING

The Coordinated Management of Meaning theorizes communication as a process that allows us to create and manage social reality. As such, this theory describes how we as communicators make sense of our world, or create meaning. Meaning can be understood to exist in a hierarchy, depending on the sources of that meaning. Those sources include:

1. raw sensory data -- the inputs to your eyes and ears, the visual and auditory stimuli you will interpret to see images and hear sounds;
2. content -- interpreted stimuli, where the words spoken are understood by what they refer to;

3. speech acts -- content takes on more meaning when it is further interpreted as belonging to a speaker who has specific communication styles, relationships with the listener, and intentions;
4. episodes -- in common terms, you may think of this as the context of the conversation or discourse where when you understand the context you understand what the speaker thinks he or she is doing;
5. master contracts -- these define the relationships the communicating participants, or what each can expect of the other in a specific episode;
6. life scripts -- the set of episodes a person expects they will participate in; and
7. cultural patterns -- culturally created set of rules that govern what we understand to be normal communication in a given episode.

Persons use two types of rules to coordinate the management of meaning among those seven levels of meaning. First, we use constitutive rules to help understand how meaning at one level determine meaning at another level. Second, we use regulative rules to help us regulate what we say so that we stay within what we consider to be normal communication in a given episode.

## THE MEANING

The first concept most students learn about the meaning of meanings is the Semantic Triangle. This label refers to the three part connection among a referent, a reference, and a symbol. The referent is the thing, such as my cat Baxter. The reference is the thought I have of Baxter, a 12 year old grey tabby who loves to lounge on my computer keyboard. The symbol is the word "Baxter." Notice that if I am talking about Baxter I have selected the referent and have control over the reference and symbol. However, if I talk to you about Baxter lounging on my keyboard you will not understand my meaning until you understand the thing (the referent) I am speaking of and the thoughts (references) I have of that thing.

The Semantic Triangle allows for some ambiguity. After all, it is not possible for you to know exactly what my thoughts are. Still, there needs to be ways for people to help make sure they are understand by others, especially when referents, references, or symbols are new to one or more of the communicators. There are four ways in which we help each other understand what we mean:

1. Definitions -- these tell others what is in our heads, or what we mean when we use a certain word;
2. Metaphors -- metaphors allow us to talk about something unfamiliar in terms of something else that is familiar. Metaphors also allow us to merge two concepts whose result is a third concept. For example, I could speak of Baxter as a furry bundle of energy.
3. Feedforward -- this is the process of providing feedback to ourselves before we even speak, so that we help ourselves choose the best way to communicate in a given situation to a given audience; and
4. Basic English -- the set of 850 words out of which any person can effectively communicate ideas, simple or complex.

## SEMIOTICS

Semiotics is concerned with signs and their relationship with objects and meaning. One way to view signs is to consider them composed of a signifier and a signified. Simply put, the signifier is the sound associated with or image of something (e.g., a tree), the signified is the idea or concept of the thing (e.g., the idea of a tree), and the sign is the object that combines the signifier and the signified into a meaningful unit. Stated differently, the sign is the relationship between the concept and the representation of that concept. For example, when I was a child I had a stuffed animal. OK, it was a stuffed green rat, but it was a smiling rat. That rat was the signifier. Think what a stuffed animal could signify to a child. In my case, it signified safety, warmth, and comfort. So, when I walked into my room and looked at my stuffed green rat it was a sign to me that everything was OK. Notice that the signifier and the signified cannot be separated and still provide a meaningful basis for the sign.

Today, that stuffed green rat is just a memory to me. I cannot even recall what I named it. In fact, as time passed that rat became a sign of something else. The rat is still a signifier but it signifies my early childhood when the world seemed calm, safe, and inviting. Now the rat could be considered a sign of my youthful innocence, long past and hard to remember, just like the name of that rat.

## SYMBOLIC INTERACTIONISM

Symbolic Interactionism is based on three assumptions:

1. communication occurs through the creation of shared significant symbols,
2. the self is constructed through communication, and
3. social activity becomes possible through the role-taking process.

You can get a basic grasp of this theory by learning its keywords and how they fit together.

I -- the active portion of the self capable of performing behaviors.

Me -- the socially reflective portion of the self, providing social control for the actions of the I.

Self -- the combination of the I and the Me. Self is a process, not a structure. The I acts and the me defines the self as reflective of others.

Self-indication -- experience and feedback as the I acts and the Me observes the I from the role of the Other. The Me then gives direction regarding future action to the I.

Generalized Other -- the typical members of a society or culture.

Specific Other -- the idea of a specific person outside the Self.

Role Taking -- putting oneself in the place of another, or waling in someone else's shoes. We learn to Role Take by Play and Games.

Play -- activity where a child is both the self and an other, without recognizing the self. The child plays both roles without recognizing the self in either role.

Game -- interaction where the child has the attitude of all the others involved in the game. The child is the self but can recognize the other's perspectives. Thus, behavior is not a response but an interpretive process. The individual can comprehend the self only through interaction with other people.

Gesture (nonsymbolic) Interaction--an impulsive and spontaneous action in the sense of a reflex response (e.g., pulling your hand away quickly when after it touches something hot).

Symbolic Interaction -- an interpretation of a symbol.

Symbol -- the representation of one thing for another thing.

Significant Symbol -- a symbol that has shared meaning (e.g., the words in a language).

Mind -- a social, behavioral process in which the human being is capable of acting toward and even creating his or her environment, or objects in the environment.

## ATTRIBUTION THEORY

Attribution Theory assumes that people try to determine why people do what they do. This search for a reason behind behavior allows people to attribute causes to behavior. A behavioral cause could be situational, where a person had to do something because of the situation they were in. A behavioral cause could also result from something unique to person. Examples of those unique attributes include, but are not limited to:

1. the person's desire to perform the behavior (e.g., they did it because they wanted to do it),
2. the person's whim (e.g., they did it because they felt like doing it),
3. the person's ability (e.g., the person is capable of doing the behavior),
4. the person's sense of obligation (e.g., the person did it because they felt they had to or should do the behavior), and
5. the person's sense of belonging (e.g., the person did it to fit in with a group of people important to the person).

A person seeking to understand why another person did something may attribute one or more causes to that behavior. However, a three-stage process leads up to the final attribution:

1. the person must perceive or observe the behavior,
2. then the person must believe that the behavior was intentionally performed, and
3. then the person must determine if they believe the other person was forced to perform the behavior (in which case the cause is attributed to the situation) or not (in which case the cause is attributed to the other person).

## CONSTRUCTIVISM

Constructivism makes three assumptions regarding communication:

1. all communication is intentional
2. communication is goal-driven
3. negotiation comes into play with shared interpretation (meaning)

Constructivism focuses on individuals rather than interactions. It tries to account for why people make the certain communicative choices. Constructs are the basis of constructivism. They are dimensions of judgment and can be thought of as filters, files, templates, or interpretive schemes. They are domain specific, almost exclusively focusing on interpersonal message variations. Constructs are assumed to change over time, following Werner's Orthogenetic Principle (impressions start globally, undifferentiated, and unorganized then get more complex, abstract, differentiated, and organized as people develop).

Constructivist research uses the Role Category Question to find constructs embedded in free response writing, often about a person the writer likes and a person the writer dislikes. The more constructs a person uses the more cognitively differentiated they are. Cognitive differentiation is a subset of cognitive complexity, which measures the organization, quantity, and level of abstractness of the constructs a person holds about another person. Cognitive differentiation measures only the quantity of constructs but still predicts the degree to which a communicator is person centered and other oriented. Constructivism claims that the more cognitively differentiated a person is the more likely they are to be a competent communicator (one who intentionally uses knowledge of shared interpretations to express meaning is such a way as to control another person's interpretations of some event, object, person, etc.).

Constructivist research shows moderately strong correlations between the organizational level of a person and cognitive differentiation, persuasive ability, and perspective taking. Smaller correlations have been found between organizational level and self monitoring.

## ELABORATION LIKELIHOOD MODEL

The Elaboration Likelihood Model claims that there are two paths to persuasion: the central path and the peripheral path. The central path is most appropriately used when the receiver is motivated to think about the message and has the ability to think about the message. If the person cares about the issue and has access to the message with a minimum of distraction, then that person will elaborate on the message. Lasting persuasion is likely if the receiver thinks, or rehearses, favorable thoughts about the message. A boomerang effect (moving away from the advocated position) is likely to occur if the subject rehearses unfavorable thoughts about the message. If the message is ambiguous but pro-attitudinal (in line with the receiver's attitudes) then persuasion is likely. If the message is ambiguous but counter-attitudinal then a boomerang effect is likely.

If the message is ambiguous but attitudinally neutral (with respect to the receiver) or if the receiver is unable or not motivated to listen to the message then the receiver will look for a peripheral cue. Peripheral cues include such communication strategies as trying to associate the advocated position with things the receiver already thinks postively towards (e.g., food, money, sex), using an expert appeal, and attempting a contrast effect where the advocated position is presented after several other positions, which the receiver despises, have been presented. If the peripheral cue association is accepted then there may be a temporary attitude change and possibly future elaboration. If the peripheral cue association is not accepted, or if it is not present, then the person retains the attitude initially held.

If the receiver is motivated and able to elaborate on the message and if there are compelling arguments to use, then the central route to persuasion should be used. If the receiver is unlikely to elaborate the message, or if the available arguments are weak, then the peripheral route to persuasion should be used.

## SOCIAL JUDGMENT THEORY

The key point of the Social Judgment Theory is that attitude change (persuasion) is mediated by judgmental processes and effects. Put differently, persuasion occurs at the end of the process where a person understands a message then compares the position it advocates to the person's position on that issue. A person's position on an issue is dependent on:

1. the person's most preferred position (their anchor point),
2. the person's judgment of the various alternatives (spread across their latitudes of acceptance, rejection, and noncommitment), and
3. the person's level of ego-involvement with the issue.

Consider the course choices available to you next term. For the sake of argument, let's say you have four required courses to finish but have one three credit hour elective remaining. What courses open to you would you definitely not enroll in, no matter what? Those courses fall in your Latitude of Rejection. Do you think anyone could persuade you to take a class that falls in that latitude? Not likely. And, the more ego-involved you are in the decision to enroll in your course (the more you care about that decision) the larger your Latitude of Rejection will be. Persuasive messages that advocate positions in your Latitude of Rejection will be contrasted by you. That is, they will appear to be further away from your anchor point than they actually are. That's not good news for the would-be persuader.

Now consider the courses that you really don't have an opinion about, that you don't have positive or negative feelings toward. Those courses fall in your Latitude of Noncommitment. It's possible that someone could persuade you to enroll in one of those courses, but you'd have to learn more about the course first, at least enough until you an opinion, or judgment, about it. Now, consider all those courses you would consider enrolling in. Those courses fall in your Latitude of Acceptance. A person with good arguments might be able to persuade you to take one of those courses, especially if, in your judgment, the course is similar to your anchor point course. Persuasive messages that advocate positions in your Latitude of Acceptance will be assimilated by you. That is, they will appear to be closer to your anchor point than they actually are. That's good news for the would-be persuader.

If you are persuaded, then the further a message's position is away from your anchor point, the larger your attitude change will be. But remember that it is very unlikely that you will be persuaded out of your Latitude of Rejection. So, once a message enters that region and moves away from your anchor point, the amount of your attitude change decreases.

## SOCIAL PENETRATION THEORY

Social Penetration Theory asserts that as relationships develop persons communication from superficial to deeply personal topics, slowing penetrating the communicators' public persona to reach their core personality or sense of self. First viewed as a direct, continuous penetration from public person to private person, social penetration is know considered to be a cyclical and dialectical. Relationships have normal ebbs and flows. They do not automatically get better and better where the participants learn more and more about each other. Instead, the participants have to work through the tensions of the relationship (the dialectic) while they learn and group themselves and a parties in a relationships. At times the relationships is very open and sharing. Other time, one or both parties to the relationship need their space, or have other concerns, and the relationship is less open. The theory posits that these cycles occur throughout the life of the relationship as the persons try to balance their needs for privacy and open relationship.

-Persons allow other people to penetrate their public self when they disclose personal information. The decision to disclose is based on the perceived rewards the person will gain if he or she discloses information. If a person perceives that the cost of disclosing information is greater than the rewards for disclosing information then no information will be disclosed. The larger the reward-cost ratio the more disclosure takes place. If you think to the relationships you have been in you will probably find that in almost all of them more disclosure took place at the outset of the relationship than at any other place. That happens because people initially disclose superficial information that costs very little if another person finds it out. It matters little if you know that I enjoy all types of music but especially enjoy listening to blues, saxophone jazz, and straightforward rock-n-roll.

It gets a bit more personal when I start explaining why I like those types of music, so I, like most people, will wait until you reciprocate and tell me your favorite types of music before I allow you more visibility into who I am. The deeper I allow you to penetrate my self, the more affective information I will disclose to you. The closer you get to my core self the higher my perceived costs will be for disclosing that information. Thus, it is not likely that I will disclose very personal information to very many people.

## UNCERTAINTY REDUCTION

The Uncertainty Reduction Theory asserts that people have a need to reduce uncertainty about others by gaining information about them. Information gained can then be used to predict the others' behavior. Reducing uncertainty is particularly important in relationship development, so it is typical to find more uncertainty reduction behavior among people when they expect or want to develop a relationship than among people who expect or know they will not develop a relationship. Consider how you try to reduce uncertainty about someone you have just met and want to spend more time with. Now consider how you try to reduce uncertainty about people you meet on an elevator.

There are three basic ways people seek information about another person:

1. Passive strategies -- we observe the person, either in situations where the other person is likely to be self-monitoring* (a reactivity search) as in a classroom, or where the other person is likely to act more naturally (a disinhibition search) as in the stands at a football game.
2. Active strategies -- we ask others about the person we're interested in or try to set up a situation where we can observe that person (e.g., taking the same class, sitting a table away at dinner). Once the situation is set up we sometime observe (a passive strategy) or talk with the person (an interactive strategy).
3. Interactive strategies -- we communicate directly with the person.

* Self-monitoring is a behavior where we watch and strategically manipulate how we present ourselves to others.

## GROUPTHINK

Groupthink occurs when a homogenous highly cohesive group is so concerned with maintaining unanimity that they fail to evaluate all their alternatives and options. Groupthink members see themselves as part of an in-group working against an outgroup opposed to their goals. You can tell if a group suffers from groupthink if it:

1. overestimates its invulnerability or high moral stance,
2. collectively rationalizes the decisions it makes,
3. demonizes or stereotypes outgroups and their leaders,
4. has a culture of uniformity where individuals censor themselves and others so that the facade of group unanimty is maintained, and
5. contains members who take it upon themselves to protect the group leader by keeping information, theirs or other group members', from the leader.

Groups engaged in groupthink tend to make faulty decisions when compared to the decisions that could have been reached using a fair, open, and rational decision-making process. Groupthinking groups tend to:

1. fail to adequately determine their objectives and alternatives,
2. fail to adequately assess the risks associated with the group's decision,
3. fail to cycle through discarded alternatives to reexamine their worth after a majority of the group discarded the alternative,
4. not seek expert advice,
5. select and use only information that supports their position and conclusions, and
6. does not make contingency plans in case their decision and resulting actions fail.

Group leaders can prevent groupthink by:

1. encouraging members to raise objections and concerns;
2. refraining from stating their preferences at the onset of the group's activities;
3. allowing the group to be independently evaluated by a separate group with a different leader;
4. splitting the group into sub-groups, each with different chairpersons, to separately generate alternatives, then bringing the sub-groups together to hammer out differences;
5. allowing group members to get feedback on the group's decisions from their own constituents;
6. seeking input from experts outside the group;
7. assigning one or more members to play the role of the devil's advocate;
8. requiring the group to develop multiple scenarios of events upon which they are acting, and contingencies for each scenario; and
9. calling a meeting after a decision consensus is reached in which all group members are expected to critically review the decision before final approval is given.

## ORGANIZING

Karl Weick writes of the process oriented organizing, rather than the structural oriented organization. Communication is key to the organizing process because it is a large factor in the sense-making process people use when they organize. The sense-making process is an attempt to reduce equivocality, or multiple meanings, in the information used by the people in the organization. When information is handled by the organizers they go through the stages of:

1. enactment -- where they define the situation and begin the process of dealing with the information,
2. selection -- where they narrow the equivocality by deciding what to deal with and what to leave along, ignore, or disregard, and
3. retention -- where they decide what information, and its meaning, they will retain for future use.

In both the selection and retention stages there are additional processes. These processes depend on double interacts. An act occurs when you say something ("Can I have a popsicle?"). An interact occurs when you say something and I respond ("No, it will spoil you dinner."). A double interact occurs when you say something, I respond, then you respond to that, adjusting your first statement ("Well, how about half a popsicle?"). Double interacts works in:

1. assembly rules -- the operating procedures (e.g., all requests for information from the media must be handled by the Corporate Communications Dept., requests for pay raises must be made through your immediate supervisor, etc.) used by the company to choose what to do maximize the likelihood of achieving the goal at hand, and in the
2. behavior cycles -- sets of double interacts the organization uses to facilitate the selection and retention process. Examples of behavior cycles include staff meetings, coffee-break rumoring, e-mail conversations, internal reports, etc.

Weick sees the the organization as a system taking in equivocal information from its environment, trying to make sense of that information, and using what was learned in the future. As such, organizations evolve as they make sense out of themselves and their environment.

## MUTED GROUP THEORY

Muted Group Theory is a critical theory because it is concerned with power and how it is used against people. While critical theories can separate the powerful and the powerless any number of ways, this theory chooses to bifurcate the power spectrum into men and women.

Muted Group Theory begins with the premise that language is culture bound, and because men have more power than women, men have more influence over the language, resulting in language with a male-bias. Men create the words and meaning for the culture, allowing expression of their ideas. Women, on the other hand, are left out of this meaning creation and left without a means to express that which is unique to them. That leaves women as a muted group.

The Muted Group Theory rests on three assumptions:

1. Men and women perceive the world differently because they have different perception shaping experiences. Those different experiences are a result of men and women performing different tasks in society.
2. Men enact their power politically, perpetuating their power and suppressing women's ideas and meanings from gaining public acceptance.
3. Women must convert their unique ideas, experiences, and meanings into male language in order to be heard.

The premise and assumptions leads to a number of hypotheses about women's communication:

1. Women have a more difficult time expressing themselves than do men.
2. Women understand what men mean more easily than men understand what women mean.
3. Women communicate with each other using media not accepted by the dominant male communicators.

4. Women are less satisfied with communication than are men.
5. Women are not likely to create new words, but sometimes do so to create meanings special and unique to women.

Muted Group Theory does not claim that these differences are based in biology. Instead, the theory claims that men risk losing their dominant position if they listen to women, incorporate their experiences in the language, and allow women to be equal partners in language use and creation. Language is about power, and men have it.

## FACE

Erving Goffman wrote about face in conjunction with how people interact in daily life. He claims that everyone is concerned, to some extent, with how others perceive them. We act socially, striving to maintain the identity we create for others to see. This identity, or public self-image, is what we project when we interact socially. To lose face is to publicly suffer a diminished self-image. Maintaining face is accomplished by taking a line while interacting socially. A line is what the person says and does during that interaction showing how the person understands the situation at hand and the person's evaluation of the interactants. Social interaction is a process combining line and face, or face work. Brown and Levinson use the concept of face to explain politeness. To them, politeness is universal, resulting from people's face needs:

1. Positive face is the desire to be liked, appreciated, approved, etc.
2. Negative face is the desire not to be imposed upon, intruded, or otherwise put upon.

Positive politeness addresses positive face concerns, often by showing prosocial concern for the other's face. Negative politeness addresses negative face concerns, often by acknowledging the other's face is threatened. Anytime a person threatens another person's face, the first person commits a face-threatening act (FTA). Face-threatening acts come in four varieties, listed below in order from most to least face threatening:

1. Do an FTA baldly, with no politeness (e.g., "Close your mouth when you eat you swine.").
2. Do an FTA with positive politeness (e.g., "You have such beautiful teeth. I just wish I didn't see them when you eat.").
3. Do an FTA with negative politeness (e.g., "I know you're very hungry and that steak is a bit tough, but I would appreciate it if you would chew with your mouth closed.").
4. Do an FTA indirectly, or off-record (e.g.; "I wonder how far a person's lips can stretch yet remain closed when eating?"). An indirect FTA is ambiguous so the receiver may "catch the drift" but the speaker can also deny a meaning if they wish.

Of course, a person can choose not to threaten another's face at all, but when a face must be threaten, a speaker can decide how threatening he or she will be.

## THE SPIRAL OF SILENCE

The Spiral of Silence is a model of why people are unwilling to publicly express their opinions when they believe they are in the minority. The model is based on three premises:

1. people have a "quasi-statistical organ," a sixth-sense if you will, which allows them to know the prevailing public opinion, even without access to polls,
2. people have a fear of isolation and know what behaviors will increase their likelihood of being socially isolated, and
3. people are reticent to express their minority views, primarily out of fear of being isolated.

The closer a person believes the opinion held is similar to the prevailing public opinion, the more they are willing to openly disclose that opinion in public. Then, if public sentiment changes, the person will recognize that the opinion is less in favor and will be less willing to express that opinion publicly. As the perceived distance between public opinion and a person's personal opinion grows, the more unlikely the person is to express their opinion.

Consider the case of Dennis Rodman, one of the stars of the Chicago Bulls basketball team. Mr. Rodman has consistently been an incredible competitor and rebounder for the Detroit Pistons, San Antonio Spurs, and Chicago Bulls. Over the years he attracted a large fan base, but watched it fall in recent years as he got "weirder" or more "individualistic" (depending on how you interpret his behavior). Fans in San Antonio welcomed Mr. Rodman when he first arrived, but vocal supporters were hard to find just before he was traded to Chicago. At the start of the 1996-1997 season Mr. Rodman's stock was high in Chicago, falling off somewhat after the "kick the cameraman" incident. I wish him well, but if the public becomes displeased with him the Spiral of Silence will strike his supporters once again.

## STANDARD FORMAT FOR A SOCIAL SCIENTIFIC JOURNAL ARTICLE

Social scientific research reports and journal articles are designed to describe what researchers did, why they did it, how they did it, what they found, and what that means. While all journals have their specific requirements, all research reports and journal articles follow the same standard format. The format is standardized to make it easy for readers to study research presented in a variety of journals. The speed with which you read journal articles and the understanding you gain from those articles will increase once you become familiar with the standard format.

1. *Title:* The title should be brief but clearly describe the focus of the research described in the article.
2. *Author(s):* The names of all authors is given. The institutional affiliation is also given, sometimes with the authors' names, sometimes at the bottom of the first page, sometimes at the end of the article, and sometimes at the end of the journal.
3. *Abstract:* The abstract is a brief summary of the article designed to give the reader an overview of what the researchers did, how they did it, what they found, and what it means.
4. *Introduction:* This section describes all prior research and theories that all relevant to the study described in

the article. That prior literature is integrated to form the basis of an argument(s) supporting why the present study was conducted. The introduction also introduces and argumentatively supports whatever research hypotheses and/or research questions are addresses in the study.

5. *Method:* This section describes what the researchers did. The section is written in sufficient detail and precision to allow a reader to replicate the study. There are exceptions to this principle of replication (e.g., lengthy surveys are not normally included, complex and detailed instructions to experimental subjects are often summarized, etc.). The method section contains as many of these five subsections as are appropriate for the study:

   *Subjects:* The demographics of the persons used in the study.

   *Apparatus:* Detailed description of special equipment used, if any, in the study.

   *Procedures:* Detailed description of what the researchers and subjects did.

   *Design:* Description of the type of experimental design used in the study.

   *Materials or Measures:* Description of which testing and measuring instruments were used, and how they were used if differently than their normal use.

6. *Results:* This section describes what the researchers found. You will often find this section to be a mixture of statistical reports, tables, and prose describing those numbers.

7. *Discussion:* This section provides the authors' the opportunity to tell what their research results mean, both to the study and to the world at large.

8. *References:* A list of all works (e.g., books, articles, personal communication, etc.) cited in the study. Most, and usually all, of the cited works will be cited and discussed in the introduction section of the article.

Readers familiar with statistical analyses and the theories, prior research, and methodologies used in field related to the article should have no problem understanding the article. Readers lacking familiarity with field related theories, research, and methodology usually have some difficulties grasping the big picture of the study, but if the article is well written the readers can understand enough to understand the gist of the study. Readers unfamiliar with statistical analyses fare worse. These readers often entirely skip the Method and Results section, relying solely on the Introduction and Discussion sections. When read alone, the Introduction and Discussion sections can work well to provide the reader with an overview of the study. However, these sections generally stay at a higher level, leaving the details for the Method and Results sections. Often, the prize is in the details.

Certainly, the Results section contains the basis for determining the validity of information in the Discussion section. Readers lacking statistical analyses expertise will be best served by taking a course on experimental design and statistical analysis, preferably in the same discipline as the journal articles they read (e.g., readers of communication articles benefit from an experimental design and statistical analysis course offered by the communication department, readers of psychology articles benefit from an experimental design and statistical analysis course offered by the psychology department, etc.).

An abstract is presented to the reader before the beginning of an article. The abstract briefly tells what the researchers did, how they did it, what they found, and what that means. More specifically, an abstract of an social scientific study will describe:

1. the problem being investigated or question being answer,
2. the subjects, along with key information about those subjects,
3. the experimental method(s) used,
4. the results of the study, including statistical significance levels; and
5. what the results mean, both in the study and with regard to prior research, theories, and the world outside the research lab.

A properly written abstract will convey all that information in about 100 to 120 words. There should be no reason to refer to the article to understand jargon, abbreviations, or other oddities in the abstract.

Use abstracts to gain a first glance into journal articles. When you are researching a particular topic you can usually tell if a journal article pertains to that topic just by reading the abstract. If you determine that the article is relevant then be sure to read the entire article. Be aware that when a journal article reports multiple significant findings only the most important four or five will be mentioned in the abstract. When writing about a journal article never rely solely on the abstract (unless you absolutely cannot find the journal article, then be sure to cite the abstract, not the article).

## MEDIA CONTROL

"The conditions associated with a particular class of conditions of existence produce habitus, systems of durable, transportable dispositions, structured structures predisposed to function as structuring structures, that is, as principles which generate and organize practices and representations that can be objectively adapted to their outcomes without presupposing a conscious aiming at ends or an express mastery of the operations necessary in order to attain them. Objectively 'regulated' and 'regular' without being in any way the product of obedience to rules, they can be collectively orchestrated without being the product of the organizing actions of a conductor" (Bourdieu, p. 53)

The above quote by Bourdieu, when viewed from the perspective of the society as the 'habitus', is quiet informing (in theory as well as in practice) of media's interplay with the social structures within which they are embedded. As we have seen throughout our course readings, media technologies-as important instruments at various levels of communication processes in the society, have encountered resistance by various cultural and social norms, and somewhat mixed response from economical and political forces because of their profit making potentials or power generation ability. More then any other type of technology, media and communication technologies have been the subject of public and scholarly debates because of their intrinsic characteristics to be able to convey (asynchronously) content across time and space (at distance), inscribed in form of data, information, images, knowledge, and wisdom, in mediums such as books, data tape drives, CD-ROMS, video and audio tapes, etc. Additionally, synchronous communication has enabled instantaneous communication among people (e.g. telephone, audio and video conferencing, online chat) enabling efficient, but not necessarily effective exchange of information, ideas, thoughts, and concepts.

The pervasive and widespread use of media technologies, often used ubiquitously for symbolic purposes, is also used by the governing elites to maintain the status quo and ensure stability. The necessity to reproduce and maintain a stable state, the habitus (to borrow from Bourdieu whose habitus concept is similar to the stable state produced and maintained by the hegemonic ideology), requires ways for disseminating cultural and political material of the dominant ideology. Similarly to how Bourdieu describes the functioning of the habitus, Gitlin defines the status quo as hegemony, "a ruling class's (or alliance's) domination of subordinate classes and groups through the elaboration and penetration of ideology (ideas and assumptions) into their common sense and everyday practice," and contends that it "is systematic (but not necessary or even usually deliberate) engineering of mass consent to established order" (Gitlin, 1980, pp. 253). Further, elaborating on the aspect of hegemony and clarifying the composition of the elite, mostly government, corporate establishment and those institutions that produce cultural artifacts, Schiller (1996) explains their economic reason for cooperation: "The American economy is now hostage to a relatively small number of giant private companies, with interlocking connections, that set the national agenda. This power is particularly characteristic of the communication and information sector where the national cultural-media agenda is provided by a very small (and declining) number of integrated private combines. This development has deeply eroded free individual expression, a vital element of a democratic society" (Schiller, 1996, p. 44).

This paper will attempt to elaborate on the interplay between media and communication technologies, and social structures and forces (social, cultural, economical, political), whether institutionalized or not, emphasizing that both the content and the channels of communication through which the content is distributed are important factors in the production, maintenance and further reproduction of the artifacts of the dominant ideology. I will argue that the content that is being represented and recorded, when conveyed via open communication (such as the Internet), can show us the liberating potentials of various media technologies. As such, communication technologies are situated as important actors in the process to displacing or shifting the status quo.

"The conditions associated with a particular class of conditions of existence produce habitus, systems of durable, transportable dispositions, structured structures predisposed to function as structuring structures, that is, as principles which generate and organize practices and representations that can be objectively adapted to their outcomes without presupposing a conscious aiming at ends or an express mastery of the operations necessary in order to attain them. Objectively 'regulated' and 'regular' without being in any way the product of obedience to rules, they can be collectively orchestrated without being the product of the organizing actions of a conductor" (Bourdieu, p. 53)

The above quote by Bourdieu, when viewed from the perspective of the society as the 'habitus', is quiet informing (in theory as well as in practice) of media's interplay with the social structures within which they are embedded. As we have seen throughout our course readings, media technologies-as important instruments at various levels of communication processes in the society, have encountered resistance by various cultural and social norms, and somewhat mixed response from economical and political forces because of their profit making potentials or power generation ability. More then any other type of technology, media and communication technologies have been the subject of public and scholarly debates because of their intrinsic characteristics to be able to convey (asynchronously) content across time and space (at distance), inscribed in form of data, information, images, knowledge, and wisdom, in mediums such as books, data tape drives, CD-ROMS, video and audio tapes, etc. Additionally, synchronous communication has enabled instantaneous communication among people (e.g. telephone, audio and video conferencing, online chat) enabling efficient, but not necessarily effective exchange of information, ideas, thoughts, and concepts.

The pervasive and widespread use of media technologies, often used ubiquitously for symbolic purposes, is also used by the governing elites to maintain the status quo and ensure stability. The necessity to reproduce and maintain a stable state, the habitus (to borrow from Bourdieu whose habitus concept is similar to the stable state produced and maintained by the hegemonic ideology), requires ways for disseminating cultural and political material of the dominant ideology. Similarly to how Bourdieu describes the functioning of the habitus, Gitlin defines the status quo as hegemony, "a ruling class's (or alliance's) domination of subordinate classes and groups through the elaboration and penetration of ideology (ideas and assumptions) into their common sense and everyday practice," and contends that it "is systematic (but not necessary or even usually deliberate) engineering of mass consent to established order" (Gitlin, 1980, pp. 253). Further, elaborating on the aspect of hegemony and clarifying the composition of the elite, mostly government, corporate establishment and those institutions that produce cultural artifacts, Schiller (1996) explains their economic reason for cooperation: "The American economy is now hostage to a relatively small number of giant private companies, with interlocking connections, that set the national agenda. This power is particularly characteristic of the communication and information sector where the national cultural-media agenda is provided by a very small (and declining) number of integrated private combines. This development has deeply eroded free individual expression, a vital element of a democratic society" (Schiller, 1996, p. 44).

This paper will attempt to elaborate on the interplay between media and communication technologies, and social structures and forces (social, cultural, economical, political), whether institutionalized or not, emphasizing that both the content and the channels of communication through which the content is distributed are important factors in the production, maintenance and further reproduction of the artifacts of the dominant ideology. I will argue that the content that is being represented and recorded, when conveyed via open communication (such as the Internet), can show us the liberating potentials of various media technologies. As such, communication technologies are situated as important actors in the process to displacing or shifting the status quo.

Evident from Gitlin's and Schiller's arguments is their emphasis on the necessity of free and open communication among the masses if there is to be any deliverance from the 'claws' of the media. On the contrary, it is the one-way communication (radio, TV, cable) utilized by the elites to achieve the subordination and dissemination of the hegemonic ideology. Fiske (1996) further elaborates this in his argument that surveillance technology is also used as means to discern the norms and regulations necessary to maintain the hegemony ideology: "Norms are crucial to any surveillance system, for without them it cannot identify the abnormal. Norms are what enable it to decide what information should be turned into knowledge and what individuals need to be monitored" (Fiske 1996, p. 220). Fiske's technologised surveillance of the physical goes hand-in-hand with surveillance of the discourse (what issues are raised on TV, radio, etc.) "because unequal access to those technologies ensures their use in promoting similar power-block interests" (Fiske 1996, p. 218). The important point brought forth here, directly or indirectly, is the identification of the closed, unidirectional (with masses on the receiving end) and restricted access of communication technology.

These aspects are identified as necessary characteristics for the maintenance and reproduction of the hegemonic ideology, enabling the elites to set the form, format and content of the public discourse (broadcasting, TV, radio, press, etc.), and as importantly decide who can participate. Therefore, it can be argued that this manifestation of communication technologies, entangled in the web of one-way communication and used by the elites for power control and dissemination of material in support of the hegemonic ideology, has shaped the traditional scholarly and public discourse, as well as their practical use, to view communication technology as intrinsically embedded with features, characteristics and functionalities, for reinforcing and aiding the hegemonic ideology.

This biased view, that communication technologies are inherently suited to help media control, is troublesome and factually wrong. For example, the scholarly and public discourse on early cable technology shows that cable access was intended for use unlike it is being used today (for dissemination popular consumer culture through its various formats with the aims of making profit). Streeter (1997) argues that cable "had the potential to rehumanize a dehumanized society, to eliminate the existing bureaucratic restrictions of government regulation common to the industrial world, and to empower the currently powerless public" (Streeter 1997, p.228). He further notes that the cable system had the potential to enable two-way communication and interactivity, but apparently failed to do so due to the social (un)response on the part of the audience: "Cable television was something that could have an important impact upon society, and it thus called for a response on the part of society; it was something to which society could respond and act upon, but that was itself outside society" (Streeter 1997, p. 225). And then adds that cable should not be viewed as an "autonomous entity that had simply appeared on the scene as the result of scientific and technical research" (Streeter 1997, p. 225). Here we see a distinction between the current social status of cable as profit making machinery and its potentials to have become socially responsible technology that would have empowered the audience with two-way open communication.

The above suggests that the communicative aspects of the production and reproduction of the dominant ideology, including the production of consent in the audience/consumer or citizen, are identified by media and communication technologies characterized by closed, one-way communication. This provides the elites with the ability to control the public discourse by selectively choosing the issues of discussion, and at the same time is able to control the access to the discourse: "But communication and information technology does not merely circulate discourse and make it available for analysts, it also produces knowledge and applies power" (Fiske 1996, p. 217). This process ensures conformity with the accepted cultural, social, economical, and political norms of the dominant ideology: "focus on communication technology both as ways of engaging in discourse struggles and, through their surveillance capability, as ways of producing a particular form of social knowledge and thus of exerting power" (Fiske 1996, p. 217)

That the various media and communication technology exhibit characteristics of closed systems with one-way communication can be hardly argued. However, the proper question to ask is: why is the communication technology so restrictive and a closed system that can be so easily controlled (deliberately or otherwise) by the elite? First, lets ask the following question regarding how does media fit in the economic system. Do the existing media/communication technologies exhibit characteristics that make them a better fit for the capitalistic free market (economy whose ultimate goal is the bottom-line, i.e. profit), rather than empowering the publics/audiences with information to better participate in representative democracy? Second, are the exhibited characteristics intrinsic to a particular technology embedded in the technology itself, or they are a result of the features and functionalities which designers embellished a particular technology?

To answer the above questions, I first turn to Schiller (1996) who argues in favor of original purpose and design: "When military or commercial advantages are the motivating forces of research and development, it is to be expected that the laboratories will produce findings that are conducive to these objectives. If other motivations could be advanced, the common good, for instance, different technologies might be forthcoming" (Schiller, p.71). Schiller's idea of the original purpose is also supported by the adaptive structurations theory

(AST) that differentiates between technology's spirit (the original intent as thought by the designers who might be operating 'outside' of the hegemonic control, relatively speaking) and its subsequent functionality due to the appropriation process as the technology becomes embedded in institutionalized social structures. As such, more then often the existing socially and politically brokered power structures reflect themselves in the structure of the technology: "Information technology is highly political, but politics are not directed by its technological features alone" (Fiske 1996, p. 219).

The AST might appear in contradiction to Schiller's argument that the social use of technology is determined by the original purpose: "What the evidence here demonstrates is the strong, if not determining, influence of the original purpose that fostered the development of each new technology. The social use to which the technology is put, more times that not, follows its originating purpose" (Schiller, p. 71). The seemingly contradictory arguments need to be scrutinized in light of the social constructionist theory and technological determinism applied together. Neither one can explain the interplay of communication technology and society alone. The argument is that if a particular technology was designed to serve the corporate interest, most of its features will be driven to maximize the profits. In contrast, if a group of people designs technology for open communication and democratic access to information, the technology in question will have such features as to enable ease of access to information and make it hard for that technology to be used for restrictive purposes.

But again, it is not the technology per se; it is the social structures that tilt the design, development, and subsequent use of the technology for particular purposes. Unfortunately, most of the communication technology in use today has been built and appropriated for profit making activities and perhaps is unfit to support activities related to participatory democracy.

For example, the development of cable as medium of communication was relatively uneventful until the media corporations saw potentials for profits via advertising. As the fight of discourses got under way between government officials, media corporations and the liberal progressive forces, the elite elements appeared on the scene controlling and moderating the discourse: "The talk about cable ... was characterized by a systemic avoidance of central issues and assumptions, and by a pattern of unequal power in the discussion of its outcomes: the discourse of the new technology was shaped not so much by full fledged debate as by the lack of it" (Streeter 1997, p.222). Thus, the future of the cable technology was affected by the social structures and institutions, striping away from its technological potential the ability to become a technology that could link the masses and bring them together.

The communication's technological determinism and social constructionism are interrelated in circular and iterative nature. It is hard to conceptualize isolated technology that is not being affected by the social structures, but constantly affects the same:

"As Raymond Williams has shown, this assumption of autonomous technology is characteristic of much though about television and society, and constitutes a false abstraction of technologies out of their social and cultural context" (Streeter 1997, p.225) "Such speculations naively assumed that telecommunication could magically resolve the power relations among people that caused racist, poverty, and international strife" (Streeter 1997, p.227)

Even when a particular communication technology changes the social structures, it does not necessarily mean that such changes will be progressive and liberating. Streeter argues that relations in social structures are created by people and can only be changed by the people themselves, suggesting that even if technology has changed some structures, the changes have been appropriated by the elite and incorporated in the production and reproduction of the dominant ideology: "The constrains were not caused by old technological limits, nor can they be eliminated by new technologies: they were caused by relationship between people and can be overcome only by changing relations between people" (Streeter 1997, p.240). Or, as Fiske has put it very succinctly: "Technology may determine what is shown, but society determines what is seen" (Fiske 1996, p. 221).

If technology's role in the society is determined both by its own characteristics and by the moderating characteristics of its social surroundings, what might be there that causes a particular technology to become a closed system, one-way communication, disseminating content which is controlled by the stakeholders whose primary concern is to advertise to the consumers or in the case of the government control its citizen through selective and strategic communications?

Arguing that one way communication by media companies (TV, cable, radio, movies) is a very important ingredient in the process of reproduction of the dominant ideology, because it is able to control the discourse by controlling the content and restricting the access to the discourse, Gitlin suggests that the centrally controlled one way communication (one-to-many) must disappear and be replaces by many-to-many communications if we wish to empower the masses (Gitlin, 1972, pp. 363). He further contends that a possible "revolutionary movement must aim to transform mass media by liberating communications technology for popular use (Gitlin, 1972, pp. 363). Apparently, Gitlin believes and posits the open communication (many-to-many) as a possible antidote to the hegemonic ideology.

Therefore, it can be argued that the communication technology, which is constantly modified and affected by the social structures in which it is embedded, while at the same time influencing and modifying those same social structures, has the potential to shift or displace the center of gravity (i.e. the status quo, the habitus) through its characteristics of open communication, which can induce mass communication amongst the masses themselves empowering them with many-to-many communication relatively outside of elites' controls.

Constrained by the historical discourse and practicality of most of the communication technology used for one way communication and for profit making purposes, Schiller is skeptical that such technology can be of any benefit to the society: "The customary argument that commerce and profit seeking go hand-in-hand with social benefit, is still to be demonstrated after hundreds of years of contrary experience" (Schiller, p.71).

At this point I would like to argue that the newest media technology, the communication facet of the Internet, exhibits characteristics of open communication that could position it as potential antidote to hegemonic ideology. As it has been argued above, whoever controls the content can control the scope of the public discourse, and whoever controls the access to the mass communication technology can practically control the voices that can debate the already restricted content/discourse. Unfortunately, TV, radio and cable technologies have been socially (various social and institutional structures) constructed such that both content and access control are in the same hands.

However, the Internet, especially the website portion of it (ability to publish) and the email discussion lists exhibit characteristics contrary to those of earlier technologies (as shaped by the social structures). For example, almost anyone can publish anything on the Internet, relatively speaking, without the fear that the server hosting firms might block the website (apart from criminally related material). In addition, the masses, can freely organize into groups of citizens, consumers, special interests groups, hobbyists, etc., and advocate their causes openly. This is partially enabled by the ability to establish many-to-many communication via email discussion lists. These two examples show that the content is not necessarily controllable by corporate power, and that the access to that content is not restricted by any corporate power. As matters of fact, both are subject to the ability to pay for Internet access, however, many libraries provide free Internet access for interested individuals. From the traditional technologies, public cable access channels resemble the above cases. However, most communities seldom use public cable access channels. When used, they are marginalized by not being included in programming listings (e.g. TV Guide) with the rest of cable and broadcast channels.

What social conditions and circumstanced led to the development of the Internet technologies which seem to exhibits open content and open communication properties, unlike the TV, radio and cable that have remained one-way communication channels? Why haven't then the same social structures and forces restricted various Internet technologies to be used for one-way communication only?

The apparent power to reach the masses, as well as the ability to interact with them, could not have escaped the elite. All of a sudden, as the number of Internet users increased manifolds each year, previously uninterested media corporations (there were repeated public claims that profit cannot be made with this new technology) invaded the Internet landscape, using it not much different than the TV: "Whether deceptively labeled as 'entertainment,' 'news,' 'culture,' 'education,' or 'public affairs,' TV programs aim to narrow and flatten consciousness-to tailor everyman's world view to the consumer mentality, to placate political discontent, to manage what cannot be placated, to render social pathologies personal, to level class-consciousness" (Gitlin, 1972, pp.345). The obviousness of the above is that almost all commercial sites support their Internet presence by online advertising. Yes, one can choose to visit a web site only to be bombarded by advertising, similar to TV advertising. However, studies have shown that web site visitors are increasingly becoming aware and do not necessarily get influenced by advertisements. This is a bit different from the TV. A visitor can still view the page without wasting time, whereas on TV you either watch the commercials or need to switch the channel.

In other words, the Internet, fueled by the open content and open communication, in its infancy and during its development until mid 90s, before it become obvious that it can be used by corporation for making profit, was truly the liberating technology alluded by Gitlin.

To think that the elites were so naive to overlook Internet's potential as mass medium is at best naivety itself. They could not have also overlooked the potential for the masses to utilize the Internet to organize themselves outside elite's control, however, perhaps the elite thought that any such conflict should be domesticated as Gitlin suggests: "What permits it to absorb and domesticate criticism is not something accidental to the liberal capitalist ideology, but rather its core" (Gitlin, 1980, pp. 256). Then, it seems that the inevitable happened, as many times before: "The hegemonic ideology changes in order to remain hegemonic; that is the peculiar nature of the dominant ideology of liberal capitalism" (Gitlin, 1982, pp. 450).

The elite moved to utilize the open communication technology, taking control over various aspect of it. Internet users still have to access the Internet via commercial entities that use online advertising as a profit stream. Various mergers and acquisition have occurred between traditional media and online industry, successfully trapping the masses to a particular content. Yet, it is still easier to escape the online advertisers than those on TV.

Corporations find this very problematic, as it is hard to centrally control a technology that was build to be managed in distributed fashion. Therefore, they have turned more than ever before to manage the access to the Internet technology and control the Internet visiting habits (through content portals) of the masses.

Despite these attempts by corporations, if a group of people wants an Internet presence, with potential readership/ viewership of all who have access to the Internet, it can do so with minimal cost. The same cannot be said for the TV, the radio or cable. Whether the possibility for inexpensive presence on the Internet and its potential mass viewership will remain so, only the future will tell.

What could change? The unimaginable could happen. Governments can for example restrict who publishes what in their country by requiring licenses to operate a website. Obviously, for it to be effective the entire world has to enact the same laws since it is easy to move website servers around the world. Next, imagine that by some 'strange' imagination a judge rules that a US firm that provides Internet access can be held responsible for the content published by its customers. If such ruling is to be enforced, it could require that a corporation first approve each websites' content.

This could potentially lead various Internet access and Internet hosting providers to utilize their central role to their advantage. Why was the Internet build with open communication in mind? Adherents of the theory of hegemony could argue that this is contrary to the theory. If the Internet contains such power that can be used as an antidote to hegemony, why did the elite allow it to be developed in the form it is? Did they intent it or is it an unintentional byproduct of government's action to create communication network that can sustains nuclear attack by creating a very distributed communication network? The Internet and its open communication and open content technologies and principles are still in the infancy. Whether the open concepts will remain part of the Internet in the future remains to be seen.

If previous communication technologies are any indication, we might expect the same with the Internet. However, as I have attempted to show in this paper, the Internet communication technologies have more or less embedded in their technology some characteristics that lend themselves to be used for open communication where the masses can communicate amongst themselves without the corporate media's oversight.

Claiming that there are embedded characteristics in a given technology sounds like technological determinism. That would be an oversight. One needs to look at the social, political, economical, and cultural factors that have helped construct those characteristics in the first place so they could be embedded in the underlying Internet technologies. Further, as time goes on, the social situatedness of the Internet technology could change and the social structures of the future might modify, change or even restricts the initially acquired and embedded open communication and open content characteristics of the Internet. Alternatively, if the open characteristics of the Internet take strong hold in society and overcomes the already entrenched hegemonic forces as they are embedded deeply in various social structures, it might empower the masses to shift and displace the status quo and thus bring forth more representative democracy.

## JARGON BUSTING

Typical of an emerging technology, the Semantic Web literature is veiled in a bewildering array of technical jargon.

So much so that a time-pressed researcher might be forgiven for concluding that the Semantic Web is something for geeks and that it has no bearing on real work and real people; that it (unrealistically) requires everyone to create all online content in the RDF (Resource Description Framework)

Semantic Web language. This, of course, could not be further from the truth. Take the Weblogs (Blogs) phenomenon as an example. Few users of Weblogs are aware that they are publishing, syndicating and aggregating data onto the Semantic Web as well as the human-readable Web. Weblog technology revolves around the RSS (Rich Site Summary or RDF Site Summary) family of languages that vary in their human-readability but are united in their machine readability.

This resultant machine processibility is exploited to connect even the most human-centric RSS vocabularies into the Semantic Web directly, or through automated transformation to RDF. Weblogs thus form a valuable (and vast) source of richly interconnected information that requires little or no knowledge of the Semantic Web in order to create and use it.

For the information researcher, the Semantic Web view of this data enables seamless fusion of Weblog data with data from completely different sources such as dictionaries, thesauri, catalogues, databases as well as the 'traditional' Web. Where all this will lead is uncertain but the jargon is no obstacle to its creation and use.

## BOTTOM-UP REVOLUTION

What seems certain is that both evolution and revolution will occur, and that the latter is all too easily overlooked. For instance, given the proliferation of data about data (metadata) that underpins the Semantic Web, it is tempting to focus in on the obvious prospect of a better-than-Google search engine. Such a "semantic search" engine is able to determine whether the query "orange" refers to the colour, the fruit, the mobile phone company, or a chemical weapon used by the United States. As clever and useful as this may be, it is only an evolutionary enhancement of something that is already possible on the Web today. By looking in a little more detail at what is happening on the Semantic Web today, it is possible to gain a deeper insight into where revolution is starting to occur. In this article we will do just that; we will take a look at one of the most exciting new developments on the Semantic Web. Joined-up information about people, emanating not from some centralistic database but from individuals themselves.

In many ways, the explosive growth of social networking software, sites and data is representative of the way the Semantic Web is emerging. Weblogs were the first wave of this evolution/revolution; they allowed individuals to publish data in a sufficiently structured format for machine processing of that data to be relatively trivial.

Communities formed around weblogs in a bottom-up fashion, defined implicitly through syndication and through the lists of other weblogs ("blogrolls") that frequently accompanied weblogs. The next step, perhaps more revolutionary than evolutionary, is to explicitly define these (and other) communities in a way that is more easily machine processible. The Friend Of A Friend (FOAF) project is one such initiative that is making this possible and, like weblogs, it does this from the bottom up. One of the aims of the FOAF project is to improve the chances of happy accidents by describing the connections between people (and the things that they care about such as documents and places).

FOAF is a vocabulary for describing people, used analogously to Dublin Core metadata for documents. The idea is to use FOAF to describe the sorts of things you would put on your homepage-your friends, your interests, your pictures-in a structured fashion that machines find easy to process. What you get from this is a network of people instead of a network of web pages: the Web now contains descriptions of real things in the world-people-and because the Semantic Web is designed to be open and extensible, information about what these people do (their calendar), what they own (cars, houses, pets), what they create (documents, pictures, weblogs), can all be described as well.

Several million FOAF documents are out there on the Web already, created both by individuals and by various social software and networking sites. FOAF documents can be created by hand, but increasingly, FOAF is being created from existing databases or by mining the existing Web. When people need to know something and the area is outside their expertise, they need a way into the information landscape. They need to find out what the main topics of interest are; who is well thought of; what where the important issues and papers in the area. People often serve as conduits for this type of information, with personal contacts serving as a way into an area and the key individuals within a field serving as a way of finding the main issues. FOAF applications cannot replace the subtle social interactions which characterise personal information exchange, but they can help to make connections that might not otherwise have occurred: for example, by enabling certain sorts of information to be accurately processed by computers and therefore much easier to search.

Privacy and trust are clearly issues in FOAF as with all digital information on the Web or elsewhere. Organisations of various sorts already intensely mine the Web for information about individuals, email spammers being the most frequent example. FOAF includes protection against email spammers but in wider terms the very network of connections described in FOAF is likely to be its greatest asset in assessing reliability and quality of digital information on the Web.

## CONCLUSION

From the perspective of the information researcher, the Semantic Web promises to provide and exploit joined-up information that goes way beyond the Web's traditional page-to-page links. Analysing the impact this will have on the day-to-day work of information professionals is not trivial. As with most new technologies, the Semantic Web is likely to create entirely new ways of working while simultaneously rendering others obsolete.

Applications like FOAF are at the vanguard of the Semantic Web, enabling a glimpse of what might be achieved. Their implicit and explicit definition of social networks offers the information researcher a wealth of new channels into the information cloud around individuals and communities.

# 5

# Making a Media List

Make up a media list and organise it into the following categories:

- wire services
- local print media
- local radio
- local TV
- national media

Record the name and title of each contact person (you may have more than one contact person for each organisation), the name of the publication or station, and the address and telephone number. For print media, get the name of the news editor (also called city editor, news director, or assignment editor), the features editor, and the person responsible for the community calendar or bulletin board.

## RELATING TO MEDIA PEOPLE

For radio or TV, you will need the name of the assignment editor, the public service director, and the people responsible for booking talkshow guests. If you don't have the names of contact people, don't be afraid to call and ask. Be sure to get their titles, since personnel turnover can be rapid. Update the list every three or four months.

Organise media information according to whether the publication is daily, weekly, or monthly. Find out the deadlines for these publications. Also, make a list of what times your local TV news is broadcast and find out which stations do live (on the scene) reports. It will help in planning times for demonstrations or actions to know what times fit into the TV station's schedule.

Try to keep profiles of your media contacts, with comments on whether they are sympathetic or hostile to certain issues and on what issues they are interested in or have covered in the past.

## MEETING DEADLINES

Reporters work against a deadline. If you call editors or reporters when they are rushing to meet a deadline, you won't get your story in the news, and you may alienate them as well.

The best time to call contacts at a morning paper is in the morning between 9:30 and 10 a.m. As it gets later, the staff will be more pressed for time. Call contacts at an evening paper in the late afternoon, when the paper has just gone out.

It is best to call radio or TV reporters as early in the day as possible if you're trying to get on an evening broadcast. Don't call after 1 or 2 p.m. for a 5 p.m. story; the staff is rushing to edit the news they already have. Talk to media people as far before deadlines as possible. Your goal is to become a resource person for the media on animal rights issues. You can do this by letting the media know you exist and by cultivating contacts.

Send a brief letter to each contact person on your media list, explaining the purpose of your group and offering information on animal rights issues. Include your group's identifying fact sheet or brochure. This alone is probably not enough to get the media to contact you-usually you have to become known in the community-but it is a start.

Try to develop and maintain professional relationships with media people in your community by being courteous and responsible. Return calls promptly-remember those deadlines! Be enthusiastic, cooperative, friendly, and always tell the truth. If you make a mistake, admit it promptly. Don't be afraid to say, "I don't know, but I can find out." Then do so.

When you send a news release to more than one person in an organisation, let each person know who else is receiving it. Nothing infuriates an editor more than to work on a story and then find that someone else at the paper is doing the same story in another section. Reporters sometimes claim that they can't cover animal rights stories because there's no new "angle," so you've got to provide it. Use interesting visuals, such as costumes and props, in your demonstrations. Focus on the local aspects by talking, for example, about what the company that employs half the people in town does to animals, or talk about local people arrested in a national demonstration.

Never speak "off the record"; there is no such thing. Also, watch out for jokes-you could be misunderstood. Don't get bullied into a simple yes-or-no answer to a complex question. Give the facts necessary to understand the issue.

Study the professionals on national interview shows. Develop a few good phrases and examples to recite that will catch a reporter's ear. When you make a press call or send out a news release, be sure that it is for something newsworthy.

Your communications should be organised and state important points clearly and briefly. It's helpful if you understand what the media consider newsworthy. Some of the characteristics of news are:

*timeliness (media are interested in what's happening today, not yesterday)*

*proximity (the closer the event is to the media, the more likely the media will consider it news)*

*prominence (if you've got well-known people involved, the media sometimes respond better)*

*conflict (the media love covering opposing factions)*

*oddity (if you're doing something for the first time, the media are more likely to respond; they get tired of the same old thing)*

*importance (how many people might be affected or interested).*

All of these "news judgments" don't have to apply before you contact the media, but your information/event should meet most of them. Remember, the media don't like to feel "used" by anyone with a cause. Reporters want to think that what they're writing about is legitimate news and not propaganda.

If your information/event isn't newsworthy, don't contact the media because you'll only anger them for wasting their time.

## WRITING A NEWS RELEASE

A news release, a short announcement of a newsworthy event, is sent to newspapers, magazines, and TV and radio stations to interest them in doing a story. Because news directors receive hundreds of releases every day, yours must look professional and present the facts quickly, or it will never be read.

Here are some guidelines: Keep it short. One page is best.

Write a concise, catchy headline that summarizes the story. It should be written in the style of a newspaper headline, using active verbs.

Use the "inverted pyramid" style to write the release: Put the most important facts in the first paragraph and supporting information in descending order, so that the least important information is last.

The first paragraph should answer the five W's: who, what, where, when, and why.

Underline the text that gives the location, time, and date of the event.

The final paragraph should describe your group and reinforce your message, with a quotation from your spokesperson.

Never editorialise. Use quotations to express opinions. The quotation should be from a specific individual, not from your group, e.g., Nafisa Kumar, a spokesperson for Animal Action, says, "....."

Proofread the release carefully for grammar and spelling. Ask someone else to read it for an objective reaction. If you have the time, set it aside and look it over again the next morning. Eliminate redundancies, use short words and phrases, and simplify complex ideas.

If you've got an exciting, relevant photo, include it. Try to use a "screened" photograph. An article showing the timeliness or significance is even better.

You may also want to include black-and-white photographs, a factsheet, or a flier. If you do, at the bottom of the last page of the release write, "Attached: (list documents)."

Make it dramatic and attention-getting, but be sure you can substantiate what you say. Double-check the facts. It is virtually impossible to correct a release once it has gone out. But if you do make a mistake-especially in the time or location of an event-be sure to call and tell those to whom you sent the release. The time you tell the press should be the ideal time for them to see your event. If your event starts at 11:00 a.m., tell the press it's a little later but ask them to arrive at the time you tell them "sharp" so that they don't arrive to find activists figuring out where to stand or discussing last week's potluck dinner and also so that they don't arrive too late.

The sample news release (click here) illustrates the proper format to use. The following tips correspond to the numbers shown on the sample.

1. Use 8 1/2" × 11" (or similar standard sized) regular weight white stationery.
2. Your letterhead should contain your group's name and address.
3. The words NEWS RELEASE should be at the top of the first page. Always refer to releases as "news releases," not "press releases." The same goes for "news conference," rather than "press conference."
4. List the name of the "contact person." Make sure that someone is always available at this number, or include both daytime and evening numbers where the contact person can be reached.
5. Type the date in the upper left-hand corner. If you have enclosed photos, note that there.
6. "FOR IMMEDIATE RELEASE" appears in the upper left-hand corner above the date.
7. The headline should be centered, underlined, and typed in capital letters. It should be placed about three inches down from the headings above it to provide space for editor's notes.

8. The body of the release should begin one-third of the way down the page.
9. Leave wide margins for reporters' and editors' notes.
10. Don't use zeroes for times (e.g., use "11 a.m.," not "11:00"), and don't use letters after numbered dates (e.g., August 22, not 22nd).
11. Indent five spaces to begin new paragraphs, and don't hyphenate words at the end of a line.
12. Never continue a release on the back of a page. Instead, end the first page with a complete paragraph and type the word "more" centered at the bottom. Number each additional page at the top. Include a topic headline and your organisation's name. Do not staple multiple pages.
13. Type all releases double-spaced using capital and lower-case letters (not all capitals).
14. At the end of the release, center any one of these closings: "-30-," "#," or "Ends."

Before deciding how and when to deliver your release, establish what you want to accomplish-do you want something printed/broadcast BEFORE the event, or do you want the media to attend and cover the event? Generally, such activities as film showings, meetings, and fund-raisers fall in the "BEFORE" category. In this case, mail your releases at least three weeks before the event. These releases are probably being sent to the "Community Calendar" or "Bulletin Board" sections.

If you're having a picket or demonstration, you want "news" coverage. In this case, try to fax or hand-deliver your news release, and distribute it only one day before the event. Schedule it to arrive around 10 a.m., and try to deliver a copy to a reporter as well as to the news editor. Be sure to note on the release who else is receiving a copy. You may need two people to hand-deliver releases-one to run inside with the releases while the driver stays with the car.

Call the news desk to inform them if you are planning a demonstration. Do not read your entire news release. Just say, "Hello, I'm calling to let you know that Action for Animals will be holding a demonstration tomorrow at 11 a.m. in front of the Leather Store at 15 MG Road. Our contact number is 011-

23232879 if you'd like more information. We've sent a release to the news desk." If you have a good relationship with a particular reporter, call to say your release is coming out, or afterwards to see if he or she got it. After the demo, assign volunteers to get the coverage. At least two people should videotape television coverage and be certain to check the newspapers for a story and/or photo. These clips can be used to send out with your next news release to show that what you're doing is "newsworthy." If a newspaper covers your event and the wires don't, call the wires afterwards to let them know that they can pick up the story from the paper. If your event is of national interest (i.e., Supreme Court Santeria ruling, animal-to-human organ transplant), call the national television news desks to let them know they can pick up footage from the local affiliate.

## MAKING A MEDIA KIT

A media kit is a packet of information to give to reporters who come to your demonstration, event, or news conference. It helps to get your message across and makes you look professional. A media kit can include any or all of the following, depending on the issue.

- a news release
- a factsheet
- black-and-white photographs and possibly colour photographs. Type the following information on a sticky label to put on the back of the photograph: what it is, where it is, when it was taken, and who took it. Never write on the back of a photograph with a pen. The ink will rub off and damage other photographs.
- background information on or history of the issue
- copies of relevant documents
- if dealing with legislation, a copy of the bill and a summary of the main points.
- biographies of key individuals and a "mug shot" photograph (i.e., a head-and-shoulders shot) with an identifying label on the back.
- background on the organisation

Package the kit in a two-pocket folder (found in office supply stores) and put a label on the cover with the group's name and the words "Media Kit." If you have a photograph, you can put it on the cover, although it is not essential.

## WORKING WITH THE WIRE SERVICES

Wire services are news-gathering agencies that sell stories to newspapers and radio stations around the country. They should be your first contact when you deliver a news release or make press calls. If you can interest the wire services, your story will be sent to all subscribing media in your area or even nationally. Popular wire services are the Associated Press (AP), United Press International (UPI), Reuters, United News of India (UNI), Press Trust of India (PTI), Agence France Press (AFP), and Deutsche Presse-Agentur (DPA). Many of the nation's largest papers-Times of India, Hindustan Times, The Indian Express, The Hindu-also have news services, which means if you interest them in your story it may be sent nationwide as well.

Getting a story "on the wire" is a valuable accomplishment. It is worth a great deal of effort to develop good relations with wire-service reporters. Many TV, radio, or print assignment editors will answer a call asking for coverage by saying, "We'll see what comes in over the wire."

To find out what wire-service bureaus are in your area, look in the telephone book or call the local newspaper office. Any reporter can tell you where the nearest bureau is. If the newspaper is a member of AP, it also submits stories to AP.

Send the bureau manager a letter describing your organisation and supply the names, addresses, and telephone numbers of your best contact people. Offer to supply information or the local angle on animal rights issues.

Always deliver two news releases to the wire services: one for the "daybook," and one for the assignment editor. Call both the daybook editor and the assignment editor.

The daybook is a listing of scheduled events for the day. Each evening and again each morning, wires like AP and UPI send the daybook to their members. Assignment editors use this list to decide how to assign reporters and camera crews. To get listed in the daybook, send your news release about one week before the event. You can still get listed in the daybook for the next day by calling the information in to the daybook editor.

You may also be able to get a photograph of your event on the wire. If you've just had a demonstration, take your roll of undeveloped black-and-white film to the photographic department of the wire-service bureau and give it to the staff along with your news release. You can come back in a few hours or the next day to pick up the negatives. If you do provide prints, they must be 8" x 10" black and white photographs-no other size will fit the machines they use to transmit the photos nationwide.

Some wires, AP and UPI for example, also have radio networks. Call the radio bureaus closest to your area. Be prepared to do an interview on the spot if they are interested. They'll tape it for use later.

## DOING RADIO AND TV TALK-SHOW INTERVIEWS

Before you can do an interview, you must get the TV station interested. It helps to know the "gatekeeper" at the station: the news assignment editor. Call the station to learn his or her name and the best time of day to call. Send your news release one or two days before your event. If you call to remind them of your event, be brief and polite and don't call in the late afternoon. Your event will be more likely to get TV coverage if it involves conflict or visual interest. You can reach thousands of people through talk shows. Call in your comments to talk shows whenever animal-related subjects are discussed or during "open phone" segments. It's even better if someone from your group can be the guest on a talk show.

If your group is expecting a visit from someone with a particular area of expertise, try to get the person on a talk show. Or, try to get yourself on one. Contact the station several weeks in advance. Send a letter to the talk show director, describing your credentials or those of your speaker, what you'd like to discuss, and why it would interest the audience. Be sure to provide your telephone number.

Prepare a list of people your speaker would feel comfortable debating, in case the show wants to present both sides.

Once-you are booked for the show, listen to it or watch it to see what style and format to expect. To prepare, do the following:

- Study the issue.
- Practice being interviewed. Tape yourself with a tape recorder or video camera.
- Anticipate difficult questions and plan your answers.
- Memorise good quotations, anecdotes, and facts.
- Have a friend ask you all the hard questions in a hostile, aggressive way so you can be prepared for a difficult interview.
- Decide on the five main points you want to make during the show. Memorise a fact or an example for each one.
- Try to make your five points even if the interviewer doesn't ask the "right" questions. Don't feel you're limited to just answering the questions. You can answer them and still take the opportunity to talk about one of your points. Practice saying, "The real question here is...." or, "That relates to a larger issue, which is...."
- If you're doing a TV show, dress carefully: no solid black, white, or bright red, and no patterns. Wear plain solid colours. Green or blue films especially well. Smile, and don't fidget or touch your face or hair.
- Try to make your point in 20 seconds or less. TV news shows look for a "sound bite"-a statement that can be plugged into a 60-second story. If you take 45 or 60 seconds to make your point, your spot won't be aired, so use short sentences.
- Speak slowly and carefully (without being too slow!) and give yourself time to think before you answer the question.
- Don't say anything you wouldn't want edited out and aired separately. The reporter may interview you for five minutes, but air only 20 seconds of it. Don't worry

about repeating yourself: It just increases the chance that what you want to be heard actually will be.

- If the reporter is hostile, don't get flustered and raise your voice or get shrill. Stay calm and concentrate on making those five points. Remember-the reporter is not your real audience!
- Talk directly to the interviewer, not to the audience or camera. If you steal side glances at the camera, you'll look nervous or shifty.

## MAKING PUBLIC SERVICE ANNOUNCEMENTS

Public service announcements, or PSAs, are 10-to 60-second notices that radio and TV stations sometimes air in order to balance the effect of paid advertisements and to present balanced coverage of issues.

They are free to nonprofit community groups.

The four standard lengths for a PSA are 10 seconds (25 to 30 words), 20 seconds (45 to 50 words), 30 seconds (60 to 75 words), and 60 seconds (120 to 150 words). Following are some sample PSA's:

**20 seconds:** More people live off research today than benefit from it. The traditional use of animals in experimentation must be replaced. Animals are not "tools for research." Their use is costly, unethical, inefficient, and old-fashioned. Sophisticated non-animal methods are available. Help us support their use. [group name and address]. (21 seconds, 48 words)

**20 seconds:** The original motto of medicine was, "First, do no harm." Yet this year millions of animals will suffer and die in U.S. laboratories. We need to encourage the use of sophisticated computers, cell and tissue cultures, clinical studies, and mathematical models. To support progress without pain, write: [group name and address]. (20 seconds, 47 words)

Besides issue-oriented PSAs such as these, radio and TV stations will air announcements of meetings or events on a "community calendar." This is an excellent way to publicise your group's event. Send several copies of your PSA with a typed, double-spaced cover letter to the public service director of the station. Explain the purpose of your organization and your activities, and state why the station should use the PSA.

On the top left side of the page, type the beginning date (the first day the PSA should be read), the kill date (the last day you want it read), and the length of the announcement in seconds and in words.

Find out the deadline for PSAs-it may be two or three weeks in advance. Make a follow-up call to be sure the station received it. Some stations may want to see proof that you're actually nonprofit, so be prepared to produce your paperwork. PETA also has television PSAs available on 3/4" videotape. If you would like to try to interest your local stations in airing them, please let us know.

## WRITING LETTERS TO THE EDITOR

You can get great exposure for animal rights issues through letters to the editor in newspapers or magazines. Make it a point to read local papers and magazines for articles that provide fuel for a letter to the editor.

Your letter must be short: 300 words is the maximum most papers or magazines will publish without cutting. It's better for you to do the cutting than for the editor to do it. The best length is 100 to 150 words (10 to 15 typed lines).

Make the first sentence catchy, so it will get the reader's attention, and stick to one issue. The letter should be timely. If possible, send it in no more than three to four days after the article you're responding to has appeared.

The letter should be typed and double-spaced. Sign it and include your home and work telephone numbers. Some papers will want to verify that you wrote it.

Don't send letters just to the biggest paper in town. The smaller the paper, the better chance you have of getting your letter printed. Small weekly papers are an excellent way to reach hundreds or even thousands of people.

Sending in regular letters to the editor should be a priority. The exposure you get is so valuable that it is worth forming a letter-writing committee just to ensure that the job gets done.

Occasionally, you may have the chance to write an opinion piece for the local paper, especially if you are involved in a controversial campaign. These are longer articles of 500 to 800 words that summarize an issue, develop an argument, and propose a solution. Send the article to the editorial page editor with a cover letter explaining why you feel it should be printed. The article has a better chance of getting printed if it is signed by someone prominent, even if you wrote it for him or her.

## APPOINTING A SPOKESPERSON

You should appoint a spokesperson for each event. Members of your group should be prepared to answer media questions with a brief sentence and then direct further questions to the spokesperson. This helps prevent the local TV station from interviewing the most inarticulate or ill-presented person.

Your group must decide ahead of time what the spokesperson should and should not say and have ready all the available facts. The group leader does not necessarily have to be the spokesperson.

The spokesperson should be well dressed and have media kits available. If the demonstration involves people wearing costumes, the spokesperson should not be in costume. Though you must appoint a spokesperson, everyone at the event/protest should be familiar with the topic, as reporters will often want a second comment from others involved.

## SETTING UP A NEWS CONFERENCE

A news conference is a good way to fall flat on your face unless you have a really important story. It's usually better to hand-deliver or mail a professional-looking media kit with a news release. Hold a news conference only when:

- The media can benefit from it more than from photographs and news releases.
- You have important or newsworthy people available to present your story.
- Experts will be available to answer questions.
- The story involves something that has to be seen to be understood.

- The press is inundating you with telephone calls, and rumours must be dispelled.

Use this format when holding a news conference:

- Start promptly-soft news at the designated hour, hard news after five minutes.
- Begin the conference with a concise statement from your spokesperson.
- Explain material available to the press.
- Call on the expert to read a short statement.
- Answer questions.
- End the conference on time. It should not last more than 30 or 40 minutes. Reporters will ask further questions if they wish.
- Hold the conference in a location convenient to the media, such as in a downtown hotel, and provide light refreshments. The best time is at 10 or 11 a.m.

If possible, issue invitations one to two weeks ahead of time by sending a "media alert." Explain the details of the conference and what will be addressed. If you are holding the conference right away, alert the media by telephone. Call the wire services to get it on the daybook.

Be careful to allow only media, not the general public, to enter the room. Assign someone to check media IDs at the door.

Be sure to have media kits prepared. Hand them out as soon as reporters arrive. If a major statement is being made, you may want to issue the news release after the statement.

After the news conference, follow up with media inquiries as quickly as possible. Make every effort to accommodate requests for personal interviews. Deliver news releases and media kits to media who were invited but did not attend. Tell radio stations that your spokesperson is available for a telephone interview.

# 6

# The Screenwriting

Screenwriting refers to the art and craft of writing screenplays for film or television. Writing for film is potentially one of the most high-profile and best-paying careers available to a writer, and as such, it is perhaps the most sought after. It is increasingly difficult to make a living as a Hollywood screenwriter, but that does not stop tens of thousands of people from trying every year, as the capricious nature of the film industry makes it possible for a complete unknown to launch a career simply by writing a commercially-appealing screenplay and getting it into the hands of the right people.

## Status of Screenwriters in the Industry

Historically, screenwriters have had a low social position in the film industry. Despite the fact that a screenwriter is often the genesis of a project, directors-not writers-frequently get their names associated with the films they make (as in, "a film by..."). Screenwriters usually do not get this honour, unless the screenwriter is also directing. Before Alfred Hitchcock, the reverse was the case.

The Writers Guild of America agreed to make an exception for Hitchcock, which other directors took advantage of (and insisted on using "a film by...") and gradually screenwriters were marginalized in this respect.

However, the situation has improved dramatically as the resurgence of the independent film in the late 20th century gave new rise to the idea of the screenwriter as the amateur, and creative generator of cinematic product. In the past few years, news of multi-million dollar screenplay deals is a sign of increased respect for the role of the screenwriter in film production.

Recently, the Writers Guild of America (WGA), the labour union representing writers in the American film and television industries, has made great efforts to limit the use of the "a film by" title in the credits of motion pictures, to preserve the respect for level of input made by the writers.

## Theories on Writing a Screenplay

Writing a screenplay requires the creativity of a storyteller and the skills of both the dramatist and the filmmaker. Because of the particular combination of skills and standards required by the motion picture industry, many writers find screenwriting more challenging than writing novels or other narrative fiction.

Fundamentally, the screenplay is a unique literary form. It is like a musical score, in that it is intended to be the basis of other artists' performance, rather than standing on its own merits. For this reason, a screenplay is often written using pre-determined technical jargon when describing stage directions. Nonetheless, a good screenwriter will use interesting visually-descriptive language when setting up a scene or its characters so as to conjure up images. There are several main screenwriting theories which help writers approach the screenplay by systematizing the structure, goals and techniques of writing a script. There are also numerous screenwriting programs available to help a screenwriter set up scenes and keep track of structure. Scenes are usually short and dialogue clipped, i.e., the way people actually speak in real life. The First Act is typically anywhere from fifteen to twenty pages leading to a major conflict. Second Act--the story--is about seventy pages. The Third Act or resolution is the rest. [See Act structure (Film) ] Screenplays are usually one-hundred-and-twenty pages in length, or two hours, a page of screenplay roughly corresponding to a minute of movie.

The most common kinds of theories are structural. Screenwriter William Goldman is widely quoted as saying "Screenplays are structure." The first, most basic theory of screenwriting is Aristotle's Poetics, which explains the Three

Act Structure. The Three Acts are Beginning, Middle and End, or more functionally, Setup, Complication and Resolution. A common way to paraphrase the Three-Act structure is "get your character up a tree, throw rocks at him, then get him down out of the tree." Many screenwriters also draw inspiration from Joseph Campbell's Monomyth which also employs a variation of the Three Act Structure.

## SYD FIELD

Screenwriting guru Syd Field wrote the seminal book Screenplay, and posited a new theory, which he called the Paradigm. Others refer to it as the "Three Act Structure".

Field noticed that in a 120-page screenplay, Act Two was notoriously boring, and was also twice the length of Acts One and Three. He also noticed that an important dramatic event usually occurred at the middle of the picture, which implied to him that the middle act was actually two acts in one.

So the Three Act Structure is noted 1, 2a, 2b, 3, resulting in Aristotle's Three Acts divided into four pieces. Field also introduced the idea of Plot Points into screenwriting theory. Plot Points are important structural functions that happen in approximately the same place in most successful movies, like the verses and choruses in a popular song.

In subsequent books, Field has added to his original list, and students of his like Viki King and Linda Seger have added to the list of Plot Points. Here is a current list of the major Plot Points that are congruent with Field's Paradigm:

**Opening Image:** The first image in the screenplay should summarize the entire film, especially its tone. Often, writers go back and redo this as the last thing before submitting the script.

**Inciting Incident:** Also called the catalyst, this is the point in the story when the Protagonist encounters the problem that will change their life. This is when the detective is assigned the case, where Boy meets Girl, and where the Comic Hero gets fired from his cushy job, forcing him into comic circumstances.

**Turning Point 1:** The last scene in Act One, Turning Point One is a surprising development that radically changes the Protagonist's life, and forces him to confront the Opponent. In Star Wars, this is when Luke's family is killed by the Empire. He has no home to go back to, so he joins the Rebels in opposing Darth Vader.

**Pinch 1:** A reminder scene at about 3/8 the way through the script (halfway through Act 2a) that brings up the central conflict of the drama, reminding us of the overall conflict. For example, in Star Wars, Pinch 1 is the Stormtroopers attacking the Millennium Falcon in Mos Eisley, reminding us that the Empire is after the stolen plans to the Death Star that R2-D2 is carrying and that Luke and Ben Kenobi are trying to get to the Rebel Alliance (the main conflict).

**Midpoint:** An important scene in the middle of the script, often a reversal of fortune or revelation that changes the direction of the story. Field suggests that driving the story towards the Midpoint keeps the second act from sagging.

**Pinch 2:** Another reminder scene about 5/8 through the script (halfway through Act 2b) that is somehow linked to Pinch 1 in reminding the audience about the central conflict. In Star Wars, Pinch 2 is the Stormtroopers attacking them as they rescue the Princess in the Death Star. Both scenes remind us of the Empire's opposition, and using the Stormtrooper attack motif unifies both Pinches.

**Turning Point 2:** A dramatic reversal that ends Act 2 and begins Act 3, which is about confrontation and resolution. Sometimes Turning Point Two is the moment when the Hero has had enough and is finally going to face the Opponent. Sometimes, like in Toy Story, it's the low-point for the Hero, and he must bounce back to overcome the odds in Act 3.

**Showdown:** About midway through Act 3, the Protagonist will confront the Main Problem of the story and either overcome it, or come to a tragic end.

**Resolution:** The issues of the story are resolved.

**Tag:** An epilogue, tying up the loose ends of the story, giving the audience closure.

### Final Thoughts

Perhaps the most daunting theory of screenwriting comes from Pulitzer Prize-winning screenwriter David Mamet, who has advised that a screenwriter should simply read Aristotle's Poetics and write a lot until they get good at it.

Professional screenwriters often recognize the importance of learning about style, craft and structure by reading the screenplays of popular/successful movies.

The time necessary to write a screenplay varies widely upon the writer and the circumstances. Professional television writers frequently are called upon to write an hour-long script in less than a week. Some major movie scripts have literally taken years of rewrites before they are ready. Most professional writers can complete two to three original screenplays in a year.

### Screenplay Format and Elements of the Screenplay

A screenplay has very rigid set of standardizations in place, beginning with proper formatting. These rules are in part to serve the practical purpose of making screenplays uniformly readable "blueprints" of movies, and also to serve as a way of distinguishing a professional from an amateur---if a screenplay doesn't follow the simple rules of formatting, it is generally disregarded as a lesser product, regardless of content.

Most screenplays are expected to be written in 12 point Courier or Courier New typeface, with no bolding or italicizing. Specific elements and formatting defined below.

### Screenplay Format

This section describes the components used to build-up a screenplay.

### Title Page

The title page of your screenplay is the first clue to a producer that you're either a professional or an amateur. The title should be about 20 lines down the page and either underlined or in quotation marks. Two lines down, in the same font, should be the words "Written By", "Adapted From (insert title here)", or just plain "By". In the bottom corners put contact information, as well as any copyright information. In shooting scripts, the title page contains in the upper right corner a list of every set of revisions distributed thus far.

Some writers are tempted to insert eye-catching fonts or images on the title page. However, such deviation from industry standards is seen as unprofessional and is not recommended.

## Scene Headings

Scene headings (or slug lines) define the beginning of a new scene in a screenplay. They either begin with "EXT."---if the scene is an exterior, or takes place outdoors---or "INT."---if the scene takes place indoors. Following this descriptor, the name of the location of the scene should appear in all caps (example: "BOB'S PLACE"). This is followed by a space, a hyphen, another space, then the time of day (example: "-DAY," "-NIGHT," "-EVENING," etc.). The finished heading should read something like "INT. HOUSE-DAY". Scene headings have a margin of 1.5 inches (37 mm) from the left, 1 inch (25 mm) from the right.

Scene numbering: It is rare that you will find a "spec script" (speculation script, the one written by a screenwriter, before it is sold) with the scenes numbered. This is a tool added later in the production as the "spec script" becomes a "shooting script." The numbers are generally found immediately to the left of the scene heading.

## Action

Two lines below the scene heading and with the same margins, the action begins. Action describes what can be seen on the screen, and is always in present tense. Here, screenwriting varies most from standard fiction writing, in that elaborate prose describing the feelings of a character is to be avoided. When introducing a character, the character's name should appear in all caps (example: "Bob turns and sees JOAN, whom he has never seen before."). Afterwards, capitalize according to standard grammar.

## Page Breaks

Scene headers, dialogue cues, and transitions-in (such as FADE IN:) should never appear at the bottom of a page. When a paragraph of action or dialogue is split across pages, the break should come between sentences and not before the second line of the paragraph. When dialogue is split, (MORE) should appear at the bottom of the first page, aligned vertically with the dialogue cue. The cue should be replicated on the subsequent page, with (CONT'D) appearing alongside it.

### Dialogue

In screenwriting, dialogue refers to anytime a character is speaking, even if it is a monologue. A dialogue "cue" is the name of the character speaking, with a margin of 4.2 inches (107 mm) from the left of the page.

The name should be in capitals letters in cues. Unless there is a parenthetical (see below), dialogue is placed one line below the cue. The standard length of a dialogue line is 35 characters starting at 3.1 inches (79 mm). Hyphenation of words in a dialogue is frowned upon.

### Parentheticals

To show minor actions or revealing body language, a parenthetical, or subtext, is placed after the cue and either above or within the dialogue, within rounded brackets. e.g:

*Jack*

*I can get a better price.*

*(to Megan)*

*Let's bounce!*

The margin for parentheticals is 3.7 inches (94 mm) left, 1 inch (25 mm) right. Many script readers prefer limited use of parentheticals. They are also looked upon unfavourably by actors and directors, especially when they become too specific about emotions or actions.

### Transitions

Transitions are short descriptions describing how the film will move from one scene (or image within the scene) to the next. They are justified to the right side of a properly formatted screenplay, and followed by a colon. Some of the most common transitions seen in screenplays are:

- CUT TO:-Indicates a direct transition (cut) to a new scene, or to a new shot within a scene. If a scene header follows the cut, this transition is usually omitted.
- DISSOLVE TO:-Indicates a dissolve, where one scene gradually fades into another. Dissolves are commonly used to indicate the passage of time.
- INTERCUT WITH/INTERCUT BETWEEN:-Indicates that a sequence of cuts back and forth between two scenes is about to begin. Subsequent transitions between the two scenes are indicated with the transition BACK TO:. Intercuts are commonly used when portraying telephone conversations, or to contrast action taking place in two locations at the same time.

Intercut example:

*INT. ADULT BOOKSTORE--DAY--INTERCUT*

*Max is on the phone by the register, ringing purchases.*

*MAX*

*(into phone)*

*Dino Velvet... yeah, he's like the*

*John Luc Godard of S+M flicks,*

*supposed to be a real weirdo.*

*WELLES (O.S.)*

*(from phone)*

*A weirdo making S+M films? Who'd*

*have thought it?*

*MAX*

*(into phone)*

*His stuff comes out of New York.*

*WELLES (O.S.)*

*Speciality product.*

## Dialogue and Description

The following is an example from an unproduced screenplay which may give the reader an idea of how a scene without camera angles can be descriptive, and perhaps even poetic, so as to convey the proper time frame (1910) and/or feeling:

*A BUNCH OF GARDENIAS*

*makes a sudden burst of BRIGHT RED. A hand removes each petal--one at a time. The petals fall on the ground.*

*Following the petals--*

*A part of a woman's SHOE is seen. It is strangely ornate with a shabby heel.*

*Giggles erupt, and the extravagantly painted face of a very young prostitute appears.*

*Her hand is at the arm of a man who is older by at least a couple of decades.*

## Imagery

Imagery can be used in many metaphoric ways. In The Talented Mr. Ripley, the title character talked of wanting to close the door on himself sometime, and then, in the end, he did.

Rain is commonly used to express a character feeling depressed, while sunny days promote a feeling of happiness and calm. Use imagery to your advantage to sway the emotions of your audience and to clue them in to what is happening.

Imagery is well defined in City of God. The opening image sequence sets the tone for the entire film. The film opens with the shimmer of a knife's blade on a sharpening stone. A drink is being prepared, The knife's blade shows again, juxtaposed is a shot of a chicken letting loose of its harness on its feet. All symbolising 'The One that got away'. The film is about life in the favelas in Rio-sprinkled with violence and games and ambition.

## Character

It is very important to develop your characters, because that is who the viewers will be relating to. Characters, especially major characters, should be original and interesting. A character's true nature is revealed by his or her actions in overcoming obstacles.

### Dialogue

Dialogue is very important to the film industry, because there are no written words to explain your characters or the plot; it all has to be explained through dialogue and imagery. If your script has weak dialogue, there is a good chance it will lose a reader's or viewer's interest. Make your dialogue sharp, snappy, and easy to follow.

### Plot

While the story is what will be told (narrative); the plot is how the story will be told (narration). This vocabulary is not indisputable, though. Sometimes in literature story and plot are used exactly the other way round. Develop your plot before you begin work, write a treatment or a short outline for a film and follow it, but feel free to branch out in other directions if you feel that it would make your script more interesting.

## ACT STRUCTURE (FILM)

Act structure explains how a plot of a film story is composed. Just like plays (Staged drama) have 'Acts', critics and screenwriters tend to divide films into acts; though films don't require to be broken down as such in reality.

Whereas plays are actual live performances that need 'breaks' in the middle for change of set, costume, or for the artists' rest; films are recorded performances shown mechanically and therefore don't need actual breaks. Still they are divided into acts for reasons that are in aesthetic and structural conformation with the original idea of Act in theatre. Act breaks in a film are usually very obscure for lay audience and only a trained person can detect the ending of one act and the beginning of the other in the progression of a movie.

The idea of Act structure is of more value while writing a Screenplay than watching a film, though the Act breaks are never actually written in the final copies of screenplays. But television scripts called Teleplays almost always include clear denotions as such.

Act is the broadest structural unit of enacted stories. The most common paradigm in theatre, and so in films, is that of the 'Three-Act structure' proposed by Aristotle. It simply means that any story has a 'beginning', a 'middle' and an 'end'. Playwrights and screenwriters divide their stories into three major parts viz. 'Set up', 'Confrontation' (alternatively called as 'conflict' or 'complication') and 'Resolution'. These form the basic three acts of any performance-staged or screened.

Though various theories have been proposed and debated, the Three-act structure stands as the most popular one. Also, this is what Hollywood has discovered and proved as the most successful. The rest of the world cinema may have its own ways of looking at the plot.

### The 'Three-Act Structure'

According to Hollywood, feature films are considered as audio-visual narrative forms which can be seen in distinct parts called 'Acts'.

It follows that the enacted story opens with the introduction of characters and situations, backdrop, locale etc. It creates interest in the audience and takes them to feel concerned as to what the real problem is and what may happen with it. Plays, and screenplays, usually revolve around main characters-the 'Protagonist' and the 'Antagonist' who engage themselves into a battle. That is "Set up".

The next part-and considered to be more important-is complication of the problem of the story. It intrigues the audience all the more, giving them more and more information and putting various points of view for imaginative comparison. This eventually leads to higher points of audience interest. Because this second Act of most screenplays adds all the possible dramatic values to the plot, this is considered to be the core of the same. The Antagonist and the Protagonist try and experiment with all their strengths (and weaknesses of the other) to win the battle. That is "Confrontation".

This takes us to the third-and the most important-act, the "Resolution". This means it tends to 'solve' the problem (-s) of the story developed so far. But this is not obvious, as it is expected to bring the 'climax' (or a series of climaxes) to give the audience the pay-off. The tool usually implemented is a 'do or die' situation where doors of escape for either or both of the two characters go on closing one by one, leaving them with only a thin chance that demands the fullest exploitation of their qualities and energies. This so called jaw-dropping, breath-taking, arm-rest-grabbing moment for the audience leads to the final outcome of the entire plot. And it is usually the triumph of the good (Protagonist) over the evil (Antagonist), with rare exceptions.

### Limitations

This framework can not be rigidly applied to all the film stories, and there are a good proportion of Hollywood movies that defy this theory. Many films follow this pattern only to a subtle extent, where their genre demands a more delicate handling. Screenwiters and Script doctors have tried to provide alternative ideas, which again are open for debate. As said earlier, cinema across the world and 20th century has evolved its own ways of putting a story. Also, this theory may not be fit for non-fiction films like documentary or corporate films, which may not have a 'plot' at their base with 'characters' and all their 'actions and speeches' predecided, like the feature films have. Such non-fiction films require their own forms of arrangement.

What is important here is that ideas of Act structure help us understand films better. More importantly, these are 'tools' of the screenplay writers who can break down the story at hand and play with various ways of presenting it to find the best possible one. Experts have gone long way ahead in dividing plot to even smaller structural units and they keep working to find the most effective formula of structuring a film story.

## BECOMING A SCREENWRITER

### Handling Writer's Block

Many writers get to the page and get stuck. Writer's block is what happens when you have the desire, but just can't think of what to write. The key to working through this kind of block is to push through it. Pick a time of day that works for you and write, write, write. Take time out. Relax. Let your screenplay ferment for a while. Watching movies, reading books of the same genre can spark that jolt of creative writing you've been looking for. Writer's block is quite common, both for new writers as well as tenured.

Some say writer's block is simply a lack of research. It is in the writer's best interest to know the world about which he or she is writing backwards and forwards. Meaning, if you don't know what to write, perhaps it's because you don't know what you're writing about.

### Editing

Every writer knows that editing is an essential part of writing. Rewrite your piece several times until you are satisfied with the final product. Not only check spelling and grammar, but rewrite scenes to develop them more fully. But always check spelling and grammar. If there is improper spelling or grammar in a piece, an agent, producer, or other person that you are submitting it to will strongly judge it. Bad spelling prejudices people against work, and they are less likely to accept it.

### Screenwriting Software

Various pieces of software are available to help screenwriters adhere to the strict formatting conventions (as described above):

- *Celtx-Free*-Open Source scriptwriting software. Linux version available.
- *Cinergy Script Editor*-Free Windows-based script editor program offered in conjunction with a full suite of non-free production management tools under the name Cinergy Motion Picture Production System.
- *Dream a Script*-All in one Screenwriting Software.
- *Final Draft*-Integrated professional scriptwriting software.
- *Montage*-Screenwriting Software for Mac OS X.
- *Movie Magic Screenwriter*-Integrated professional screenwriting software.
- *NTCore Screenwriter*-A little freeware software with autocompletion.

- *Practical Scriptwriter*-Requires no knowledge of script formats.
- *Rough Draft*-A simple script and creative writing word processor. Free (donationware).
- *Scenario*-Modern, intuitive interface with full 30-day trial.
- *Scriptbuddy*-Web-based screenwriting software.
- *Script Right Mobile Edition*-screenwriting software for Pocket PC and Palm OS
- *Scriptware*-The first scriptwriting word processor with real-time formatting/pagination
- *Sophocles*-Screenplay and production management software.
- *Script Smart*-Microsoft Word templates.
- *Totally Write Development Suite*-A four-module program created by professional writer Jeffrey Alan Schechter to streamline the story development and screenplay structure process.

The first screenwriting software was SmartKey, a macro program that sent strings of commands to existing word processing programs, such as WordStar, WordPerfect and Microsoft Word. SmartKey was popular with screen writers from 1982-1987, after which word processing programs had their own macro features.

## COPYRIGHT PROTECTION FOR SCREENPLAYS

In the United States, completed works may be copyrighted, but ideas and plots may not be. Any document written after 1978 in the U.S. is automatically copyrighted even without legal registration or notice. However, The U.S. Library of Congress will formally register a screenplay, and some sources claim that if a work is not registered with the Library of Congress, then it is not possible to file for copyright infringement. For the purpose of establishing evidence that a screenwriter is the author of a particular screenplay (but not related to the legal copyrighting status of a work), The Writer's Guild of America registers screenplays. Since this service is one of record keeping and it is not regulated by law, other organizations can register screenplays as well, such as The Creators Vault. While there are benefits to registering a screenplay, it is considered amateurish and a faux-pas to include mention of copyright or guild-registered status anywhere on the screenplay itself.

## Screenplay

A screenplay or script is a blueprint, written by a screenwriter, for a film or television program. Screenplays can be original works or adaptations from existing works such as novels. A screenplay differs from a script in that it is more specifically targeted at the visual, narrative arts, such as film and television, whereas a script can involve a blueprint of "what happens" in a comic, an advertisement, a theatrical play and other "blueprinted" creations.

The major components of a screenplay are action and dialogue, with the "action" being "what we see happening" and "dialogue" being "what the characters say". The characters, when first introduced in the screenplay, may also be described visually. Screenplays differ from traditional literature conventions in ways described below; however, screenplays may not involve emotion-related descriptions and other aspects of the story that are, in fact, visual within the end-product. For more details on the contents of screenplays, see Screenwriting.

In the United States, the Writers Guild of America (WGA) has final control on who may be awarded screenwriting credit for a screenplay in a union production. The WGA is one of several organizations in the U.S. and worldwide which recognize screenplays with awards.

A script for television is sometimes called a teleplay.

## Screenplay Format

There is no unique "rule" for the writing of a screenplay, but throughout the world, within the relevant industries, several conventions are adhered to.

### Film

Motion picture screenplays intended for submission to mainstream studios, whether in the US or elsewhere in the world, are expected to conform to a standard typographical format known widely as studio format which stipulates how elements of the screenplay such as scene headings, action, transitions, dialogue, character names, shots and parenthetical matter should be presented on the page, as well as the font size and line spacing.

One reason for this is that, when rendered in studio format, most screenplays will transfer onto the screen at the rate of approximately one page per minute. This rule of thumb is widely contested-a page of dialog usually occupies less screen time than a page of action, for example, and it depends enormously on the literary style of the writer-and yet it continues to hold sway in modern Hollywood.

There is no single standard for studio format. Some studios have definitions of the required format written into the rubric of their writer's contract. The Nicholl Fellowship, a screenwriting competition run under the auspices of the Academy of Motion Picture Arts and Sciences, has a useful and accurate guide to screenplay format. There is also a compact, quick-reference chart with format specifications and examples called the Screenplay Format Guide from ScriptBuddy. Most screenwriting software comes with a set of templates for various screenplay formats which are more or less standard. A detailed description of correct screenplay format can be found here.

Traditionally, a screenplay should be 90-110 pages long. Comedies and children's films tend to weigh in at the lower end.

Screenplays are almost always written using a monospaced font, often a variant of Courier although other fonts are sometimes seen, including those intended to resemble the output of an old battered typewriter such as a Remington Portable.

### Television

For American TV shows, the format rules for hour dramas, like CSI, and single-camera sitcoms, like Scrubs, are essentially the same as for motion pictures. The main difference is that TV scripts have act breaks. Multi-camera sitcoms, like Two and a Half Men, use a different, specialized format that derives from radio and the stage play. In this format, dialogue is double-spaced, action lines are capitalized, and scene headings are capitalized and underlined.

The script format for documentaries and audio-visual presentations which consist largely of voice-over matched to still or moving pictures is different again and uses a two-column format which can be particularly difficult to achieve in standard word processors, at least when it comes to editing.

## PHYSICAL FORMAT

American screenplays are printed single-sided on three-hole-punched letter sized (8.5 x 11 inch) paper, and held together with two brass brads in the top and bottom hole. The middle hole is left empty. In the UK, double-hole-punched A4 paper is often used, although some UK writers use the US letter paper format, especially when their scripts are to be read by American producers, since otherwise the pages may be cropped when printed on US paper. Despite the use of double-punched paper, it is common to see scripts in the UK held together by a single brad punched in the top left hand corner. This makes it easy to flip from page to page during script meetings and may have something to do with the taller page of A4.

Screenplays are usually bound with a light card stock cover and back page, often showing the logo of the production company or agency submitting the script.

Increasingly, reading copies of screenplays (that is, those distributed by producers and agencies in the hope of attracting finance or talent) are distributed printed on both sides of the paper (often professionally bound) to cut down on paper waste out of environmental concerns. Occasionally they are reduced to half-size to make a small book which is convenient to read or put in a pocket; this is generally for use by the director or other production crew during shooting.

Although most writing contracts continue to stipulate physical delivery of three or more copies of a finished script, it is common for scripts to be delivered electronically via email. Although most production companies can handle scripts in most formats, it is better practice to supply scripts as a PDF file where possible. This is because it gives the writer final control over the layout of the script, which may otherwise vary depending on what fonts and/or paper size the recipient uses to print the script out. The formatting software programs listed at the bottom of this article produce industry formatted standard screenplays in PDF.

## WRITING ON SPEC OR ASSIGNMENT

Screenplays can be written either on "spec" (speculative) or as assignment ("Commissioned"). The Variety language dictionary defines "spec script" as "a script shopped or sold on the open market, as opposed to one commissioned by a studio or production company."

### Writing on Assignment

Assignments are commissioned by production companies or studios on the basis of pitches from producers or writers, or literary properties they already own. Most established writers do most of their work on assignment and will only "spec" scripts which they think no-one will pay them to write, or if they cannot find assignment work.

There are exceptions: some very famous writers only write on spec because they know that they can get a better price for their work this way. Other writers spec scripts that they care deeply about so that they do not have to bend to the whims of executives and producers.

An assignment may be for an original screenplay, or for an adapted screenplay based on another work such as a novel, film, short story, comic book, magazine article or, increasingly, video game. It may also, however, be for a rewrite of an existing script, and in fact this is how a large proportion of writers in the modern studio system make their living. Rewriting scripts is an art in itself and an extremely lucrative one at that: it is not unknown for trusted writers in the higher echelons of the industry to receive $200,000 a week (2004 numbers) for their efforts. $50,000 per week is not uncommon.

Rewriting is difficult because executives often have very clear ideas about what is wrong with a script, however, they are usually unable to provide detailed prescriptions for ways it can be fixed. This is not surprising, because screenwriting is not the expertise of the executive, but of the screenwriter. The writer is therefore usually expected to come up with a detailed prescription for how the script can be improved, and then execute this in a timely fashion. During the process of choosing a writer to rewrite a script the executives may ask several writers for their 'take' and choose the one who appears to have the greatest likelihood of moving the script forward to the point where it may be granulite for production.

Before 'going to script' a writer may be asked to write a treatment, an outline, or a step outline describing the script in various granularities of detail. Some writers resist this process and will do anything to avoid it and get down the writing the script itself; others embrace the process and even deliver fairly elaborate treatments, the so-called scriptments. It is fair to say that producers tend to be wary of the former and pleasantly surprised by the latter.

## SPEC SCRIPTS

A spec script is a "speculative" screenplay, one that the Variety language dictionary defines as being "shopped or sold on the open market, as opposed to one commissioned by a studio or production company."

Spec scripts are written for various reasons:

- by writers, who hope to have a script optioned and eventually purchased by producers or studios;
- by writer/directors, who want to direct a film themselves;
- by amateur writers hoping to convince a literary agent to represent them or a producer to hire them.

### Attracting Producers

The process of 'going out' with a spec script can be an extremely tense and nerve-wracking one for a writer. The writer's agent will identify a number of prospective buyers who may range from small independent producers to executives working in the major studios, and attempt to build up 'heat' under the script. The script is sent out simultaneously to all the prospective buyers, usually to be read over the weekend, in the hope of attracting a bidding war. Within a few days it is abundantly clear whether the script is going to sell or not. If it does, the writer may receive a payment of anything from a few tens of thousands of dollars to several million. If not, the script is often dead in the water because it is now in the databases of the studios and development executives, and has been marked as having been 'passed' on.

## Sample Script

A sample script is usually not intended for production, but to showcase the screenwriting skills of the author, in hopes of attracting the attention of an agent or producer. Often a spec script which fails to sell goes on to be a sample script

Many Spec scripts (short for speculative) are written independently by screenwriters in hopes of optioning and eventually outright selling them to producers or studios. Other spec scripts are written by writer-directors who plan to direct the film themselves. Many so-called "arthouse" films fall into this latter category, whereas the former category tends to be filled with "high-concept" scripts-mostly action or comedy, to which a star or A-list director can be attached.

## Script Costs

Script costs can include adaptation rights, but often story rights are listed separately in the development section of a budget.

The cost of screenplays vary enormously, and there are often many different writers involved, some of which are uncredited. For example, Quentin Tarantino did uncredited rewrites for Silver Surfer and It's Pat (see Jami Berhard's Quentin Tarantino: The Man and His Movies).

Jurassic Park was adapted by the book's author, Michael Crichton, for a large undisclosed sum. His salary for Twister was 2.5 million, but there were many writers involved, not just him.

Out of a $72 million budget for the film Signs, writer-director M. Night Shyamalan was paid $5 million, most of which were however license fees for the story rights. For the film The Village (total budget: $71 million) Shyamalan received $327,500 for all writing costs including the screenplay fees for his production company Blinding Edge Pictures and costs for materials, supplies, script duplication as well as fringes. An additional $7.2 million were payed to Shyamalan for the story rights, almost three times the amount Shyamalan earned for his work as producer and director on the film.

Although the highest paid names are stars and directors and sometimes novelists who get their film adapted, a good screenwriter can command-and is worth-a large salary. Total script costs can easily be ten percent of the film's budget but, like other areas of a film, unless the writer is a star, it is unlikely for a big budget film to spend more than 5% in the script department.

For a movie with a script budget of $500,000 that is not an adaptation, written on assignment, the payments might break down as follows (referred to as "300,000 against 500,000"):

- First draft: $150,000
- First draft revisions: $50,000
- Second draft: $75,000
- Second draft revisions: $25,000
- Production bonus: $200,000

The first four payments are paid half on commencement of the writing step and half on completion. The final payment, the production bonus, is paid only if the script goes into production and becomes due on the first day of principal photography. If a script is approved for production before all the steps have been completed, the production bonus could be bigger. This means there may be an incentive for the writer not to drag out the process.

### The Development Process

Once a studio has purchased or commissioned a script, it goes through the process of revisions and rewriting until all stakeholders are satisfied and ready to proceed. It is not uncommon for a script to go through many, many drafts on its journey to production. Very few scripts improve steadily with each draft, and when a certain avenue has been exhausted the writer will often be replaced and another brought in to do a rewrite. Occasionally it becomes impossible to satisfy all such parties, and the project enters development hell.

If a studio decides it does not wish to proceed to production with the script, the project enters 'turnaround'. Another studio may purchase the script from its original owner, but the script is encumbered with the development costs the studio has already incurred. At a certain point, it may simply be uneconomic for anyone to purchase the script, even if it is a very good one. This goes part of the way to explaining why some of the best scripts in Hollywood remain unproduced.

## The Shooting Script

Once a script has been approved for production, camera directions and notes may be inserted by the Director, and each scene is assigned a number to provide a convenient way for the various production departments to reference individual scenes. When a scene is omitted, its number is retained labelled with "OMITTED", so that it won't be assigned to any newly added scenes.

When the shooting script is distributed, its pages are locked, meaning that any subsequent revisions will apply to the first set of revision pages. When revisions are distributed, the pages are swapped into the outstanding drafts, and the script is once again locked. The process is repeated for each new round of revisions.

Each round of revisions is distributed on different coloured paper. The progression of colours varies from one production to the next. Since rewrites often continue throughout principal photography, most shooting scripts evolve into a rainbow of gold, pink, blue, green and cherry pages.

## Transcripts

A screenplay is different from a transcript. A transcript is simply a copy of what dialogue finally appeared on-screen, without regard to the original script, the stage directions or action. A full post-production transcript may also include descriptions of the action on-screen, but since it is generally not written by a professional writer but either a production assistant or a fan, it may not be particularly entertaining to read. Many published screenplays available at booksellers or downloaded from the internet are in fact glorified post-production transcripts rather than shooting scripts. Transcripts and screenplays often differ radically because scenes are frequently re-ordered or dropped entirely during the editing process. Moreover, actors may change lines or simply improvise dialog, and many directors will make their own changes to the script on the fly during rehearsal or shooting.

It can be extremely revealing to compare a shooting script with the film as finally distributed.

### Screenwriting Software

Detailed computer programs are designed specifically for screenplays, and many have templates for teleplays and stageplays. These programs have been designed to create industry standard screenplays and are used by professional screenwriters. What should be remembered is that all such software is an aid in 'formatting' of a screenplay and not the actual 'creation' of it. A number of these programs offer access to on-line screenwriter communities where you can publish your work for feedback from fellow screenwriters. Furthermore, screenwriting software is available for handheld devices (Palm OS, and Windows Mobile / Pocket PC).

## SCREENWRITER'S SALARY

A typical writer's deal usually comprises:

- *Option:* Monies paid in exchange for the right (the "option") to produce--and therefore to purchase outright--a screenplay, treatment or other work within a certain period.
- *Guarantee:* Literally, the monies the writer is guaranteed to receive, whether the script is produced or not. This amount is usually divided into payments for multiple drafts (commonly, a draft and a "set," a set being a rewrite and a polish). The guaranteed monies are sometimes referred to as the "front-end."
- *Bonus/Bonuses:* Also known as the "back-end." Typically, a production bonus is paid once the script goes into

production, or, if there has been more than one writer, after the final credit has been determined. A typical contract will specify a smaller production bonus for shared credit. There may also be bonuses contingent upon budget (e.g. "if the movie's budget is greater than x...") or grosses. The cousin of the bonus is the "penalty," which might be paid by the writer if, for example, the script has not been put into production by a set date. Penalties are rarely included in writer's deals, however.

**Definitions**

- Five figures: under $100,000
- Low-six figures: under $300,000
- Mid-six figures: between $300,000 and $600,000
- High-six figures: over $600,000
- Seven figures: Over $1 million
- *Spec Script:* Short for "speculative." The writer writes the script without being paid, and, subsequently, tries to sell it.
- *Pitch:* The writer works up a five-to-twenty minute presentation of a prospective movie and presents it to buyers in a short meeting.
- *Assignment:* A rewrite-for-pay of someone else's script. The writer pitches his "take" much like he would an original pitch.

**History of Screenwriters' Pay**

- 1900: One of America's first screenwriters, New York journalist Roy McCardell, is hired to write ten scenarios (each about 90 seconds long) for $15 each (has the buying power of about $332 today).
- 1947: The original screenplay Woman of the Year is bought by MGM for $100,000 (about $950,000 today).
- 1949: Ben Hecht is paid $10,000 a week (about $77,000 today). Claims David O. Selznick paid him $3,500 a day (about $27,000 today).

- 1967: William Goldman's original screenplay Butch Cassidy and the Sundance Kid is bought for $400,000 (about $2.25 million today).
- 1972: Leonard and Paul Schrader's spec script The Yakuza is sold for $350,000 (about $1.6 million today). Paul Schrader and his agent receive 40% each; novelist Leonard Schrader, who conceived the idea for the story, is persuaded to take just 20% and a story credit.
- 1984: Shane Black sells the screenplay to Lethal Weapon for $250,000, ushering in the modern spec market.
- 1985: Ex-fireman Gregory Widen sells his university thesis screenplay Highlander for $500,000.
- 1990: Kathy McWorter-promoted by her agent as a 21 year-old wunderkind, though she was in fact 28-sells her sex comedy The Cheese Stands Alone for $1 million. This was followed by nuclear-terrorist technothriller The Ultimatum by Laurence Dworet and Robert Roy Pool and WWII action comedy Hell Bent... and Back! by Doug Richardson, both of which sold for a million dollars.
- 1990: Brian Helgeland and Manny Coto sell their nuclear-armed robot spec The Ticking Man for $1.2 million. The script was sent out with a ticking alarm clock attached.
- 1990: Shane Black is paid $1.75 million for The Last Boy Scout.
- 1990: Joe Eszterhas sells Basic Instinct to Carolco for $3 million, but is replaced by Total Recall scribe Gary Goldman when he argues with director Paul Verhoeven over explicit content. There will not be another million dollar spec script for over two years.
- 1991: Front page of Variety mourns the end of the modern spec market, announcing "the candy store is closed."
- 1992: Sherry Lansing is hired to run Paramount and spends $3.6 million in less than a week, $2.5 million for a two-page outline of Jade by Joe Eszterhas, and $1.1 million for the for the script Milk Money by John

Mattson. At the time, both deals are records, respectively, for outlines and romantic comedy specs.

- 1994: After a bidding war, Shane Black is paid $4.5 million by New Line for The Long Kiss Goodnight.
- 1999: M. Night Shyamalan-who received $2.5 million for breakout script The Sixth Sense-is paid $5 million for Unbreakable, plus another $5 million to produce and direct. Later receives same sum for Signs.
- 2003: M. Night Shyamalan is paid $7.5 million for The Woods, later renamed The Village, but with a reduced fee of $3.21 million for producing and directing.
- 2004: Peter Jackson is paid the higher of $20 million aggregate or 20% of the gross to write, produce and direct King Kong. Jackson wrote the screenplay with his wife, Fran Walsh, and Phillipa Boyens.
- 2004: Bobby Florsheim and Josh Stolberg are paid $1.5 million against $2.5 million + 2% for "The Passion Of The Ark", later becoming Evan Almighty. Daily Variety reports this as the highest price paid for a spec script by unproduced writers.

### Current Records

Some of the highest amounts paid to writers for spec screenplays:

$4 million:

- The Long Kiss Goodnight by Shane Black

$3 million:

- Basic Instinct by Joe Eszterhas
- Medicine Man by Tom Schulman
- The Ugly Americans (Eurotrip) by Alec Berg, David Mandel and Jeff Schaffer
- Bad Dog (unproduced) by Dale Launer
- Married in the Morning (unproduced) by Harry Elfont and Deborah Kaplan
- Panic Room by David Koepp. $2 million against $3 million.

$2.75 million:

- Mozart and the Whale (The Newports) by Ronald Bass. $2 million-against $2,750,000.

$2.5 million:

- The Sixth Sense by M. Night Shyamalan
- Twister by Michael Crichton and Anne-Marie Crichton
- Jade by Joe Eszterhas
- A Knight's Tale by Brian Helgeland
- Untitled Will Davies Romantic Comedy (unproduced) by Will Davies
- Jackson (unproduced) by Brandon Camp and Mike Thompson
- The Superconducting Supercollider of Sparkle Creek, Wisconsin (unproduced) by David Koepp and John Kamps. '$2.5 million against $3.25 million with an additional deferred bonus of $1.5 million for Koepp.
- Deja Vu by Terry Rossio and Bill Marsilii. $2 million against $5 million.

$2.25 million:

- Untitled Disney Family Comedy (unproduced) by Kevin Bisch
- They Came From Upstairs (unproduced) by Mark Burton
- You, Me and Dupree by Mike LeSieur
- The Break-Up by Vince Vaughn, Jeremy Garelick and Jay Lavender

$2 million:

- The Arrangement (unproduced) by Kevin Bisch
- Stalker: A Love Story (unproduced) by Michael Carnes and Josh Gilbert
- The Worst Man (unproduced) by Michael Carnes and Josh Gilbert
- Manhattan Ghost Story (unproduced) by Ronald Bass, based on the novel by T.M. Wright.
- Radio Flyer by David M. Evans
- Forever Young by Jeffrey Abrams

- Showgirls by Joe Eszterhas
- Sacred Cows (unproduced) by Joe Eszterhas
- Reliable Sources (unproduced) by Joe Eszterhas
- Courage Under Fire by Patrick Sheane Duncan
- Tennessee (Pearl Harbor) by Randall Wallace
- River Road (unproduced) by Andrew Niccol
- The Mark (unproduced) by Rob Liefield
- Untitled Tim Herlihy Comedy (unproduced) by Tim Herlihy
- The Game by John D. Brancato and Michael Ferris
- Untitled Firestein-Pesce Action Project (unproduced) by Les Firestein and PJ Pesce
- Executive Search (unproduced) by Gerald Di Pego
- Going West (Switchback) by Jeb Stuart
- Untitled Michael McCullers Buddy Comedy (unproduced) by Michael McCullers
- Alpha (unproduced) by David Benioff
- Ghost Town by David Koepp and John Kamps
- Male Pattern Baldness (unproduced) by Joe Eszterhas. $2 million against 4.5 million.

$1.8 million:

- RPM (unproduced) by J.H. Wyman
- Stay by David Benioff

$1.5 million:

- The Passion of the Ark by Bobby Florsheim and Josh Stolberg. $1.5 million against 2.5 million.

$1.25 million:

- 99 Problems (unproduced) by Deborah Kaplan and Harry Elfont. $1.25 against $2 million.

$1.1 million:

- Milk Money by John Mattson, bought outright by Paramount in 1992.

$1 million:

- Foreplay (unproduced) by Joe Eszterhas. $1 million against $3.5 million.

- The Cheese Stands Alone (unproduced) by Kathy McWorter.

$750,000:

- Steinbeck's Point of View (unproduced) by Brandon Camp and Mike Thompson. $750,000 against $3,750,000 with an additional potential $2 million bonus cast contingent.
- Man-Witch by Bobby Florsheim and Josh Stolberg. $750,000 against $1.5 million.

## ACT STRUCTURE (FILM)

Act structure explains how a plot of a film story is composed. Just like plays (Staged drama) have 'Acts', critics and screenwriters tend to divide films into acts; though films don't require to be broken down as such in reality.

Whereas plays are actual live performances that need 'breaks' in the middle for change of set, costume, or for the artists' rest; films are recorded performances shown mechanically and therefore don't need actual breaks. Still they are divided into acts for reasons that are in aesthetic and structural conformation with the original idea of Act in theatre. Act breaks in a film are usually very obscure for lay audience and only a trained person can detect the ending of one act and the beginning of the other in the progression of a movie. The idea of Act structure is of more value while writing a Screenplay than watching a film, though the Act breaks are never actually written in the final copies of screenplays. But television scripts called Teleplays almost always include clear denotions as such. Act is the broadest structural unit of enacted stories. The most common paradigm in theatre, and so in films, is that of the 'Three-Act structure' proposed by Aristotle. It simply means that any story has a 'beginning', a 'middle' and an 'end'. Playwrights and screenwriters divide their stories into three major parts viz. 'Set up', 'Confrontation' (alternatively called as 'conflict' or 'complication') and 'Resolution'. These form the basic three acts of any performance-staged or screened.

Though various theories have been proposed and debated, the Three-act structure stands as the most popular one. Also, this is what Hollywood has discovered and proved as the most successful. The rest of the world cinema may have its own ways of looking at the plot.

## THE 'THREE-ACT STRUCTURE'

According to Hollywood, feature films are considered as audio-visual narrative forms which can be seen in distinct parts called 'Acts'.

It follows that the enacted story opens with the introduction of characters and situations, backdrop, locale etc. It creates interest in the audience and takes them to feel concerned as to what the real problem is and what may happen with it. Plays, and screenplays, usually revolve around main characters-the 'Protagonist' and the 'Antagonist' who engage themselevs into a battle. That is "Set up".

The next part-and considered to be more important-is complication of the problem of the story. It intrigues the audience all the more, giving them more and more information and putting various points of view for imaginative comparison. This eventually leads to higher points of audience interest. Because this second Act of most screenplays adds all the possible dramatic values to the plot, this is considered to be the core of the same. The Antagonist and the Protagonist try and experiment with all their strengths (and weaknesses of the other) to win the battle. That is "Confrontation".

This takes us to the third-and the most important-act, the "Resolution". This means it tends to 'solve' the problem (-s) of the story developed so far. But this is not obvious, as it is expected to bring the 'climax' (or a series of climaxes) to give the audience the pay-off. The tool usually implemented is a 'do or die' situation where doors of escape for either or both of the two characters go on closing one by one, leaving them with only a thin chance that demands the fullest exploitation of their qualities and energies. This so called jaw-dropping, breath-taking, arm-rest-grabbing moment for the audience leads to the final outcome of the entire plot. And it is usually the triumph of the good (Protagonist) over the evil (Antagonist), with rare exceptions.

### Limitations

This framework can not be rigidly applied to all the film stories, and there are a good proportion of Hollywood movies that defy this theory. Many films follow this pattern only to a subtle extent, where their genre demands a more delicate handling. Screenwiters and Script doctors have tried to provide alternative ideas, which again are open for debate. As said earlier, cinema across the world and 20th century has evolved its own ways of putting a story. Also, this theory may not be fit for non-fiction films like documentary or corporate films, which may not have a 'plot' at their base with 'characters' and all their 'actions and speeches' predecided, like the feature films have. Such non-fiction films require their own forms of arrangement.

What is important here is that ideas of Act structure help us understand films better. More importantly, these are 'tools' of the screenplay writers who can break down the story at hand and play with various ways of presenting it to find the best possible one. Experts have gone long way ahead in dividing plot to even smaller structural units and they keep working to find the most effective formula of structuring a film story.

## PLOT POINT

In television and film, a plot point is a significant event within a plot that digs into the action and spins it around in another direction. Noted screenwriting teacher Syd Field teaches that the 'ideal' movie plot has the first plot point occurring around the 30th minute of the film, then the second one around the 90th minute. See screenwriting theories for an overview list of plot points.

### Monomyth

The monomyth (often referred to as "the hero's journey") is a description of a basic pattern found in many narratives from around the world. This universal pattern was described by Joseph Campbell in his book The Hero with a Thousand Faces (1949). A noted scholar of novelist James Joyce, Campbell borrowed the term monomyth from Joyce's Finnegans Wake.

Campbell's work has been consciously applied by a wide variety of modern writers and artists, for example, in creating screenplays for movies. The best known is perhaps George Lucas, who has acknowledged a debt to Campbell regarding both the original Star Wars trilogy and its prequels.

In addition, leaders in the men's movement, notably Robert Bly and Michael J. Meade, have used Campbell's insight as a guide for personal spiritual growth.

Campbell's insight was that important myths from around the world which have survived for thousands of years, all share a fundamental structure. This fundamental structure contains a number of stages, which includes

1. A call to adventure, which the hero has to accept or decline
2. A road of trials, regarding which the hero succeeds or fails
3. Achieving the goal or "boon," which often results in important self-knowledge
4. A return to the ordinary world, again as to which the hero can succeed or fail
5. Application of the boon, in which what the hero has gained can be used to improve the world

In a well-known quote from the introduction to The Hero with a Thousand Faces, Campbell wrote:

> *"A hero ventures forth from the world of common day into a region of supernatural wonder: fabulous forces are there encountered and a decisive victory is won: the hero comes back from this mysterious adventure with the power to bestow boons on his fellow man."*

The classic examples of the monomyth relied upon by Campbell and other scholars include the Buddha, Moses, and Christ stories, although Campbell cites many other classic myths from many cultures which rely upon this basic structure.

### Summary of the Monomyth

In the monomyth, the hero starts in the ordinary world, and receives a call to enter an unusual world of strange powers and events. If the hero accepts the call to enter this strange world, the hero must face tasks and trials, and may have to face these trials alone, or may have assistance. At its most intense, the hero must survive a severe challenge, often with help earned along the journey.

If the hero survives, the hero may achieve a great gift or "boon." The hero must then decide whether to return to the ordinary world with this boon. If the hero does decide to return, the hero often faces challenges on the return journey. If the hero is successful in returning, the boon or gift may be used to improve the world. The stories of Osiris, Prometheus, Moses, Buddha, and Christ, for example, follow this structure very closely.

Campbell describes some seventeen stages or steps along this journey. Very few myths contain all seventeen stages-some myths contain many of the stages, while others contain only a few; some myths may have as a focus only one of the stages, while other myths may deal with the stages in a somewhat different order. These seventeen stages may be organized in a number of ways, including division into three sections: Departure (sometimes called Separation), Initiation and Return. "Departure" deals with the hero venturing forth on the quest; "Initiation" deals with the hero's various adventures along the way; and "Return" deals with the hero's return home with knowledge and powers acquired on the journey.

### Other Formulations

Campbell's proposed structure has been expanded and modified since its conception. Many modern characterizations of it add in new steps (such as the hero having a miraculous birth) or combine or prune others. For instance, Phil Cousineau, in his book, The Hero's Journey, divides it up into the following eight steps:

1. The Call to Adventure
2. The Road of Trials
3. The Vision Quest
4. The Meeting with the Goddess
5. The Boon

6. The Magic Flight
7. The Return Threshold
8. The Master of Two Worlds

Another eight-step formulation was given by David Adams Leeming in his book, Mythology: The Voyage of the Hero:

1. Miraculous conception and birth
2. Initiation of the hero-child
3. Withdrawal from family or community for meditation and preparation
4. Trial and Quest
5. Death
6. Descent into the underworld
7. Resurrection and rebirth
8. Ascension, apotheosis, and atonement

## Use of the Monomyth by Modern Artists

The monomyth has influenced a number of artists, musicians, poets, and filmmakers, including Bob Dylan and George Lucas. Mickey Hart, Bob Weir and Jerry Garcia of the Grateful Dead had long noted Campbell's influence and agreed to participate in a seminar with him in 1986 entitled From Ritual to Rapture.

### *George Lucas and Star Wars*

George Lucas's deliberate use of Campbell's theory of the monomyth in the making of the Star Wars movies is well-documented. In addition to the extensive discussion between Campbell and Bill Moyers broadcast in 1988 on PBS as The Power of Myth (Filmed at "Skywalker Ranch"), on Campbell's influence on the Star Wars films, Lucas, himself, gave an extensive interview for the biography Joseph Campbell: A Fire in the Mind (Larsen and Larsen, 2002, pages 541-543) on this topic.

In this interview, Lucas states that in the early 1970's after completing his early film, American Graffiti, "it came to me that there really was no modern use of mythology...so that's when I started doing more strenuous research on fairy tales, folklore and mythology, and I started reading Joe's books. Before that I hadn't read any of Joe's books.... It was very eerie because in reading The Hero with A Thousand Faces I began to realize that my first draft of Star Wars was following classical motifs"(p.541).

Twelve years after the making of The Power of Myth, Moyers and Lucas met again for the 1999 interview, the Mythology of Star Wars with George Lucas & Bill Moyers, to further discuss the impact of Campbell's work on Lucas' films. In addition, the National Air and Space Museum of the Smithsonian Institution sponsored an exhibit during the late 1990s called Star Wars: The Magic of Myth which discussed the ways in which Campbell's work shaped the Star Wars films. A companion guide of the same name was published in 1997.

### *Chris Vogler, The Writer's Journey, and Hollywood Films*

Christopher Vogler, a Hollywood film producer and writer, created a now-legendary 7-page company memo, A Practical Guide to The Hero With a Thousand Faces, based on Campbell's work which inspired films such as Disney's 1994 film, The Lion King. Vogler's memo was later developed into the late 1990s book, The Writer's Journey: Mythic Structure For Writers, This story structure is evident in a vast number of successful Hollywood films including the Matrix series.

## Orson Scott Card and Ender's Game

In his book, Ender's Game, Orson Scott Card gives a very complete example of the monomyth structure, with the main character, Ender Wiggin, fulfilling all eight primary stages of it:

- *Miraculous Birth*-In a world where only two children are normally allowed, Ender is born as the third child by special government decree
- *Initiation*-Ender shows remarkable intelligence at a young age
- *Withdrawal*-Ender is removed from his family and sent to Battle School

- *Trial and Quest*-Ender learns of the threat to humanity from the Buggers
- *Death*-Ender grows despondent after his unit is broken up, and he is sent back to Earth
- *Descent into the underworld*-Ender's sister helps him feel like part of humanity once again
- *Resurrection and rebirth*-Ender refuses to play the "simulations" anymore, and ends the "game" by destroying the Buggers' homeworld
- *Ascension, apotheosis, and atonement*-Ender realizes that the simulations were in fact real and has to cope with this

The narrative structure within Ender's Game doesn't follow this structure perfectly linearly. Many elements of it are actually repeated throughout the book. For instance, the latter four steps can also describe the psychological states Ender went through after his realization of what he'd done to the Buggers.

## Modern Applications of the Monomyth

Each of the seventeen stages of the monomyth (below) can be found in popular works, including movie series such as the Star Wars movies, The Matrix movies and even the anime Fortune Dogs.

## DEPARTURE (OR SEPARATION)

### The Call to Adventure

The adventure begins with the hero receiving a call to action, such as a threat to the peace of the community, or the hero simply falls into or blunders into it. The call is often announced to the hero by another character who acts as a "herald". The herald, often represented as dark or terrifying and judged evil by the world, may call the character to adventure simply by the crisis of his appearance.

Campbell: The Call To Adventure-"A blunder-apparently the merest chance-reveals an unsuspected world, and the individual is drawn into a relationship with forces that are not rightly understood" (Joseph Campbell, The Hero With A Thousand Faces, 51).

**Modern Applications:** In Star Wars, Luke Skywalker, the hero, begins the story in frustration over being unable to leave home. The heralds are the two droids who carry a message from Princess Leia. In The Matrix, the call comes in the form of Morpheus and his followers who encourage the hero, Neo, to question reality. Morpheus literally calls Neo using a cell phone.

**Classic Examples:** Sometimes the call to adventure happens of the character's own volition. In the story of the Minotaur, Theseus learns the tale of the beast and the terrible sacrifice to appease it, which sets him on a quest to destroy it. In Herman Hesse's book Siddhartha the main character, Siddhartha, becomes weary of his way of life and decides he must venture away from his accustomed life in order to attain spiritual enlightenment. Most Buddhist myths describe the Buddha as becoming bored with his royal life and venturing into the world. Other times, the hero is plunged into adventure by unforeseen events. In Homer's Odyssey, Odysseus is caught in the terrible winds of the angered god Poseidon and sent off to distant lands.

## REFUSAL OF THE CALL

In some stories, the hero initially refuses the call to adventure. When this happens, the hero may suffer somehow, and may eventually choose to answer, or may continue to decline the call.

**Campbell:** Refusal of the Call-"Refusal of the summons converts the adventure into its negative. Walled in boredom, hard work, or 'culture,' the subject loses the power of significant affirmative action and becomes a victim to be saved" (Joseph Campbell, The Hero With A Thousand Faces, 59).

**Modern Applications:** In Star Wars, Luke is refused adventure by his uncle, a man who seeks to protect Luke from the inevitable dangers of fate. Subsequently, Luke's family is killed by stormtroopers. In The Matrix, Neo refuses to take the window washing scaffold to escape and is captured by the Agents.

**Classic Examples:** Myth and history are rife with examples of what happens to those who refuse the call too long or do not take it seriously. A Persian city was turned to stone, inhabitants and all, for refusing the call of Allah. Daphne was pursued by the Greek god Apollo (a herald), but refused his advances at all costs. She prayed to her father, Peneus, to take away her beauty to be rid of Apollo; Peneus turned the nymph into a tree, the only semblance left of her past self being her beauty. In Judeo-Christian mythology, Lot's wife is turned into a pillar of salt for looking back with longing to her old life when she had been summoned forth from her city by Yahweh. One of the clearest references to the refusal and its consequences comes in the voice of Yahweh in Proverbs 1:24-27 and 32:

Because I have called, and ye refused... I also will laugh at your calamity; I will mock when your fear cometh; when your fear cometh as desolation, and your destruction cometh as a whirlwind; when distress and anguish cometh upon you.... For the turning away of the simple shall slay them, and the prosperity of fools shall destroy them.

**SUPERNATURAL AID**

After the hero has accepted the call, he encounters a protective figure (often elderly) who provides special tools and advice for the adventure ahead, such as an amulet or a weapon.

Modern applications: In Star Wars, Luke encounters the Jedi Master Obi-Wan Kenobi who presents Luke with a lightsaber and teaches him the ways of the Force. In The Matrix Neo meets with The Oracle who gives him advice which proves invaluable in his journey.

In The Hitchhikers Guide to the Galaxy, Ford Prefect gives Arthur Dent the copy of the guide.

Classic example: In Greek mythology, Ariadne gives Theseus a ball of string and a sword before he enters the labyrinth to confront the minotaur.

## THE CROSSING OF THE FIRST THRESHOLD

The hero must cross the threshold between the world he is familiar with and that which he is not. Often this involves facing a "threshold guardian", an entity that works to keep all within the protective confines of the world but must be encountered in order to enter the new zone of experience.

Modern applications: In Star Wars, the threshold is Mos Eisley, a spaceport that acts as a doorway between Luke's home planet and the wider universe; Luke must avoid capture by the threshold guardians, the Imperial stormtroopers. In The Matrix, Neo must choose the red pill to leave the Matrix and enter the real world.

### Rebirth

The hero, rather than passing a threshold, passes into the new zone by means of rebirth. Appearing to have died by being swallowed or having their flesh scattered, the hero is transformed and becomes ready for the adventure ahead.

Biblical applications: In the gospels, John the Baptist baptizes Jesus before Jesus begins his public ministry.

Modern applications: In Star Wars, it is the Death Star, in which Luke is engulfed and in which he learns how to be a hero. In The Matrix, Neo finds himself waking up in a bio-electric cell where he is one of the humans being harvested by the machines.

## INITIATION

### The Road of Trials

Once past the threshold, the hero encounters a dream landscape of ambiguous and fluid forms. The hero is challenged to survive a succession of obstacles and, in so doing, amplifies his consciousness. The hero is helped covertly by the supernatural helper or may discover a benign power supporting him in his passage.

### Marriage

The ultimate trial is often represented as a marriage between the hero and a queenlike, or mother-like figure. This represents the hero's mastery of life (represented by the feminine) as well as the totality of what can be known. When the hero is female, this becomes a male figure.

**Modern Applications:** In The Matrix, Neo confronts the Oracle. In The Matrix Reloaded, Neo takes Trinity as a lover.

### Woman as Temptress

His awareness expanded, the hero may fixate on the disunity between truth and his subjective outlook, inherently tainted by the flesh. This is often represented with revulsion or rejection of a female figure.

**Modern Applications:** In The Matrix Reloaded, Persephone attempts to seduce Neo. In Star Wars, there is tension between Luke and Han Solo over their love for Princess Leia--this is resolved in Episode VI, Return of the Jedi when Luke finds out that Leia is actually his sister. Luke is also tempted by the dark side itself, as demonstrated by his vision in the cave on Dagobah.

### Atonement with the Father

The hero reconciles the tyrant and merciful aspects of the father-like authority figure to understand himself as well as this figure.

**Biblical Applications:** In the gospels, Jesus wrestles with his impending death in the Garden of Gethsemane, before submitting to his Father's will.

Modern applications: In The Empire Strikes Back, Luke confronts Darth Vader and learns that he is his father and a former Jedi; in Return of the Jedi, he is reconciled with the reformed Vader. In The Matrix Revolutions, the Oracle explains to Neo that she and the Architect are two programs that work together to keep the Matrix working, the latter to "balance the equation" and the former to "unbalance" it.

## APOTHEOSIS

The hero's ego is disintegrated in a breakthrough expansion of consciousness. Quite frequently the hero's idea of reality is changed; the hero may find an ability to do new things or to see a larger point of view, allowing the hero to sacrifice himself.

Modern applications: In The Empire Strikes Back, Luke sacrifices a part of himself (losing his hand) rather than turn to the dark side. In The Matrix, Neo faces off against Agent Smith resulting in his death and resurrection as the One.

## THE ULTIMATE BOON

The hero is now ready to obtain that which he has set out, an item or new awareness that, once he returns, will benefit the society that he has left. Modern applications: In the climactic scene of Star Wars, Luke uses the Force to successfully destroy the Death Star by firing torpedoes down a narrow ventilation shaft of the Death Star.

## RETURN

### Refusal of the Return

Having found bliss and enlightenment in the other world, the hero may not want to return to the ordinary world to bestow the boon onto his fellow man.

**Classic Examples:** After obtaining Nirvana, Buddha doubted whether he could communicate the path to enlightenment. (Actually, some Buddhist traditions hold that this was only cunning politics by Buddha: by saying this he gave people the impression that he didn't want to teach them, which made them curious and eager to hear all about it).

### The Magic Flight

When the boon's acquisition (or the hero's return to the world) comes against opposition, a chase or pursuit may ensue before the hero returns.

**Classic Examples:** In many fairy tales and folktales, it is literally a magic flight, with the hero or heroine transforming objects to stop the pursuit (The Master Maid, The Water Nixie) or transforming himself and any companions to hide themselves (Farmer Weathersky or Foundling-Bird).

**Modern Examples:** In the Metroid video game series, Samus Aran frequently has to outrun the destruction of a collapsing structure after defeating the final boss.

### Rescue from Without

The hero may need to be rescued by forces from the ordinary world. This may be because the hero has refused to return or because he is successfully blocked from returning with the boon. The hero loses his ego.

**Modern Application:** In The Empire Strikes Back, Luke is rescued by the Millennium Falcon as he hangs on an antenna beneath Cloud City after a battle with Darth Vader. In The Matrix: Revolutions, Neo is physically trapped in the limbo-like Mobil Avenue subway station construct, and Morpheus and Trinity have to help him escape.

### The Crossing of the Return Threshold

The hero returns to the world of common day and must accept it as real.

### Master of Two Worlds

Because of the boon or due to his experience, the hero may now perceive both the divine and human worlds.

**Modern Application:** In Return of the Jedi, Luke becomes a Jedi. He has mastered the force and defeated the one true temptation, the Dark Side. In The Matrix Neo returns from death now able to see and control the world of The Matrix, stopping bullets and defeating the Agents. In The Matrix Reloaded, Neo destroys several Sentinels in the real world using only his mind.

**Classic Example:** In the Christ story, Jesus is able to return to the ordinary world after resurrection.

### Freedom to Live

The hero bestows the boon to his fellow man.

**Modern Application:** In "The Return of the Jedi" Luke has overcome the Empire and his rebellion is free to live and thrive, the ending scene establishes the peace restored by Luke's victory.

In The Matrix Revolutions, Neo realizes that machine life is as valid as human life and gives his own life in order to reconcile the worlds of man and machine.

According to the Gospels, Christ returns to the ordinary world after his resurrection, but not as an ordinary man. He can seem to be as others are and interact with them, but his body is a "glorified" body, capable of assuming visible and palpable form, but freed from the bonds of space and time; he is able to appear and disappear at will, for example.

Other traditional examples of something similar, are Elijah, Enoch, and Khidr, the "immortal prophet" of the Sufis.

## Use of the Monomyth by the Men's Movement

Poet Robert Bly, Michael J. Meade, and others involved in the men's movement have applied and expanded the concept of the hero's journey and the monomyth as a metaphor for personal spiritual and psychological growth, particularly in the mythopoetic men's movement.

Characteristic of the mythopoetic men's movement is a tendency to retell fairy tales and engage in their exegesis as a tool for personal insight.

Using frequent references to archetypes as drawn from Jungian analytical psychology, the movement focuses on issues of gender role, gender identity and wellness for modern men. Advocates would often engage in storytelling with music, these acts being seen as a modern extension to a form of "new age shamanism" popularized by Michael Harner at approximately the same time.

Among its most famous advocates were the poet Robert Bly, whose book Iron John: A Book About Men was a best-seller, being an exegesis of the fairy tale "Iron John" by the Brothers Grimm.

The mythopoetic men's movement spawned a variety of groups and workshops, led by authors such as Bly and Robert L. Moore. Some serious academic work came out of this movement, including the creation of various magazines and non-profit organizations, such as the Mankind Project.

## "The Hero's Journey"

The phrase, "the hero's journey," to describe Campbell's theories first entered into popular discourse through two documentaries. The first, released in 1987, The Hero's Journey: The World of Joseph Campbell was accompanied by a 1990 companion book, The Hero's Journey: Joseph Campbell on His Life and Work (with Phil Cousineau and Stuart Brown, eds.). The second was Bill Moyer's series of seminal interviews with Campbell, released in 1988 as the documentary (and companion book) The Power of Myth.

The phrase was then referenced in the title of a popular guidebook for screenwriters released in the 1990's, The Writer's Journey: Mythic Structure For Writers, by Christopher Vogler. Though they used the phrase in their works, Cousineau, Moyers, and Vogler, all attribute the phrase and the model of The Hero's Journey to Joseph Campbell.

### Criticism

Thoughtless use of monomyth structure is often blamed for lack of originality and clichés in popular culture, especially big-budget Hollywood films. In addition to the popularity of Campbell-influenced guides such as The Writer's Journey, the influential book Screenplay by Syd Field also proposed an ideal three-act structure, which is easily compatible with modern screenwriters' attempts to craft a monomyth.

However, since the peak popularity of cinematic monomyth narratives in the 1990s, some would-be blockbuster movies that have been seen as conscious attempts to follow the structure have met with indifference from critics and often disappointing performance at the box office, as in the case of Cinderella Man and George Lucas' three Star Wars prequels.

## THE HERO WITH A THOUSAND FACES

The Hero with a Thousand Faces (1949) is the seminal work of comparative mythologist Joseph Campbell. In this text Campbell discusses his theory of the journey of the archetypal hero found in world mythologies and religions.

Since publication of The Hero with a Thousand Faces, Campbell's theory has been consciously applied by a wide variety of modern writers and artists. The best known is perhaps George Lucas, who has acknowledged a debt to Campbell regarding the stories of the Star Wars films.

### Summary

Campbell's insight was that important myths from around the world which have survived for thousands of years, all share a fundamental structure, which Campbell called the monomyth.

This fundamental structure contains a number of stages, which include: (1) a call to adventure, which the hero has to accept or decline, (2) a road of trials, regarding which the hero succeeds or fails, (3) achieving the goal or "boon," which often results in important self-knowledge, (4) a return to the ordinary world, again as to which the hero can succeed or fail, and finally, (5) application of the boon in which what the hero has gained can be used to improve the world.

In a well-known quote from the introduction to The Hero with a Thousand Faces, Campbell wrote:

> *"A hero ventures forth from the world of common day into a region of supernatural wonder: fabulous forces are there encountered and a decisive victory is won: the hero comes back from this mysterious adventure with the power to bestow boons on his fellow man."*

The classic examples of the monomyth relied upon by Campbell and other scholars include the Buddha, Moses, and Christ stories, although Campbell cites many other classic myths from many cultures which rely upon this basic structure.

While Campbell offers a discussion of the hero's journey by using the Freudian concepts popular in the 1940s and 1950s, the monomythic structure is not tied to these concepts. Similarly, Campbell uses a mixture of Jungian archetypes, unconscious forces, and Arnold van Gennep's structuring of rites of passage rituals to provide some illumination.

However, this pattern of the hero's journey influences artists and intellectuals worldwide, suggesting a basic usefulness for Campbell's insights not tied to academic categories and mid-20th century forms of analysis.

# 7

# The Structure of Monomyth

In the monomyth, the hero starts in the ordinary world, and receives a call to enter an unusual world of strange powers and events. If the hero accepts the call to enter this strange world, the hero must face tasks and trials, and may have to face these trials alone, or may have assistance. At its most intense, the hero must survive a severe challenge, often with help earned along the journey. If the hero survives, the hero may achieve a great gift or "boon." The hero must then decide whether to return to the ordinary world with this boon. If the hero does decide to return, the hero often faces challenges on the return journey. If the hero is successful in returning, the boon or gift may be used to improve the world. The stories of Osiris, Prometheus, Moses, Buddha, and Christ, for example, follow this structure very closely.

Campbell describes a number of stages or steps along this journey. Very few myths contain all of these stages-some myths contain many of the stages, while others contain only a few; some myths may have as a focus only one of the stages, while other myths may deal with the stages in a somewhat different order.

These stages may be organized in a number of ways, including division into three sections: Departure (sometimes called Separation), Initiation and Return. "Departure" deals with the hero venturing forth on the quest; "Initiation" deals with the hero's various adventures along the way; and "Return" deals with the hero's return home with knowledge and powers acquired on the journey.

The Hero with a Thousand Faces has influenced a number of artists, musicians, poets, and filmmakers, including Bob Dylan and George Lucas. Mickey Hart, Bob Weir and Jerry Garcia of the Grateful Dead had long noted Campbell's influence and agreed to participate in a seminar with him in 1986 entitled From Ritual to Rapture.

George Lucas' deliberate use of Campbell's theory of the monomyth in the making of the Star Wars movies is well-documented. In addition to the extensive discussion between Campbell and Bill Moyers, broadcast in 1988 on PBS as The Power of Myth (filmed at "Skywalker Ranch"), on Campbell's influence on the Star Wars films, Lucas gave an extensive interview for the biography Joseph Campbell: A Fire in the Mind (Larsen and Larsen, 2002, pages 541-543) on this topic.

Christopher Vogler, a Hollywood film producer and writer, wrote the book The Writer's Journey: Mythic Structure For Writers, which became the basis for a number of successful Hollywood films and is believed to have been used in the development of the Matrix series.

Matthew Amerling, who had a severe case of writer's block, completed his first novel The Midknight after reading this book.

## INTRODUCTION

Campbell used the work of early 20th century theorists to develop his model of the hero (see also structuralism), including Freud (particularly the Oedipus complex), Carl Jung (archetypal figures and the collective unconscious), and Arnold Van Gennep (The three stages of The Rites of Passage, translated by Campbell into Departure, Separation, and Return). Campbell also looked to the work of ethnographers James Frazer and Franz Boas and psychologist Otto Rank.

Campbell called this journey of the hero, the monomyth. Campbell was a noted scholar of James Joyce (in 1944 he had authored A Skeleton Key to Finnegans Wake with Henry Morton Robinson), and Campbell borrowed the term Monomyth from Joyce's Finnegans Wake. In addition, Joyce's Ulysses was also highly influential in the structuring of The Hero with a Thousand

Faces. The Princeton University Press published all editions of this text. Originally issued in 1949, The Hero with a Thousand Faces has been reprinted a number of times. Reprints issued after the release of Star Wars Episode IV: A New Hope in 1977 used the image of Mark Hamill as Luke Skywalker on the cover. The 2004 Commemorative Edition has both a new introduction by Clarissa Pinkola Estés and a new cover.

**Quotes**

- "There are of course differences between the numerous mythologies and religions of mankind, but this is a book about similarities; and once they are understood the differences will be found to be much less great than is popularly (and politically) supposed. My hope is that a comparative elucidation may contribute to the perhaps not-quite disparate causes of those forces that are working in the present world for unification, not in the name of some ecclesiastical or political empire, but in the sense of human mutual understanding" (Third edition, page VIII).
- "As we are told in the Vedas: 'Truth is one, the sages speak of it by many names,' " (Third edition, page VII).

**Criticism**

- Clyde W. Ford (2000) was initially distressed by the opening lines of the prologue to The Hero with a Thousand Faces. He eventually returned to the text, in order to synthesize what was of value to him: "Several months passed before I mustered the courage to challenge Campbell again...I was rewarded for my persistence. Campbell's shortsightedness about Africa could not obliterate his immense contributions to mythology, and his omission gave me an opportunity to explore African mythology in a novel and meaningful way" (p. 12).
- Marc Manganaro (1992), argues that Campbell's theories violate the expectations of poststructuralism: "Campbell's reading of mythology as text hardly aligns with post-structuralist notions of 'world as text,' as a realm of

constantly shifting signifiers having no provable reference to a ground of signified meaning...on the contrary Campbell's trope of 'text'...functions as a shell that covers the true interior of the myth" (p. 159).

- Pearson and Pope (1981) claim that Campbell's model discounts the possibility of female heroes: "The great works on the hero--such as Joseph Campbell's The Hero With A Thousand Faces...all begin with the assumption that the hero is male" (p. vii).
- Novelist David Brin has been openly critical of his theories.
- Novelist David Foster Wallace in the short story Another Pioneer (part of the collection, Oblivion, 2004) critiques Campbell's journey of the hero.
- American novelist Kurt Vonnegut satirized Campbell's views on the monomyth as being excessively complicated by offering his interpretation, called the "In The Hole" theory; loosely defined as "The hero gets into trouble. The hero gets out of trouble."
- American philosopher John Shelton Lawrence and American religious scholar Robert Jewett have discussed an "American Monomyth" in many of their books, The American Monomyth, The Myth of the American Superhero, and Captain American and the Crusade of Zealous Nationalism.

## STORYBOARD

Storyboards are graphic organizers such as a series of illustrations or images displayed in sequence for the purpose of previsualizing a motion graphic or interactive media sequence, including website interactivity.

## ORIGINS

The storyboarding process, in the form it is known today, was developed at the Walt Disney studio during the early 1930s, after several years of similar processes being in use at Walt Disney and other animation studios. In the biography of her father, The Story of Walt Disney (Henry Holt, 1956), Diane

Disney Miller explains that the first complete storyboards were created for the Disney short the Three Little Pigs (film). According to John Canemaker, in Paper Dreams: The Art and Artists of Disney Storyboards (1999, Hyperion Press), the first storyboards at Disney evolved from comic-book like "story sketches" created in the 1920s to illustrate concepts for animated cartoon short subjects such as Plane Crazy and Academy Award winner Steamboat Willie.

According to Christopher Finch in The Art of Walt Disney (Abrams, 1973), Disney credited animator Webb Smith with creating the idea of drawing scenes on separate sheets of paper and pinning them up on a bulletin board to tell a story in sequence, thus creating the first storyboard.

One of the first live action films to be completely storyboarded was Gone with the Wind. William Cameron Menzies, the film's production designer, was hired by David Selznik to design every shot of the film. Many large budget silent films were also storyboarded but most of this material has been lost during the reduction of the studio archives during the 1970's.

Storyboarding became popular in live-action film production during the early 1940s, and grew into a standard medium for previsualization of films: "We can see the last half century... as the period in which production design was largely characterized by adoption of the storyboard," wrote curator Annette Michelson in a 1993 catalog for the Pace Gallery exhibit Drawing into Film: Director's Drawings, which featured storyboards of popular films. Storyboarding's most recent use is outlining websites and other interactive media projects during the design phase.

## USAGE

### Film

A film storyboard is essentially a large comic of the film or some section of the film produced beforehand to help film directors, cinematographers and television commercial advertising clients visualize the scenes and find potential problems before they occur. Often storyboards include arrows or instructions that indicate movement. In creating a motion picture with any degree of fidelity to a script, a storyboard provides a visual layout of events as they are to be seen through the camera lens. And in the case of interactive media, it is the layout and sequence in which the user or viewer sees the content or information. In the storyboarding process, most technical details involved in crafting a film or interactive media project can be efficiently described either in picture, or in additional text.

Some live-action film directors, such as Joel and Ethan Coen, used storyboard extensively before taking the pitch to their funders, stating that it helps them get the figure they are looking for since they can show exactly where the money will be used. Other directors storyboard only certain scenes, or not at all. Animation directors are usually required to storyboard extensively, sometimes in place of doing a script.

### Animatics

In animation and special effects work, the storyboarding stage may be followed by simplified mock-ups called "animatics" to give a better idea of how the scene will look and feel with motion and timing. At its simplest, an animatic is a series of still images edited together and displayed in sequence. More commonly, a rough dialogue and/or rough sound track is added to the sequence of still images (usually taken from a storyboard) to test whether the sound and images are working effectively together.

This allows the animators and directors to work out any screenplay, camera positioning, shot list and timing issues that may exist with the current storyboard. The storyboard and soundtrack are amended if necessary, and a new animatic may be created and reviewed with the director until the storyboard is perfected. Editing the film at the animatic stage can avoid animation of scenes that would be edited out of the film. Animation is usually an expensive process, so there should be a minimum "deleted scenes" if the film is to be completed within budget.

Often storyboards are animated with simple zooms and pans to simulate camera movement (using non-linear editing software). These animations can be combined with available animatics, sound effects and dialog to create a presentation of how a film could be shot and cut together. Some feature film DVD special features include production animatics.

### Business

Storyboards were adapted from the film industry to business, purportedly by Howard Hughes of Hughes Aircraft. Today they are used by industry for planning ad campaigns, commercials, a proposal or other projects intended to convince or compel to action.

A "quality storyboard" is a tool to help facilitate the introduction of a quality improvement process into an organisation.

Design comics are a type of storyboard used to include a customer or other characters into a narrative. Design comics are most often used in designing web sites or illustrating product usage scenarios during design.

### Interactive Media

More recently the term "storyboard" has been used in the fields of web development, software development and instructional design to present and describe interactive events as well as audio and motion, particularly on user interfaces, electronic pages and presentation screens. An interactive media storyboard may be used in the graphical user interface for the user experience design of a website or interactive project as well as a visual tool for planning the content. In contrast, a site map or flow chart may be better to plan the information architecture, navigation, links, organization and total user experience, especially when the sequence of events is less predictable or the audiovisual change between events is of little design importance.

### Benefits

One advantage of using storyboards is that it allows (in film and business) the user to experiment with changes in the story-line to evoke stronger reaction or interest. Flashbacks, for instance, are often the result of sorting storyboards out of chronological order to help build suspense and interest. The process of visual thinking and planning allows a group of people to brainstorm together, placing their ideas on storyboards and then arranging the storyboards on the wall. This fosters more ideas and generates consensus inside the group.

## ANIMATION

Animation is the rapid display of a sequence of images of 2-D artwork or model positions in order to create an illusion of movement. It is an optical illusion of motion due to the phenomenon of persistence of vision. This could be anything from a flip book to a motion picture film.

### Early Animation

There is no single person who can be considered the "creator" of the art of animation, as there were several people doing several projects which could be considered various types of animation all around the same time. (Short, hand-drawn animation scenes could be presented with the Phenakistoscope, the Zoetrope, and other optical "toys" already in the early 1800s.) The following is a brief listing on those who are often acknowledged as significant to the development of animation. Note that this list is by no means a comprehensive list of contributors to early animation.

Georges Méliès was a creator of special effect films, such as A Trip to the Moon. He used many techniques-one of which was to stop the camera rolling, change something in the scene, and then continue rolling the film. This is a very similar idea to that of stop-motion animation. Méliès accidentally happened upon the technique when his camera broke down while shooting a bus driving by. When the camera was fixed, a horse happened to be passing by just as Méliès continued to film. The result was that the bus appeared to change into a horse.

J. Stuart Blackton was possibly the first filmmaker in America to use the techniques of stop-motion and hand-drawn animation. Introduced to film-making by Edison, he pioneered these concepts at the turn of the 20th century, with his first copyrighted work dated 1900. Émile Cohl began drawing cartoon strips and created a film in 1908 called Fantasmagorie. The film largely consisted of a stick figure moving about and encountering all manner of morphing objects, such as a wine bottle that transforms into a flower. There were also sections of live action where the animator's hands would enter the scene. The film was created by drawing each frame on paper and then shooting each frame onto negative film, which gave the picture a blackboard look.

Winsor McCay created detailed animations that required a team of artists and painstaking attention for detail. Each frame was drawn on paper, requiring backgrounds to be redrawn, as well characters to be animated. His films such as Gertie the Dinosaur (1914) and The Sinking of the Lusitania (1918) were of an impressive scale, although The Sinking of the Lusitania used cells.

Otto Messmer, in 1919, created the character of Felix the cat for Pat Sullivan's animation studios. The importance of Felix lies in the character's strong personality, created largely through gesture and actions.

### Animation Techniques

Animation techniques are incredibly varied and difficult to categorize. Techniques are often related or combined. The following is a brief on common types of animation. Again, this list is by no means comprehensive.

### Traditional Animation

Also called cel animation, the frames of a traditionally animated movie are hand-drawn. The drawings are traced or copied onto transparent acetate sheets called cels, which are then placed over a painted background and photographed one by one on a rostrum camera. Nowadays, the use of cels (and cameras) is mostly obsolete, since the drawings are scanned into computers, and digitally transferred directly to 35 mm film. The "look" of traditional cel animation is still preserved, and the character animator's work has remained essentially the same over the past 70 years. Because of the digital influence over modern cel animation, it is also known as tradigital animation.

*Examples:* The Lion King, Spirited Away, Les Triplettes de Belleville.

### Full Animation

The most widely-known style in animation, known for its realistic and often very detailed art.-

**Examples:** All Disney feature length animations, The Secret of NIMH, The Iron Giant

### Limited Animation

A cheaper process of making animated cartoons that does not follow a "realistic" approach.

**Examples:** The Flintstones, Yellow Submarine

### Rubber Hose

The characters are usually very "cartoony", and the animators have a lot of artistic freedom as rubber hose doesn't have to follow the laws of physics and anatomy to the same degree as the other main styles of animation.

**Examples:** Early Mickey Mouse cartoons, Popeye, Ren and Stimpy

### Rotoscoping

A technique where animators trace live action movement, frame by frame, either by directly copying an actors outlines into an animated drawing (e.g. Ralph Bakshi), or use rotoscoped material as a basis and inspiration for a more fluid and expressive animation (e.g. Disney).

**Examples:** Snow White and the Seven Dwarfs, Gulliver's Travels, American Pop

### Stop Motion

Stop-motion animation is any type of animation which requires the animator to physically alter the scene, shoot a frame, again alter the scene and shoot a frame and so on, to create the animation. There are many different types of stop-motion animation. Some notable examples are listed below.

#### *Clay Animation*

Often abbreviated to claymation, this is a type of stop-motion animation using figures made of clay or a similar malleable material. The figures may have an armature or wire frame inside of them, similar to puppet animation (below). Alternatively, the figures may be made entirely of clay, such as in the films of Bruce Bickford where clay creatures morph into a variety of different shapes.

**Examples:** Morph, Wallace and Gromit; Jan Svankmajer's Dimensions of Dialogue; The Amazing Mr. Bickford; The Trap Door

### *Cutout Animation*

A type of stop-motion animation formed by moving 2-dimensional pieces of material such as paper or cloth.

**Examples:** Terry Gilliam's animated sequences of Monty Python's Flying Circus; Fantastic Planet; Tale of Tales; pilot episode of South Park

### *Silhouette Animation*

A monochrome variant of cutout animation in which the characters are only visible as black silhouettes.

**Example:** The Adventures of Prince Achmed; Princes et princesses

### *Graphic Animation*

**Model animation:** In this form of animation, model animated characters interact with, and are a part of, the live-action world.

**Examples:** The films of Ray Harryhausen (Jason and the Argonauts) and Willis O'Brien (King Kong)

Go motion

Object animation

Pixilation

**Examples:** Neighbours

### *Puppet Animation*

Puppet animation typically involves puppet figures interacting with each other in a constructed environment, in contrast to the real-world interaction in model animation (above). The puppets generally have an armature inside of them to keep them still and steady as well as constraining them to move at particular joints.

**Examples:** The Tale of the Fox, the films of Jirí Trnka, The Nightmare Before Christmas, Robot Chicken

Brickfilm

Puppetoon

*Computer Animation*

Like stop motion, computer animation encompasses a variety of techniques, the unifying idea being that the animation is created digitully on a computer.

**2D Animation:** Figures are created and/or edited on the computer using 2D bitmap graphics or created and edited using 2D vector graphics. This includes automated computerized versions of traditional animation techniques such as of tweening, morphing, onion skinning and interpolated rotoscoping.

**Examples:** A Scanner Darkly, Jib Jab

- Analog computer animation
- Flash animation
- PowerPoint animation

**3D Animation:** Figures are created in the computer using polygons. To allow these meshes to move they are given a digital armature (sculpture). This process is called rigging. Various other techniques can be applied, such as mathematical functions (gravity), simulated fur or hair, effects such as fire and water and the use of motion capture to name but a few.

**Examples:** The Incredibles, Shrek, Finding Nemo.

- Cel-shaded animation
- Morph target animation
- Skeletal animation
- Motion capture
- Crowd simulation

*Less Common Techniques*

**Drawn on Film Animation:** A technique where footage is produced by creating the images directly on film stock.

**Paint-on-glass Animation:** A technique for making animated films by manipulating slow drying oil paints on sheets of glass.

**Pinscreen Animation:** Makes use of a screen filled with movable pins, which can be moved in or out by pressing an object onto the screen.

The screen is lit from the side so that the pins cast shadows. The technique has been used to create animated films with a range of textural effects difficult to achieve with traditional cel animation.

**Sand Animation:** Sand is moved around on a backlighted or frontlighted piece of glass to create each frame for an animated film.

## OTHER TECHNIQUES AND APPROACHES

**Character Animation:** Character animation is the animation of a character to create the illusion of life, usually as one aspect of a larger production, and often to complement voice acting.

Character animation is artistically unique from other animation in that it involves the creation of apparent thought and emotion, in addition to physical action.

Historically, Winsor McCay's Gertie the Dinosaur, 1914, is often considered the very first example of true character animation.

Otto Messmer imbued his Felix the Cat with an instantly recognizable personality during the 1920s. The following decade, Walt Disney made character animation a particular focus of his animation studio, best showcased in productions such as Three Little Pigs, Snow White and the Seven Dwarfs, Pinocchio, and Dumbo.

Disney animation artists such as Bill Tytla, Grim Natwick, Fred Moore, Ward Kimball, Les Clark, John Sibley, Marc Davis, Wolfgang Reitherman, Hal King, Hamilton Luske, Norm Ferguson, Eric Larson, Johnny Lounsbery, Milt Kahl, Frank Thomas and Ollie Johnston all became masters of the technique.

Other notable figures in character animation include the Termite Terrace/Warner Bros. directors (Tex Avery, Chuck Jones, Bob Clampett, Frank Tashlin, Robert McKimson, and

Friz Freleng), independent animator Richard Williams, John Lasseter at Pixar, and latter-day Disney animators Andreas Deja and Glen Keane. Character animation is not limited to Hollywood studios, however. Some of the finest examples of character animation can be found in the work of Nick Park of Aardman Animations and Russian independent animator Yuri Norstein.

Character animation is augmented by special effects animation, which creates anything that is not a character; most commonly vehicles, machinery, and natural phenomena such as rain, snow, and water.

# 8

# Cinematography

## INTRODUCTION

### *1896-1910*

Cinema was introduced to India on July 7, 1896. It began with the Lumiere Brothers' Cinematography, unveiling six silent short films at the Watson Hotel in Bombay, namely Entry of Cinematographe, The Sea Bath, Arrival of a Train, A Demolition, Ladies & Soldiers on Wheels and Leaving the Factory. The Times of India carried details of the "Living Photographic Pictures in Life-Size Reproductions by Mssrs. Lumiere Brotheres". In thc same year, the Madras Photographic Store advertised "animated photographs". Daily screenings of films commenced in Bombay in 1897 by Clifton and Co.'s Meadows Street Photography Studio.

In 1898, Hiralal Sen started filming scenes of theatre productions at the Classic Theatre in Calcutta, inspired by Professor Stevenson (who had brought to India the country's first bioscope)'s, film presentation alongside the stage production of The Flower Of Persia; his debut was a contribution to this presentation. He continued making similar films to complement theatrical productions, which were shown as added attractions during intermission, in private screenings for high society households or taken to distant venues where the stage performers could not reach.

Harischandra Sakharam Bhatavdekar (H. S. Bhatavdekar) alias Save Dada, who had attended the show, imported a cine-camera from London at a price of 21 guineas and filmed the first Indian documentary, a wrestling match in Hanging

Gardens, Bombay, in 1897. In 1901, he recorded the return from Cambridge of 'Wrangler' Ragunath P. Paranjpye, who had secured a distinction in mathematics from Cambridge University, and M M Bhownuggree, considered the first Indian news film.. He also filmed Lord Curzon (the Viceroy of India)'s Delhi Durbar that marked the enthronement of Edward VII in 1903.

The commercial potential of cinema was also tested during the time. F.B. Thanewala's "Grand Kinetoscope Newsreels" is one successful case. J.F. Madan was another highly successful film producer, who released hit films like Satyavadi Raja Harishchandra and Bilwamangal; also, he launched Madan Theatres Limited, which became India's largest film production-distribution-exhibition company and the biggest importer of American films after World War I. His films were marked by a high degree of technical sophistication, facilitated by his employment of experienced foreign directors like Eugenio De Liguoro and Camille Legrand. This expertise was complemented by grand sets and popular mythological storylines which ensured good returns.

Cinema houses were set up in major Indian cities in this period, like one in Madras (in 1900 by Major Warrick), the Novelty Cinema in Bombay (where newsreels from the Boer Wars were shown) and the Elphinstone Picture Palace in Calcutta (set up by J.F. Madan in 1907). Apart from these, a number of film shows were arranged in tents; examples are: shows arranged by two Italians, Colourello and Cornaglia, in tents at the Azad Maidan Bombay, J.F. Madan's tent cinema at the Calcutta Maidan. Another popular mode of broadcasting films was the touring cinema. In 1904, Manek Sethna started the Touring Cinema Co. in Bombay and a year later, Swamikannu Vincent, a draughtsman for the railways set up a touring cinema going around small towns and villages in the South of India. Pathe, the famous film production company set up an Indian Office in 1907.

### *1910-1920*

The first feature film made in India was a narrative named Pundalik, by N.G. Chitre and R.G. Torney. The first full-length

Indian feature film was Raja Harishchandra (3700 feet as compared to 1500 for Pundalik), made in 1913 and released commercially in May that year, by Dadasaheb Phalke. Phalke had attended a screening of The Life of Christ at P.B. Mehta's American-Indian Cinema and was inspired to make films himself. He was convinced of the possibility of establishing an indigenous film industry by focussing on Indian themes. In this regard, he said Like the life of Christ, we shall make pictures on Rama and Krishna. The film was about an honest king who for the sake of his principles sacrifices his kingdom and family before the gods, who are impressed with his honesty and restore him to his former glory. The film was a success, and Phalke went on to make more mythological films till the advent of talkies, and commercialization of Indian films lessened his popularity.

In 1916, Universal Pictures set up Hollywood's first Indian agency (see Hollywood meets India, below). The first South Indian feature was Rangaswamy Nataraja Mudaliar's Keechaka Vadham, released in 1918. The following year, he made the film Draupadi Vastrapaharanam, featuring Anglo-Indian actress Marian Hill who played the role of Draupadi.

## REGIONAL FILM INDUSTRIES

India is a large country where many languages are spoken. According to the 1991 Census of India there are about 10,400 'raw mother tongues' in India. If closely related and mutually comprehensible dialects are grouped, the number can be reduced to 1576 'rationalised' mother tongues, or with even more consolidation, 114 main languages. These 114 languages are the ones surveyed in the Indian census. Indian film producers have made films in thirty of the largest languages. However, only the very largest language groups support major regional industries. These are: Hindi, Bengali, Marathi, Kannada, Tamil, Telugu, Odiya, Malayalam. Official statistics categorise Indian films according to the languages in which they are distributed.

There is a great deal of mobility between the regional industries. Many workers in other regional industries, once their talent and popularity is established, move on to work in other film industries, nationally as well as internationally. For example, A. R. Rahman, one of the best known film music composers in Indian cinema, started his career in Tamil cinema in Chennai but has since worked in Bollywood, London, and New York. Similarly, films that succeed in one language are often remade or dubbed in others. Films like Padosan and Roja, for example, were re-made or dubbed from their original Bengali and Tamil versions respectively, into Hindi.

### Bengali (Bangla) Film Industry

The Bengali film industry has long centred in the Tollygunge district of Kolkata (Calcutta). Its most famous film director is Satyajit Ray, who won an Oscar for lifetime achievement in cinema.

### Hindi Film Industry

The Hindi film industry, based in Mumbai (formerly Bombay), is the largest branch of Indian cinema. Hindi film Industry is often called 'Bollywood' (a melding of Hollywood and Bombay). The word "Bollywood" is sometimes applied to Indian cinema as a whole, especially outside South Asia and the South Asian diaspora, but this usage is incorrect. Bollywood has been recently greatly criticized for what critics see as a violation of Indian cultural values and its discussion of controversial topics. It is considered the most liberal out of the Indian language film industries.

Regional movies are distinctively different from Bollywood (Hindi) movies, as the stories and themes of these movies portray the culture of the region from which they originate, while most Bollywood movies nowadays are greatly influenced by Western culture.

Although Bollywood does not distribute a lot of films, it can be considered to be largest in terms of viewers. It is believed that 95% of the Indian population watches Bollywood. It also has international recognition, especially in Western countries such as the UK, USA and Australia where there is a large South Asian community. Despite having the widest coverage, Bollywood movies fail to impress South Indians especially in Tamil Nadu & Kerala because of a very strong local film industry which arguably produces movies of much superior quality.

## Kannada Film Industry

The Kannada film industry, based in Karnataka, is sometimes called 'Sandalwood', as Karnataka is known for its sandalwood; however, this term does not seem to be in widespread use. The Gubbi Veeranna Company, or Veeranna's Sri Chennabasaveshwara Krupa Poshita Nataka Sangha and other groups established themselves first as theatre troupes, and later went on to dominate kannada cinema into the 1960s. "They provided all its key directors like H.L.N. Simha, B. R. Panthulu and G. V. Iyer, its stars led by Rajkumar and Leelavathi and most of its early commercial hits: Bedara Kannappa (1953), for instance. The first big success in Kannada cinema adapted a Gubbi Company stage play written by G. V. Iyer to introduce the mythological adventure movie into that language.". Kannada films has become very popular after the recent hits like Jogi (2005) & Mungaru Male (2007).

## Kashmiri Film Industry

The Kashmiri film industry, which had been lying dormant since the release of Habba Khatoon in 1967, was revived after a 39-year hiatus with the release of Akh Daleel Loolech in 2006. Cinema halls had been shut down for a long time in Kashmir, by militants protesting against the New Delhi based Government. There are few cinema halls and a handful of directors have been returning to shoot in the region. Though the region was favoured by many producers as a scenic locale in pre-militancy era Bollywood movies as a romantic backdrop, the regional industry was not very strong, due to lack of finances and infrastructure.

## Malayalam Film Industry

The Malayalam film industry, based in Kerala. Malayalam movies are known for their artistic nature and they frequently figure in the national film awards. It is also currently known for being the most conservative out of the different film industries in India, despite the fact that it went through a liberal phase in the 80's. Notable personalities: filmmakers, Padmavibhushan Adoor Gopalakrishnan, Bharathan, Aravindan, Padmarajan, John Abraham; scriptwriter,

M.T. Vasudevan Nair, Sreenivasan; cinematographer, Azhagappan, Santhosh Sivan, Shaji; actors, Bharath Gopi, Tilakan, Padmabhushan Prem Nazeer, Satyan, Padmasree Bharath Mammootty, Padmasree Bharath Mohanlal, Padmasree Bharath Balachandra Menon; playback singers, Padmabhushan Dr. K.J Yesudas, Padmasree K.S. Chitra and Sujatha.

The first 3D film which has produced in India was in Malayalam. Its name is My Dear Kuttichatthan produced by Navodaya. Padayottam, the first 70MM film which has done its full work in India was in Malayalam which was also produced by Navodaya. The fist Cinemascope film in the world was produced in Malayalam. Chemmeen is the first film which bring a gold medal from the President in South India. Mohanlal's "Guru", directed by Rajiv Anchal, is the only malayalam film which is nominated for Oscar Award.

Malayalam film Industry has been nicknamed as Malluwood. Mohanlal's "Narasimham" has got the highest profit till 2005. Mammootty has got 3 times National Award for best actor with Kamal Hasan. The industry contributed many best directors, actors, writers etc. A.R. Rahman's first film which he give music was in Malayalam. Vanaprastham produced by Mohanlal is the first Indo-French production movie. It has been dubbed into English (International & Europe), French & German. Mohanlal's Kalapani tells the story about the life of people in Indian prison in Andaman.

## Marathi Film Industry

The Marathi Film industry is based in Maharashtra. Marathi film industry is one of the oldest in India. Dadasaheb Falke was one of the pioneers of the films in Marathi. Every year there is an award given in the name of "Dadasaheb Falke Award" for exceptional contribution to India cinema. Marathi film industry is now a days overshadowed by presence of Bollywood, but is evolving due to some off-beat movies like Shwaas, Uttarayan, and so on.. Old marathi film songs are popular even today also. Old songs are remixed and presented now-a-days. Also actors like Dilip Prabhavalkar are making more difference in growing marathi film industry. Films like Chavkat Raja, Jhapatlele, Phachadlela, etc are excellent movies.

## Tamil Film Industry

The Tamil film industry (Kollywood), based in the Kodambakkam area of Chennai is one of biggest film-industries in India. Tamil films have enjoyed consistent popularity among Tamil speakers in India, Sri Lanka, Singapore, Malaysia and Mauritius.

In the Tamil film industry, directors such as K. Balachander, Shankar, Bharathiraja, Balu Mahendra, Santhana Bharathi, Cheran, and Mani Ratnam have achieved box-office success whilst producing films that balanced art and popular elements. The Tamil film industry accounts for approximately 1% of the gross domestic product of the state of Tamil Nadu. Costs of production have grown exponentially from just under Rs.4 million in 1980 to over Rs.110 million by 2005 for a typical star-studded big-budget film. Similarly, costs of processing per print have risen from just under Rs.2,500 in 1980 to nearly Rs.70,000 by 2005. There has been a growing presence of English in dialogue and songs as well. It is not uncommon to see movies that feature dialogue studded with English words and phrases, or even whole sentences. Some movies are also simultaneously released in two or three languages (either using subtitles or several soundtracks). Contemporary Tamil movies often feature Madras Bashai, a colloquial version of Tamil spoken in Madras.

## Telugu Film Industry

The Telugu film industry is based in Andhra Pradesh's capital city, Hyderabad. After Bollywood, more movies are produced every year in Telugu than any other language. The state also has what is claimed to be the largest film studio in the world, Ramoji Film City. The first studio for Telugu talkies was Vel Pictures, constructed in 1934 by P.V. Das, located at Madras. The first film made here was Sita Kalyanam. The first film made by a Telugu person, R.S. Prakash, was Bhishma Pratigna (The Pledge of Bhishma, 1922). Another important Telugu personality of this era was Y.V. Rao (1903-1973), an actor and director, whose silent film (directing) credits include Pandava Nirvana (1930), Pandava Agnathavaas (1930) and Hari Maya (1932). The first big movies in Telugu were made by the Surabhi Theatres troupes. They produced the first Telugu talkie, Bhakta Prahlada, directed by Hanumappa Munioappa Reddy in 1931. In the first few years of Telugu talkies, films were all mythological stories, taken from the stage. In 1936, Krittiventi Nageswara Rao made the first Telugu film not based on mythology, Premavijayam. The film influenced other Telugu film-makers into making such films. Some popular themes of these films (often called 'social' films) were the feudal zamindari system (Raitu Bidda, 1939), untouchability (Maala pilla, 1938), and widow remarriage. Since then, there have been both social (contemporary) and mythological or folk stories in Telugu cinema.

Telugu films are released in Andhra Pradesh, Tamil Nadu, Karnataka, East Maharastra, Orissa and few parts of West Bengal. Telugu movies are released world wide in United States, Canada, parts of Europe, South Africa, Malaysia and Singapore.

The film Pokiri (Actor-Mahesh Babu) was released in 2006 collected 67 crores in India which is second heighest in India.

## CONVENTIONS OF COMMERCIAL FILMS

The principal difference between American and Indian commercial cinema is that Indian films usually feature periodic song-and-dance routines which, in a good movie, are expected to move the story forward (in mediocre movies, they are poorly integrated into the story). The uniqueness of Indian Cinema is that songs in Indian films play a role. In generic films, they serve as fillers, often amusing distractions. In artistic commercial films, songs convey emotions and passions of the protagonist or of the situation-ranging from love and pathos to triumph and celebration. The lyrics in the latter type are usually well written and set to music with catchy tunes, that go on to become popular. Songs are sung by professionals play-back singers and lip-synched by dancing actors and actresses. Most non-Indians would consider the ordinary Indian film a musical, but this would be a mistake. The music and song industry associated with Indian Cinema is a major contender in determining box office hits.

Indian commercial films, in whatever regional centre they are made, tend to be long; they are usually two to three hours long, often with an intermission. They tend to be melodramatic, sentimental, and formulaic, but may also feature romance, comedy, action, suspense, and other generic elements. Unlike commercial Western films, there is almost no nudity at all in Indian films. Such scenes are classified as obscene in the Constitution of India and are usually removed by the Indian Censor Board.

## ART CINEMA IN INDIA

In addition to commercial cinema, there is also Indian cinema that aspires to seriousness or art. This is known to film critics as "New Indian Cinema" or sometimes "the Indian New Wave" (see the Encyclopedia of Indian Cinema), but most people in India simply call such films "art films". These films deal with a wide range of subjects but many are in general explorations of complex human circumstances and relationships within an Indian setting.

From the 1960s through the 1980s, art films were subsidised by Indian governments: aspiring directors could get federal or state government grants to produce non-commercial films on Indian themes. Many of these directors were graduates of the government-supported Film and Television Institute of India. Their films were showcased at government film festivals and on the government-run TV station, Doordarshan. These films also had limited runs in art house theatres in India and overseas. Since the 1980s, Indian art cinema has to a great extent lost its government patronage. Today, it must be made as independent films on a shoestring budget by aspiring amateurs, much as in today's Western film industry.

The art directors of this period owed more to foreign influences, such as Italian neorealism or the French New Wave, than they did to the genre conventions of commercial Indian cinema. The best known New Cinema directors were Bengali: Satyajit Ray, Ritwik Ghatak, and Bimal Roy. Some well-known films of this movement include the Apu Trilogy by Ray (Bengali), Meghe Dhaka Tara by Ghatak (Bengali) and Do Bigha Zameen by Roy (Hindi).

Of these film-makers, Satyajit Ray was arguably the most well-known: his films obtained considerable international recognition during the mid-twentieth century. His prestige, however, did not translate into large-scale commercial success. His films played primarily to art-house audiences (students and intelligentsia) in the larger Indian cities, or to film buffs on the international art-house circuit in India and abroad.

Art cinema was also well-supported in the South Indian state of Kerala. Some outstanding Malayalam movie makers are Adoor Gopalakrishnan, G. Aravindan, T. V. Chandran, Shaji N. Karun, and M. T. Vasudevan Nair. Some of their films include National Film Award-winning Elippathayam, Piravi (which won the Camera d'Or at the Cannes Film Festival), Vaanaprastham and Nizhalkkuthu (a FIPRESCI-Prize winner).

Starting in the 1970s, Kannada film makers from Karnataka state produced a string of serious, low-budget films. Girish Kasaravalli is one of the few directors from that period who continues to make non-commercial films. He is the only Indian director after Satyajit Ray to win the Golden Lotus Awards four times.

From the 1970s onwards Hindi cinema produced a wave of art films. The foremost among the directors who produced such films is Shyam Benegal. Others in this genre include Govind Nihalani, Mani Kaul, Kumar Shahani, M.S. Sathyu.

Many cinematographers, technicians and actors began in art cinema and moved to commercial cinema. The actor Naseeruddin Shah is one notable example; he has never achieved matinee idol status, but has turned out a solid body of work as a supporting actor and a star in independent films such as Mira Nair's Monsoon Wedding.

## GLOBALIZATION OF INDIAN CINEMA

Contact between Indian and Western cinemas was established in the early days of film in India itself. Dadasaheb Phalke was moved to make Raja Harishchandra after watching the film Life of Christ at P.B. Mehta's American-Indian Cinema. Similarly, some other early film directors were inspired by Western movies.

In India at least 80 percent of films shown in the late 1920s were American, even though twenty-one studios manufactured local films, eight or nine of them in regular production. American serials such as Perils of Pauline and Exploits of Elaine, and the spectacular sets of films like Quo Vadis and Cabira were popular and inspiring during the World War I era.

Universal Pictures set up an Indian agency in 1916, which went on to dominate the Indian distribution system. J. F. Madan's Elphinstone Bioscope Company at first focussed on distribution of foreign films and organization of their regular screenings Additionally, J.P. Madan, the prolific producer, employed Western directors for many of his films.

A number of Indian films have been accused of plagiarising from Hollywood Movies. Due to the long time taken by courts to decide a case, few cases relating to copyright violations are brought up.

One of the reasons Bollywood hesitates in purchasing rights is the assumption that these would run into millions of dollars, though according to some like screenwriter-director Anurag Kashyap, this is incorrect; He argues that while the films may cost millions of dollars in the west, the rights would be less expensive for Hindi remakes because the price would be based on the audience's buying power, the economy and the number of bidders.

In 2003, best-selling fiction writer Barbara Taylor Bradford brought a copyright infringement suit against Sahara Television for allegedly making a television series (Karishma: A miracle of destiny) out of her book, A Woman of Substance, without acquiring the legal rights to do so.

Today, Indian cinema is becoming increasingly westernised. This trend is most strongly apparent in Bollywood. Newer Bollywood movies sometimes include Western actors (such as Rachel Shelley in Lagaan), try to meet Western production standards, conduct filming overseas, adopt some English in their scripts or incorporate some elements of Western-style plots.

Bollywood also produces box-office hit like the films Dilwale Dulhaniya Le Jayenge and Kal Ho Naa Ho, both of which deal with the overseas Indian's experience.

However, the meeting between west and India is a two-way process: Western audiences mostly of Indian origin are becoming more interested in India, as evidenced by the mild success of Lagaan and Bride and Prejudice.

As Western audiences for Indian cinema grow, Western producers are funding maverick Indian filmmakers like Gurinder Chadha (Bride and Prejudice) and Mira Nair (Monsoon Wedding). Both Chadha and Nair are of Indian origin but do not live in India, and who made their names in Western independent films; they have now been funded to create films that "interpret" the Indian cinematic tradition for Westerners. A similar filmmaker is Deepa Mehta of Canada, whose films include the trilogy Fire, Earth and Water.

Indian cinema is also influencing the English and American musical; Baz Luhrmann's Moulin Rouge! (2001) incorporates a Bollywood-style dance sequence; The Guru and The 40-Year-Old Virgin feature Indian-style song-and-dance sequences; A. R. Rahman, a film composer, was recruited for Andrew Lloyd Webber's Bombay Dreams; and a musical version of Hum Aapke Hain Koun has played in London's West End.

## AWARDS

The Filmfare Awards ceremony is one of the oldest and most prominent film events given for Hindi films in India and is sometimes referred to as the "Indian Oscars." The Filmfare awards were first introduced in 1954, the same year as the National Film Awards and gave awards to the best films of 1953. The ceremony was referred to as the Clare Awards after the magazine's editor. A dual voting system was developed in 1956. Under this system, "in contrast to the National Film Awards, which are decided by a panel appointed by Indian Government, the Filmfare Awards are voted for by both the public and a committee of experts."

Since 1973, the Indian government has sponsored the National Film Awards (which first began in 1954), awarded by the government run Directorate of Film Festivals (DFF). The DFF screens not only Bollywood films, but films from all the other regional movie industries and independent/art films. These awards are handed out at an annual ceremony presided over by the President of India.

Additional-ceremonies held within India are:

- Stardust Awards
- Star Screen Awards

Ceremonies held overseas are:

- Bollywood Movie Awards-Long Island, New York, United States
- Global Indian Film Awards-(different country each year)
- IIFA Awards-(different country each year)
- Zee Cine Awards-(different country each year)

Most of these award ceremonies are lavishly staged spectacles, featuring singing, dancing, and lots of stars and starlets.

## WRITING FOR RADIO

The purpose of this website is to help radio journalists improve their skills as writers and anchors. Journalism education has greatly declined over the past two decades as colleges and universities have either closed journalism programs or transformed them into "Communications Departments." Radio journalism has been especially hard hit, with diminished teaching resources given over to television instruction because TV is the more attractive broadcast medium.

Consequently, many journalists starting out in radio lack basic knowledge on how to communicate effectively though the medium. In the past, much of that knowledge was learned on the job, but consolidations, cutbacks and downsizing in radio have reduced news staffs to the point where news directors can afford little time to training those new in the profession. In this sink-or-swim environment, far too many radio journalists have figured out only how to float.

They haven't been introduced to the wide range of possibilities in preparing radio news and are often frustrated either by not being able to move up to a larger market or by not having the satisfaction of becoming respected journalists within their communities.

## FEATURES

This discussion is intended for those who are early in their radio careers, whether in a first or second job or still in college or an internship. The pages assume some experience in radio, but visitors unfamiliar with some of the terminology may consult a small glossary. Although the Newswriting for Radio website has been extensively used in college journalism courses, the website is not meant to replace a broadcast newswriting textbook. The Newswriting for Radio website is a supplement to coursework, and especially to on-the-job experience.

The site is organized into four major sections. In The Basics, you learn fundamental lessons and characteristics of broadcast newswriting. Three different newscast formats are examined in The Styles. You'll examine some of the questions surrounding what deserves coverage in the section on News Judgment. Finally, The Newsroom teaches you about creating an organized environment that allows you to be better prepared for stories. There's also a collection of links to other radio journalism websites.

On several of the pages, sample news scripts are accompanied on the right side of the page by the speaker symbol (shown on the right side of this paragraph). The appearance of the symbol next to a script indicates that you can listen to a sound file (in the WAV format) containing the words of the script. Listening to these files will allow you to hear and practice the patterns of voice modulation regularly used in radio newscasts. Just click on the symbol to hear the script.

Here are some common terms in radio journalism used throughout the Newswriting for Radio website and their definitions:

**Actuality:** Recorded segment of a newsmaker speaking, generally lasting from 10 to 20 seconds; this is what people outside of radio journalism often call a "sound bite"

**Clock:** Schedule of a broadcast hour, with precise time in minutes and seconds allotted for the various programming segments; for example, a clock might begin "00:00-01:30--news,"

"01:30-02:30--spots," and so forth; often represented as a pie chart resembling an analog clock

**Cut:** Tape containing the recording of a voicer, wrap, actuality or nat sound; networks feed cuts to affiliates via satellite

**Hourly:** Network newscast beginning at the top of the hour; the cast generally contains a commercial break at two and a half or three minutes past the hour and resumes a minute or a minute and a half later; most hourlies conclude at five minutes past the hour

**IQ:** "in cue"--the first words recorded on a cut

**Lead:** First sentence of a news story, which should concisely reveal the story's basic events and provide an introduction to the details given in the rest of the story

**Live Shot:** Report introduced by an anchor that has not been recorded but is read live by another journalist, often at a news scene

**Lockout:** Final words of a report spoken by a journalist in which the journalist's name and station call letters or frequency are given, such as "Corrie Carpenter, 990 News"; often a location is given as well: "In Middleville, Corrie Carpenter, 990 News"

**MOS:** Abbreviation for "Man On the Street" interviews; that is, interviews of passers-by chosen at random in a public place and asked their opinions of events or people in the news

**Nat or Natural or Raw Sound:** A "raw sound" is recorded sound that is not of a newsmaker speaking, such as the sound of an airplane landing or a marching band playing or a crowd cheering; sometimes known as "natural sound" or "nat sound," especially when the source of the sound is from nature, such as frogs croaking or geese honking

**OQ:** "out cue"--the last words recorded on a cut

**Reader:** Script of a news story in which no actualities are to be played; this script is read live on the air by the anchor; the recording of a reader by a reporter is called a "voicer"

**Script:** Written-out version of a news story, the text of which is read on the air; a newscast is made up of a collection of scripts read by an anchor

**Slug:** Title of a script; used for reference purposes; wire-service stories are each given one

**Sounder:** Recorded tune used to introduce segments of the broadcast, such as at the beginning of a traffic report or sports; the networks use sounders at the beginning of the hourlies

**Spot:** Recorded commercial advertisement

**Tease:** Brief phrase spoken by the anchor immediately before playing a spot or going to traffic (or some other interruption of the newscast) to tell the listener about a story coming up later; the tease should intrigue the listener without either misrepresenting the story or revealing it entirely

**Voicer:** Recorded report containing only the journalist's voice--there is no actuality; can be understood as a recorded reader

**Wrap:** Recorded report in which a journalist's voice occurs at the beginning and end, and an actuality is played in between; the report is "wrapped around" the actuality

**Zinger:** Unusual and generally humorous feature story often placed at the end of a newscast

## AVOIDING "COP TALK"

Many of the stories we report involve crimes and police attempts to apprehend those responsible. The importance of these stories to our listeners, as well as the often complex and uncertain nature of police investigations, can be quite intimidating for young reporters, with the result that they frequently repeat verbatim the description of a crime given to them by a police official.

## DON'T "DO THE POLICE IN DIFFERENT VOICES"

Police officers are taught to describe their investigations in a way that provides specific details of events with the vaguest possible discussions about those whom police believe responsible. This "cop talk" developed from the legal requirements that enforcement officials need to meet in order to make arrests and gain convictions. But "cop talk" is inadequate for reporting on radio. Here's an example of "cop talk," a story only slightly modified from what was broadcast on a small-market station:

- TWO MEN ARE UNDER ARREST FOR ROBBING A JEWELLERY STORE. POLICE SAY THE MEN ENTERED THE VILLAGE PAWN SHOP AT 1407 MAIN STREET AT APPROXIMATELY 10:15 YESTERDAY MORNING. AFTER WAITING INSIDE THE STORE FOR A FEW MINUTES, ONE OF THE MEN DISPLAYED A GUN AND ORDERED TWO EMPLOYEES TO PLACE INTO A DUFFEL BAG ALL THE CASH FROM THE REGISTER AS WELL AS SEVERAL ITEMS OF JEWELLERY. THERE WAS NO ONE ELSE IN THE STORE AT THE TIME. THE MEN LEFT THE STORE, AND ONE EMPLOYEE WAS ABLE TO SEE THE MEN DRIVE OFF IN A BLUE DODGE ARIES. THE EMPLOYEES NOTIFIED POLICE, AND AT APPROXIMATELY 11 O'CLOCK A VEHICLE MATCHING THE DESCRIPTION OF THE GETAWAY CAR WAS SPOTTED PARKED IN AN ALLEY IN BACK OF A HOUSE AT 684 WILLOW STREET. POLICE ENTERED THE HOUSE WHERE THEY FOUND TWO MEN, AN AMOUNT OF MONEY, AND ITEMS OF JEWELLERY LATER IDENTIFIED AS HAVING BEEN TAKEN FROM THE STORE. A COMPUTER CHECK OF THE VEHICLE DETERMINED THAT IT WAS STOLEN. THE MEN WERE IDENTIFIED AS 34-YEAR-OLD MILES STANDISH OF MIDDLEVILLE AND 28-YEAR-OLD JOHN ALDEN OF SMALLTOWN. THE MEN WILL FACE A VARIETY OF CHARGES.

### CUT IRRELEVANT DETAILS

This script (which runs about 54 seconds) is far too long, with irrelevant details such as the make and model of the getaway car, while the identification of the suspects isn't revealed until the very end. It is obvious that the reporter merely repeated the words of a police officer or of a police press release. Here's a brief rewrite of the script (which now runs 31 seconds):

- TWO MEN ARE BEHIND BARS THIS MORNING AFTER AN ARMED ROBBERY OF A MIDDLEVILLE PAWN SHOP. POLICE SAY 34-YEAR-OLD MILES STANDISH OF MIDDLEVILLE AND 28-YEAR-OLD JOHN ALDEN OF SMALLTOWN ROBBED THE VILLAGE PAWN SHOP ON MAIN STREET YESTERDAY, FORCING TWO WORKERS AT GUNPOINT TO STUFF A DUFFEL BAG WITH MONEY AND JEWELLERY. THE SUSPECTS WERE LATER ARRESTED IN A HOUSE ON WILLOW STREET AFTER POLICE SAY THEY SPOTTED THE GETAWAY CAR BEHIND THE HOME AND ITEMS TAKEN IN THE HEIST WERE FOUND INSIDE THE HOUSE. STANDISH AND ALDEN ARE EXPECTED TO FACE A VARIETY OF CHARGES.

The new version has the police making the allegations against the two suspects (as is legal and proper), but many details unnecessary to the main point of the story have been removed.

### DON'T MAKE THE OPPOSITE MISTAKE OF BEING TOO INFORMAL

"Cop talk" is predominantly a problem in small-market stations in stories by inexperienced reporters, but the opposite extreme seems to be taking hold in larger markets. Big-city reporters are becoming exceedingly colloquial in their language when covering police stories. Here's an example that aired on a major-market station in New England. The story concerned a stolen minivan in which a mother had left two babies inside. In telling the story the reporter said:

- ...A WOMAN LEFT TWO INFANTS IN THE VAN WHILE SHE DROPPED OFF AN OLDER CHILD AT DAYCARE. THE VAN WAS STILL RUNNING, AND MEANWHILE SOME GUY MUST HAVE JUMPED IN AND DROVE OFF. WHEN HE REALIZED THERE WERE TWO INFANTS IN BACK, HE DITCHED THE VAN, AND POLICE ARE NOW SEARCHING FOR THE GUY IN SOME NEARBY WOODS.... BUT THANKFULLY THE KIDS ARE OKAY.

This script does not clearly report what police believe to have happened. In fact, the script seems to indicate that this version of events is merely speculation on the part of the reporter. There was no indication of any witness seeing who drove the minivan away. Perhaps the driver was a woman. Moreover, there is no evidence for the alleged motivation of this mystery driver to have abandoned the minivan. Maybe the driver saw the babies, maybe the driver didn't.

Just as troubling as the sloppiness with which this script was put together was the overly conversational tone. A suspect of unknown sex should be called a "suspect." If an unidentified suspect is a man, he should be called a "man"--not "some guy." Being too chatty damages the credibility of the reporter to be an authoritative source of information.

Radio reporters need to strike a balance in the language they use. Scripts cannot be ploddingly detailed and dull, yet being too colloquial may lead to sloppiness and lack of credibility.

Journalism instructors often state that broadcast newswriting is supposed to sound just like everyday speech. In essence, however, writing broadcast news is more akin to writing song lyrics. Both tasks involve constructing language in a visual form (writing) for communication in an oral form (speaking or singing). Like song lyrics, broadcast newswriting adheres to patterns of language use (such as appropriate vocabulary and formulaic sentence-structure) that the audience expects to hear and will use in interpreting the communication.

Even though commercial broadcasting has been around for less than a century, radio listeners have come to expect their newscasts to be written in a particular way. Learning about broadcast sentence-structure is one of the foundations for developing effective skills at radio newswriting.

## KEEP IT SIMPLE

Grammarians distinguish between three types of sentences: simple, compound and complex. A simple sentence contains a subject and a verb. A compound sentence is composed of two simple sentences joined by a coordinating conjunction ("and," "but," "or," "nor"). A complex sentence is composed of two simple sentences joined by a subordinating conjunction (which may be temporal, such as "when"; causal, such as "because"; or concessive, such as "although"). You probably remember this lesson from elementary school, but the distinctions remain quite relevant to broadcast newswriting. In your scripts, simple sentences are best. You will, of course, regularly use compound and complex sentences, but the clarity achieved through the use of simple sentences can rarely be surpassed.

Linguists describe English as a highly asyndetic language--which means that clauses in the same train of thought do not always need to be connected by conjunctions or connecting particles. Such particles in English include the words "moreover," "furthermore," and "however," words that should be avoided in broadcast newswriting. Listeners are themselves capable of connecting the elements of a story if the story is presented clearly and concisely, and these listeners expect important news to be reported in simple sentences. This expectation is especially true of leads, which generally should be written as simple sentences. When a lead begins with a subordinating conjunction, listeners discount the story's urgency. This is why such leads almost always appear in feature stories or zingers.

## AVOID YOUR RELATIVES

Relative clauses, which begin with a relative pronoun or adverb such as "who," "which" or "where," provide additional information about a noun in a sentence. Those relative clauses which interrupt the flow of the sentence should not be used in broadcast newswriting. In a text communicated visually, a reader has the words on a page or screen to help guide him back to the story after the detour of a relative clause. Listeners do not have such a guide and must rely on the speaker to provide information in readily understood clauses that are concise and uninterrupted. A sentence with an interrupting relative clause should be rewritten into two simple sentences. Take the following example:

- FRED GRANDY...WHO PLAYED "GOPHER" ON THE ORIGINAL "LOVEBOAT" T-V SERIES...LATER SPENT 8 YEARS AS A CONGRESSMAN FROM IOWA.

A clearer means of expressing the same information is through two simple sentences:

- FRED GRANDY PLAYED "GOPHER" ON THE ORIGINAL "LOVE BOAT" T-V SERIES. HE LATER SPENT 8 YEARS AS A CONGRESSMAN FROM IOWA.

Recognize that apposition--the placing of a noun or phrase after another noun and marked off only by commas or, in this very example, dashes--is like a relative clause without the relative pronoun. Long, interrupting oppositions, like interrupting relative clauses, should be avoided in broadcast newswriting.

Relative clauses and oppositions can be used at the end of a sentence. This placement is especially useful for clauses beginning with the adverb "where," as in

- FIRE DESTROYED THE HISTORIC HOME, WHERE GEORGE WASHINGTON ONCE SLEPT.

Clauses beginning with "who" or "which" are acceptable when placed at the end of a sentence, but sometimes it may be preferable to write two simple sentences instead. For example,

- SIMMONS IS SUING FOR RETURN OF THE "BARBIE"-DOLL COLLECTION, WHICH HE SAYS IS WORTH A QUARTER-OF-A-MILLION DOLLARS.

could also be written

- SIMMONS IS SUING FOR RETURN OF THE "BARBIE"-DOLL COLLECTION. HE SAYS THE COLLECTION'S WORTH A QUARTER-OF-A-MILLION DOLLARS.

## BE ACTIVE

Finally, two very common writing faults made by beginning reporters also appear nowadays in all other types of English writing, namely the overuse both of the passive voice and of the existential "there is," "there are" construction. Use the active voice. Write sentences with subjects that are doing things and not subjects that are merely receiving actions upon them. Do not waste time stating an object's existence (this is what the "there is" construction shows). Describe that object doing something. Simple sentences with active verbs form the basis of effective writing for radio. All other broadcast newswriting techniques are built upon the foundation laid by this type of sentence structure.

During the initial flurry of stories concerning President Clinton's relationship with former White House intern Monica Lewinsky, the late ABC-TV news anchor Peter Jennings interviewed humourist and social commentator P. J. O'Rourke.

Jennings asked O'Rourke to discuss "the alleged age difference between the President and Ms. Lewinsky," to which O'Rourke wittily replied, "Yes, Peter, we haven't yet determined whether there actually is an age difference between President Clinton and Monica Lewinsky. There is only an alleged age difference."

Jennings smiled at the reply, realizing that he had misused the word "alleged." The word allows journalists to discuss claims that have not been proved, but it is a word easily open to abuse.

## SAY, SAY, SAY

The best way to use the words "allege," "alleged" and "allegedly" is not to use them at all. Instead, have your scripts reveal who is making the claim by using phrases such as "police say" or "prosecutors say" followed by the substance of the allegation. For example, a story about a bank-robbery suspect that contains the sentence

- ...34-YEAR-OLD MILLARD FILLMORE ALLEGEDLY ROBBED THE "BANK NOW" BRANCH ON CHURCH STREET....

should be rewritten so that the sentence reads

- ...POLICE SAY 34-YEAR-OLD MILLARD FILLMORE ROBBED THE "BANK NOW" BRANCH ON CHURCH STREET....

As another example, if a sentence in a story about a local government official facing trial for corruption reads

- ...ZONING BOARD PRESIDENT DOLLY MADISON IS ALLEGED TO HAVE TAKEN BRIBES FROM DEVELOPERS....

rewrite the script into something like

- ...PROSECUTORS SAY ZONING BOARD PRESIDENT DOLLY MADISON TOOK BRIBES FROM DEVELOPERS....

Always use the verb "say" in such scripts. Avoid the temptation to employ other verbs (such as "claim," "state" or "charge") when reporting allegations. Other verbs bring connotations that will colour your reporting. For example, if your script has police claiming that an individual committed a crime, your listeners may well interpret the script as indicating that you the reporter do not believe the police. To speak of someone charging an allegation implies legal actions--charges--have been filed. To maintain as unbiased and accurate a report as possible, stay with the neutral verb "say."

## J'ACCUSE

Learn the distinction between "accused" and "alleged." When legal charges have been filed against an individual, that individual becomes accused of the behaviour detailed in those charges. The individual can then be described as an "accused rapist," "accused murderer," "accused embezzler," and so forth. In scripts, the use of the adjective accused should be limited to one occurrence at or near the beginning of the script in order to describe a suspect quickly and efficiently. Notice the use of the word in this story about a homicide trial:

- ACCUSED MURDERER AARON BURR HAS BROKEN DOWN IN TEARS AT HIS TRIAL, TELLING JURORS THAT HE DID NOT KILL HIS FRIEND ALEX HAMILTON LAST JULY. TAKING THE STAND IN HIS OWN DEFENSE, BURR CRIED YESTERDAY AS HE WAS TALKING ABOUT HIS INITIAL INTERROGATION BY SHERIFF'S DEPUTIES. BURR SAID INTIMIDATING QUESTIONING CAUSED HIM TO GIVE CONFLICTING STORIES TO INVESTIGATORS. PROSECUTORS HAVE SAID THAT BURR KILLED HAMILTON AFTER AN ARGUMENT OVER MONEY IN HAMILTON'S MOHICAN SPRINGS APARTMENT. BURR IS EXPECTED TO FACE CROSS-

EXAMINATION WHEN THE TRIAL RESUMES AT THE HANOVER COUNTY COURTHOUSE LATER TODAY.

In the above script, the adjective "accused" appears once and only once. Multiple use may lead listeners to believe that you the reporter want them to think a suspect is guilty because the adjective "accused" is weaker than the powerful nouns it regularly accompanies (such as "murderer" or "rapist").

## CHARGED UP

As has already been mentioned, the verb "charge" implies that legal actions have been filed against an individual or company. The verb should be used only to describe the process of filing the action:

- POLICE HAVE CHARGED 32-YEAR-OLD LIZZIE BORDEN WITH TWO COUNTS OF FIRST-DEGREE MURDER FOR THE PICK-AXE SLAYINGS OF HER FATHER AND STEP-MOTHER....

The specific legal charge should also be named, such as the "two counts of first-degree murder" of the previous example. Pay careful attention to the specific charge. Prosecutors may say that an individual is a murderer and organized-crime boss but charge him with only tax evasion. The defendant could then be described as being "accused of tax evasion" but not as an "accused murderer and crime boss"--the murders and organized-crime connections are allegations, not charges.

## PROPER ALLEGATIONS

Occasions do exist for the use of "allege," "alleged" or "allegedly." When claims are made concerning an individual but no legal charges have been publicly filed, and the source of the claims is complicated to identify, then "alleged" becomes an acceptable option for describing the individual and the claims. For example, a community group holds a press conference calling for the firing of the deputy chief of police. Earlier that week, three former civilian employees of the police department told a newspaper reporter that they have heard the deputy chief use racial slurs. The reporter was investigating a tip that the deputy chief had recently faced a closed-door, disciplinary hearing with the public safety director and the civil service commission.

The complex nature of the story can lead to extremely tortured syntax in your script. In this situation, a sentence such as:

- ...THE "TOGETHER COALITION" IS ANGRY OVER RACIST COMMENTS ALLEGEDLY MADE BY DEPUTY CHIEF FRANKLIN PIERCE....

might be the most efficient way of succinctly explaining the story. As with "accused," forms of "alleged" should be used only once in a given script.

Finally, remember the mistake of Peter Jennings and ensure that you place the word "alleged" in front of what is actually being alleged. Rewriting the previous script example to read

- ...THE "TOGETHER COALITION" IS ANGRY OVER ALLEGEDLY RACIST COMMENTS MADE BY DEPUTY CHIEF FRANKLIN PIERCE....

significantly changes the meaning of the sentence. Now the question is not whether the deputy chief made comments, but rather whether the particular words he used were racist. If, however, it has not yet been determined what, if anything, the deputy chief may have said, the allegations concern the making of the comment and not the sense of the comments themselves. The earlier version of the sentence is then the correct one.

Finally, until a judicial authority has rendered a decision, a suspect or defendant has not been proved guilty of the charges or allegations against him. Not only is it unethical to describe this individual as, say, a "murderer" or "embezzler" without the qualification of words like "accused" and "alleged," but such descriptions could turn you into a defendant yourself--for libel.

Getting listeners to keep their radios tuned to your entire newscast...that's the function of leads and teases. (Incidentally, the first phrase of the previous sentence is itself a tease.) Despite the importance of leads and teases, many radio journalists do not understand how to fashion effective "hooks" to keep listeners listening.

## REPETITION IS THE MOST COMMON MISTAKE

Repetition is the most common mistake made in leads and teases. As you may have experienced when recognizing the identity of the first six words of the subhead with those at the beginning of this paragraph, repetition of words or ideas is tedious.

Listeners understandably come to believe that there is far less news than meets the ear. Yet repetition is a far-too-frequent feature of news writing, especially between the lead-in to tape (be it voicer, wrap or actuality) and the first sentence on that tape. Here's one such example:

- EMBATTLED STATE LOTTERY DIRECTOR SAMANTHA WU HANDED IN HER RESIGNATION TO GOVERNOR FREDERICK DOUGLASS. REPORTER SUSAN STARR SAYS WU TOLD THE GOVERNOR THAT SHE HAD BECOME A POLITICAL DISTRACTION.
- IQ: "IN HER RESIGNATION LETTER TO THE GOVERNOR, WU SAID THAT SHE HAD BECOME A DISTRACTION...

The second sentence of the lead provides information that is immediately given again by the first sentence of the tape. This is not, however, the only problem with this lead.

## KEEP IT FRESH

Tenses of the past should be avoided in leads and teases. The preterite, or simple past tense, must almost never be used. Any past action should be described in the perfect tense--"have/has" + past participle, which often ends in "-ed." The stative quality of the perfect tense can make it seem like the present.

Better still is the use of the present progressive tense--"am/are/is" + present participle ending in "-ing"--to describe an event that has just taken place. In the story above, it would have been better to write:

- EMBATTLED STATE LOTTERY DIRECTOR SAMANTHA WU IS CALLING IT QUITS. REPORTER SUSAN STARR SAYS WU FEARS THE CONTROVERSY SURROUNDING HER HUSBAND'S

BUSINESS DEALINGS IS HARMING GOVERNOR DOUGLASS.

- IQ: "IN HER RESIGNATION LETTER TO THE GOVERNOR, WU SAID THAT SHE HAD BECOME A DISTRACTION...

Present tenses give immediacy and energy to news writing, allowing listeners to feel that they are hearing about the news as it is taking place. Moreover, in the course of the day leads should be advanced to freshen the story...even though the same tape is being used. In the example story given above, a later lead for the same tape could be as follows:

- GOVERNOR DOUGLASS MUST FIND A NEW LOTTERY DIRECTOR. REPORTER SUSAN STARR SAYS EMBATTLED CURRENT DIRECTOR SAMANTHA WU IS GIVING UP THE JOB.
- IQ: "IN HER RESIGNATION LETTER TO THE GOVERNOR, WU SAID THAT SHE HAD BECOME A DISTRACTION...

The changing lead shifts the emphasis of the story to a future event, the appointment of a new lottery director. The tape then functions as background information for this future event, and so the package of lead and tape together remain fresh.

**ABSENT ANTECEDENT ALERT!**

A frequent error in teases is the use of pronouns without any reference to identify the pronouns. The pronouns' antecedents are absent. This error leads to teases such as:

- HE WANTED TO DIE BUT THEY SAID NO. THE STORY NEXT ON 990 NEWS.

Who is "he"? Who are "they"? (The story concerns a convicted murderer who asked the jury to sentence him to death, but the jury decided instead on a sentence of life in prison without parole.) Some might claim that this lead has mystery, and this mystery will compel listeners to stay tuned. There certainly is mystery, but confusion seems the only result in the minds of listeners. A better tease gives listeners information, not a guessing game:

- LIFE WITHOUT PAROLE FOR CHILD-KILLER WALT THOMAS. THE DETAILS NEXT ON 990 NEWS.

Teases should not tell the entire story, but teases are only a sentence long. Even the most information-packed short sentence can rarely give all the necessary details to satisfy listeners. The tease whets the appetite of listeners, who will want the completeness of hearing the full script if they have an idea of what the story is about. Deliberately confusing or gimmicky teases only frustrate listeners and drive them away.

Radio reporters spend as much time rewriting scripts as writing them. Stories are rewritten from three types of sources: newspapers, press releases and other radio news scripts. The first two of these sources are not written in broadcast style, and radio reporters need to be aware of the differences between print and broadcast.

## DIFFERENCES IN STYLE

One obvious difference involves numbers. In print style, numbers can be written out to exactitude, while on the radio numbers are reduced to two significant digits. Ages in the newspaper are written between commas after an individual's name; in broadcast style, ages are given as adjectival phrases preceding the name.

Newspaper stories also display a greater use of the past tense. Print is a distancing medium, separating events through the filter of the written word from the immediacy of their occurrence. Newspapers are also written hours before they are read, so the events described seem "old news." Radio, on the other hand, has an intimate, "you-are-there" quality that is enhanced by the use of the present tense. Newsmakers spoke to newspaper reporters ("Bush said...."); they speak to a radio audience ("BUSH SAYS....").

### The Art of Condensing

The greatest difference involves story length and detail. Print reporters write hundreds, even thousands of words for a particular story. Few, if any, of your stories as a radio reporter should have even a hundred words. Rewriting newspaper stories becomes an art of condensing. Take the following example of a newspaper story from the imaginary Middleville Times:

- The crumbling Salt Creek bridge on Old Route 9, considered one of Middle County's most historically significant bridges, will receive a $200,000 grant for repairs from the state Department of Transportation, according to county engineer Squire Whipple.

The funding comes from the state's Transportation Enhancement Fund, Whipple said.

Built of sandstone in 1834, the bridge is a 285-foot span made up of three arches over Salt Creek on the old route from Middleville to Greenfield. Deterioration of the bridge in recent years has been a worry to local preservationists. The bridge was closed to traffic in 2002.

The $200,000 infusion will cover the estimated cost to stabilize the bridge until money can be found to restore it. Permanent repairs could cost as much as $1,750,000, Whipple said.

The example above is quite short by print standards, but it's far too long for radio. Remember, a radio story without an actuality (a "reader") should generally run about 20 seconds. Get to the heart of your story and leave the additional details out, as in the following 21-second rewrite:

- A CRUMBLING HISTORIC BRIDGE IS GETTING SOME LONG-NEEDED REPAIRS TO KEEP IT FROM COLLAPSING INTO SALT CREEK. THE MIDDLEVILLE TIMES REPORTS THE STATE WILL PROVIDE TWO HUNDRED THOUSAND DOLLARS TO PRESERVE THE OLD-ROUTE 9 BRIDGE BETWEEN MIDDLEVILLE AND GREENFIELD UNTIL MORE MONEY CAN BE FOUND FOR PERMANENT REPAIRS. THE 170-YEAR-OLD STONE BRIDGE HAS BEEN CLOSED FOR THREE YEARS.

Unless you have spoken to individuals involved in the story yourself, you must attribute your rewritten story to its newspaper source. The attribution generally begins the second sentence of the script ("THE MIDDLEVILLE TIMES

REPORTS...."). Not only is it ethical to credit the news organization that discovered the story, but if the newspaper gets it wrong (a not infrequent occurrence), the error and any of its consequences will generally not fall on you or your station.

## PLEASE RELEASE ME

Most of the press releases a newsroom receives concern community groups trying to gain publicity for themselves or their events. Usually these press releases are of minor news value. In smaller communities, however, listeners expect to be informed of such events, and program directors may well inform the newsroom that a story must be aired. Generally, though, if a news or program director believes a press release is worth a story, a reporter will make a phone call or visit an event, with the result that the reporting is original rather than a rewrite.

Businesses and organizations often use press releases...through mail though increasingly through the fax machine or PR Newswire...to tout promotions, reorganizations, mergers, hirings, layoffs and other activities. These press releases are the first, and sometimes the only official contact the business or organization will make with the media. Press releases are an essential aspect of business reporting. Let's say your fax machine spits out the following press release from an out-of-town bank announcing a deal for it to buy a local bank:

- Heron Bank, Inc., of Lyons, has entered into a definitive agreement to acquire the Middleville Savings Bank, Inc., of Middleville, in a cash transaction for $8,375,000.

Mary Gonzales, President and Chief Executive Officer of Heron Bank, announced, "We are very pleased with opportunities afforded by our prospective acquisition of Middleville Savings Bank. We are looking forward to serving the Middleville community."

The closing of the acquisition transaction is subject to the completion by Heron Bank of its due diligence investigation of Middleville Savings Bank, as well as regulatory approval by federal and state banking officials.

Middleville Savings Bank has assets of $65,000,000 and operates three branches, two in Middleville and the third in

Smalltown. Heron Bank operates in seven markets in two states and has assets of $1,880,000,000. Heron Bank provides a full range of banking services to individuals and small-to-medium businesses.

This press release is full of legalese and large numbers. Bring the story close to home for your listeners by referring to something that will directly affect their lives, as in the lead to this 16-second reader:

- YOU MAY SOON SEE A NEW SIGN OUTSIDE YOUR BANK. MIDDLEVILLE SAVINGS BANK IS ACCEPTING A BUYOUT OFFER FROM LYONS-BASED HERON BANK. THE EIGHT-POINT-FOUR MILLION DOLLAR DEAL WOULD ADD MIDDLEVILLE TO THE SEVEN OTHER CITIES SERVED BY HERON. THE DEAL STILL NEEDS THE OKAY FROM REGULATORS.

Remember that press releases are primary sources of information, like the tape from an interview. The information in a press release contains the bias of the organization that sent it out. Be aware of that bias and show the same prudence in dealing with press releases as you show with other forms of newsgathering.

### Keep Stories Current

In the course of the day, stories you or other reporters have written need to be rewritten. Rewriting is essential not just because each time you tell a story it should sound different and fresh, but also because situations change. Keep the focus on what is current. An early-morning house fire will bring stories about the blaze, the firefighters and any injuries or fatalities. By midday, the lead concerns the amount of damage to the building. In the evening, the focus shifts to the family that might be homeless that night. The shifts in focus require rewriting the story several times in the course of the day.

Rewriting is an important aspect of radio journalism. Knowing how to adapt stories to your medium and to current situations will aid you in informing the public and gaining respect as a timely provider of news.

One of the catch-phrases in teaching broadcast newswriting is that scripts should be "just like speaking"--in other words, you should write the words and phrases you would use if you were talking to a friend. This is not quite correct, and it is especially not the case when it comes to numbers.

### Not Exactly Like Speaking

Take ages, for example. Ages in broadcast scripts are given as adjectival phrases placed in front of the person's name or other identifying feature, such as "66-year-old Dick Cheney," or "the 66-year-old Vice President." This type of construction is not, of course, conversational. The purpose for it is to make the use of numbers in scripts as clear as possible to our listeners. This same desire for clarity should govern other appearances of numbers in our stories, such as in the following script on economic data:

- THE NATION'S HOMEBUILDERS ARE KEEPING BUSY. THE GOVERNMENT REPORTS HOUSING STARTS CLIMBED ONE-POINT-FOUR PERCENT IN AUGUST AFTER A THREE-POINT-FIVE PERCENT RISE THE PREVIOUS MONTH. ECONOMISTS WELCOME THE NEWS, SAYING IT'S ANOTHER SIGN OF STEADY YET SUSTAINABLE GROWTH.

This story is economic--so to speak--in its use of numbers. Only two numbers are given, the percentages of increase for the months of July and August. Listeners aren't faced with statistical overload, and the script ends with expert explanation of these numbers' significance.

### TWO DIGITS ONLY

This story also follows the "two digits only" rule of newswriting: every number must be reduced to two significant digits. This involves rounding the numbers so that they don't end up taxing the short-term memories of listeners. For example, "six point eight three" becomes "six point eight," and "527" becomes "roughly 530." In addition, the descriptive words "half" and "quarter" are generally preferable to "point five" and "point two five." Here's a story that fails to follow the "two digits" rule:

- UNIONS REPRESENTING THE 1284 CLERICAL AND MAINTENANCE WORKERS AT MIDDLE STATE UNIVERSITY HAVE REJECTED PROPOSED CONTRACT CONCESSIONS. UNIVERSITY OFFICIALS WANTED THE UNIONS TO DELAY THEIR SCHEDULED THREE-POINT-SEVEN-FIVE-PERCENT PAY RAISE TO HELP THE SCHOOL DEAL WITH ITS ESTIMATED FOUR-POINT-SIX-ONE-MILLION-DOLLAR DEFICIT. ALTHOUGH LAYOFFS HAVE BEEN THREATENED IF THE CONCESSIONS WERE NOT APPROVED, WORKERS VOTED AGAINST THE PROPOSAL 1090 TO 89, WITH 105 FAILING TO VOTE.

This script is quite bad in its use of numbers, which are too large and appear too often. A better approach is to simplify and follow the "two digits rule":

- UNIONS REPRESENTING NEARLY 13-HUNDRED CLERICAL AND MAINTENANCE WORKERS AT MIDDLE STATE UNIVERSITY HAVE REJECTED PROPOSED CONTRACT CONCESSIONS. UNIVERSITY OFFICIALS WANTED THE UNIONS TO DELAY A SCHEDULED PAY RAISE TO HELP THE SCHOOL DEAL WITH AN ESTIMATED FOUR-AND-A-HALF-MILLION-DOLLAR DEFICIT. ALTHOUGH LAYOFFS HAVE BEEN THREATENED IF THE CONCESSIONS WERE NOT APPROVED, WORKERS VOTED OVERWHELMINGLY AGAINST THE PROPOSAL.

Keeping track of numbers is a difficult task even for the most attentive of listeners. If your station broadcasts lottery results, you may already have discovered that the newsroom telephone rings immediately after the numbers have been read on the air, and on the other end of the line is a listener who became confused or was unable to remember the lottery numbers by the time he or she found paper and pencil to write them down. Our purpose as journalists is to impart information in a helpful manner. Being judicious in the use of numbers should allow listeners a clearer understanding of the events affecting their lives.

## THREE STYLES OF RADIO NEWSWRITING

These pages provide hints on creating three different types of newscast through changes in writing. The topics include an in-depth style appropriate to many formats, a style similar to that heard on the network hourlies, and a vivid style that fits well with younger formats.

### The In-Depth Style

Many stations run local news-talk during drive time, often with a longtime, well-respected, pillar-of-the-community talker--especially in morning drive.

The newsroom needs not only to inform listeners of the important events of the day, but also to give them...and the talker...something to talk about. Stories need to have enough detail to allow the talker to make cogent arguments and hold intelligent conversations with listeners. Here the in-depth style can help.

### Asking and Answering Questions

We all remember the six essential questions a news story should answer: Who? What? When? Where? Why? and How? An in-depth story needs to pay special attention to the last two: the Why and the How...as in, Why is this politician proposing this plan? How will the plan work?, or Why is this researcher's work important? How will the research help people? When writing your stories, ensure that your script tries to provide some answers.

For example, a press release arrives from State University heralding better chickens. A researcher in the agriculture school says she's discovered that hens fed a special enzyme produce offspring less prone to disease. When you do your phone interview, ask about the implications for the person in the street in order to get tape that will be comprehensible to those listeners who are not poultry scientists. In your script, emphasize the general value of having healthier chickens while including a few details of the research with, say, a sentence like this:

- ...HENS GIVEN THE ENZYME TOBLERONE IN THEIR FEED PRODUCED LARGER CHICKENS LESS LIKELY TO PICK UP DISEASES THAT COULD BE

PASSED ON TO HUMAN CONSUMERS IF THOSE CHICKENS AREN'T PROPERLY COOKED....

The story also gives your-talker an issue, food safety. The talker can even extend the issue to question whether there's been too much manipulation of nature through all these research studies.

### Thorough doesn't Mean Long

Story length in the in-depth style will be longer than in other styles, but not by that much. Stories without tape should run 25-30 seconds....stories with tape, 40-45. Shorter, 20-second stories should also be used both to increase story count (giving a wider sense of news coverage) and to provide listeners with some variety.

Since story count is relatively low, the in-depth style is not suitable for 90-second casts. This style is best suited for stations with a 5-minute news hole at the top of the hour and 3:30 at the bottom.

### STORY PLACEMENT

Hierarchy is especially significant for the in-depth style. Length is often used by listeners to judge the importance of a story, but when many of the stories run at least half a minute, length no longer helps listeners figure out what's important. Story placement becomes the only means. The most important stories should come at the beginning of the cast....the less important stories towards the end.

You may want to end the cast with a zinger--a humorous or unusual piece that gives the talker something immediately to play with and helps the talker's phone lines light up. Use common sense, however, in choosing a zinger. A longtime, well-respected, pillar-of-the-community talker is not going to want to offend listeners. Also keep in mind that you're supposed to be a journalist, not a comedian.

### The Network Style

Credibility can often be a problem in medium-sized markets, where communities are too large for listeners to be personally familiar with most of the people or places making news, yet the resources of the station rarely allow for a newsroom staff of more than half a dozen reporter/anchors (if that)--and this small staff often means few stories are produced and listeners perceive a "reporting gap."

One way to restore station credibility is to make the cast resemble the network hourlies, regardless of whether your station replaces the hourly with a local cast or does a 90-second local after the hourly.

### High Story Count

The hallmark of the network style is high story count. Listen to a network hourly and notice how many different events are related. This variety gives listeners a sense of completeness....they feel they know all the major stories. This feeling helps build trust between your listeners and the station, and it gives your newsroom credibility.

A 90-second cast should aim for seven stories. You might be wondering, "My staff is so small to begin with, how am I to get seven different stories?" Odds are you're already taking some of your stories from press releases and the local newspaper. The two or three stories you've taken haven't exhausted their source....there are still plenty of press releases on your desk and dozens of pages left in the newspaper. Certainly there are stories your listeners want to know about.

### Short Story Length

Of course high story count means short story length. A 90-second cast with seven stories works out to an average of 13 seconds per story. This doesn't mean every story should be 13 seconds....rather, important stories should be given adequate time (20-25 seconds, though certainly no more), but less important stories need only a sentence or two.

For example, let's say city council has been in a dispute with the mayor over cuts in the police budget. This story has been in the news on and off for a couple of weeks, and today at City Hall council members are holding a special meeting with the mayor to reach some sort of compromise. Here's all you need (and it runs roughly 7 seconds):

- MIDDLEVILLE CITY COUNCIL MEMBERS ARE HUDDLING WITH MAYOR JANE SMITH TODAY, WITH BOTH SIDES HOPING TO RESOLVE THEIR DISPUTE OVER POLICE CUTS.

There should be some variation in story length throughout the cast...don't give listeners five 7-second stories followed by three 20-second ones. But there should be some progression, with the more important, longer stories at the beginning of the cast and the shorter, less important stories towards the end. One way of producing variation is to stick a 20-second-long humorous or feature story near or at the end of the cast.

### Tape and the Network Style

You might think it impossible to incorporate much tape into a cast with such a high story count, but listen to the hourlies, which often have half a dozen or more tape pieces (both actualities and voicers/wraps). There's little difference in editing actualities for the network style. Keep them under 15 seconds or so, as you probably would for a more discursive style. The difference is in the copy surrounding the act. Two sentences in front, one sentence at the most (and quite often none at all) after.

For example, let's say the governor is proposing eliminating parole for those convicted of using a firearm when committing a crime. Your State News Network has fed you a 9-second cut, which runs as follows:

- IF YOU USE A GUN WHEN COMMITTING A CRIME, YOU SHOULD DO THE TIME...AND THAT MEANS ALL THE TIME...BEFORE YOU ARE ALLOWED BACK IN SOCIETY.

Here's a script to make the cut fit within your time constraints:

- PAROLE COULD BE A THING OF THE PAST FOR CONVICTS WHO USED A GUN IN THEIR CRIMES....THAT'S IF GOVERNOR DOUGLASS GETS HIS WAY.
- Douglass act...OQ: "IN SOCIETY."

- LEGISLATORS WOULD HAVE TO APPROVE DOUGLASS'S PLAN.

This entire story runs 18 seconds. In summary fashion it includes the important facts: the concept behind the governor's proposal, an actuality, and that the legislature would have to pass a bill for the proposal to become reality. For voicers and wraps, station reporters should be instructed to keep stories short (though reporters often have difficulty with the concept of limiting the time their voices are on the air). For voicers in general...and network tape in particular...edit the cut down to 20-25 seconds. Start either from the beginning or, even better so long as the story remains coherent, with the second sentence of the piece, and continue for 20 seconds or so until there's a natural break (which there usually is). Leave off the lockout. In other words, transform the tape into what's often called a "correspondent's" cut.

If you leave out the first sentence of the original report, the information should be incorporated into your lead-in. You do not need to identify the reporter at the front....the differences in the sound of the voice will tell listeners there's a new reporter. When the cut ends, get out of the story only through identifying the reporter, such as:

- ABC'S SUSAN STARR.

Cutting down wraps is far more difficult, and often wraps can't be coherently reduced under 30 seconds (especially if they contain a 20-second-long actuality). Nonetheless by editing voicers and wraps down to 20-25 seconds, you'll be able to include several pieces of tape into your network style cast.

## THE NETWORK STYLE

Two popular radio formats are political talk and the FM Zoo. In political talk, the talker spends time generally warning listeners that Armageddon is upon us. Many political talkers are syndicated, but there are plenty of local versions as well.

The FM Zoo is a morning drive format on FM stations that during other dayparts play various shades of popular music (contemporary hit radio, adult contemporary, hot country, oldies, and so forth). In morning drive there is some music played, but much of the time is spent in sophomoric banter (often of a sexual nature) among the hosts, a traffic reporter, a sports reporter and a news anchor. You may recognize that the so-called "shock jocks" are merely the Zoo without music.

Tedium is fatal to these formats, and news anchors must employ a vivid writing style to keep listeners engaged.

## Choosing Stories

Story selection differs wildly between political talk and the FM Zoo. Violent crime, natural disasters and, of course, politics are the mainstay of the political talk newscast. The FM Zoo prefers stories about celebrities (which often include politicians) and about the humorous or unusual. Generally the news in the FM Zoo format should give listeners an excuse to be happy. The news in political talk gives listeners an excuse to be unhappy. In both formats, however, the same vivid style of newswriting applies.

### *Content, Sentence Structure, Word Choice*

Vivid writing brings out unusual elements in everyday stories. For example, contract negotiations between the city and its workers have made little progress. A strike is possible, though the current contract still has a few weeks to run and no strike vote has been taken. The mayor has repeatedly said that any pay increase would lead to layoffs. The unions say the pay raise can be met by cutting fat in the city administration.

At the biweekly city council meeting, union leaders make a presentation. One council member tells the leaders in a matter-of-fact style, "I think it's a shame the way you've been treated. I want you to know that I support your efforts to improve your standard to living, and I support your right to strike. I hope it doesn't come to this, but shut down the city if you must. It's the mayor who's the only city worker who ought to be losing her job."

A standard reader on the story, lasting 18 seconds, might run like this:

- CITY WORKERS IN MIDDLEVILLE HAVE TAKEN THEIR CONTRACT DISPUTE TO CITY COUNCIL. UNION LEADERS GOT A SYMPATHETIC HEARING

AT LAST NIGHT'S COUNCIL MEETING IN THEIR ATTEMPTS FOR A PAY RAISE AND JOB GUARANTEES. MAYOR JANE SMITH HAS SAID THERE'S NO MONEY IN THE BUDGET FOR A PAY INCREASE, AND CONTRACT TALKS SO FAR HAVE MADE LITTLE PROGRESS.

The vivid writer notices that a city council member has told the unions, albeit conditionally, to "shut down the city." This becomes the lead of a more vivid reader lasting 21 seconds:

"SHUT DOWN THE CITY"--THAT'S WHAT ONE MIDDLEVILLE CITY COUNCILMAN IS ADVISING CITY WORKERS IN THEIR SIMMERING CONTRACT DISPUTE WITH MAYOR JANE SMITH. DON JONES TOLD UNION LEADERS AT LAST NIGHT'S CITY COUNCIL MEETING THAT HE SUPPORTS THEIR RIGHT TO STRIKE FOR BETTER PAY AND JOB SECURITY, ADDING THAT IF ANY CITY WORKER'S TO LOSE A JOB, IT OUGHT TO BE THE MAYOR.

Content isn't the only difference between these two readers. The vivid reader is more conversational in sentence structure, beginning with a quotation that is back-referenced and ending with a conditional ("if...then") clause. The standard reader is prosaic, with simple sentence followed by simple sentence. There are also differences in word choice. The standard reader contains the bland adjective "sympathetic," in contrast to the vigorous "simmering" of the vivid reader. Notice also that "better pay" has a stronger sound than "pay increase."

### Short and Spare

Don't confuse vividness with verbosity. The vivid style is generally spare, with few adjectives ever used. Readers should run about 20 seconds. Wraps should last about 30 seconds. Far too often reporters fall in love with their own cleverness and give newscasts that sound like second-rate Victorian novels. The fault is especially evident in reporting violent crime, when we hear of "city sidewalks drenched with crimson stains from tepid pools of blood," or of "the languid evening interrupted by the sudden patter of semi-automatic weapons."

Violent crime is usually dramatic enough as it is. A simple telling of the event will be far more powerful than any re-creation compiled with the assistance of Roget's Thesaurus.

## NEWS JUDGMENT

These pages allow you to grow as a journalist by getting you to think about how to cover events and what sorts of events should be covered. The topics involve reporting public meetings, analyzing polls and studies, how and whether to broadcast profane speech, as well as tips on avoiding bias, and on becoming an enterprise reporter who finds the stories other reporters miss.

### Avoiding Bias

As politics has become more polarized and the radio audience more fragmented, listeners are now quite sensitive to perceived biases in broadcast journalism. Radio talk-show hosts are frequently highly partisan in their comments on current events, and program directors may choose to promote controversial talkers in order to attract a particular demographic for a particular station. With media consolidation, many markets are now dominated by a single ownership group, which programs deliberately distinct formats and political viewpoints on the different frequencies in that market under the group's management.

Reporters must take particular care to ensure that their stories are free from bias. Of course, journalists are expected to discover the truth about events in their communities and report that information to their audience. Journalists are not supposed to be politicians or entertainers. Under the rules of classical rhetoric, the three tasks of the public speaker are to inform, to entertain and to persuade. Let your talk-show host concentrate on the final two tasks. You are responsible for the first task: to inform. This is especially true if your reports are used on multiple stations with different formats and demographics.

## SIGNIFICANCE OF THE STORY

Story selection is one area where listeners are quick to perceive bias. From my own experience, I remember criticisms

I received from listeners upset at the attempts by a mayor to fire the city's police chief. Supporters of the police chief complained that the media highlighted negative news about the police department but gave little attention when the police successfully solved cases. One example brought up by these supporters was the greater prominence given to the story that a city police officer had been expelled from a statewide drug-enforcement task force because of drunken behaviour at an out-of-state convention, than what was given to the capture of a local burglary ring and the recovery of many of the items stolen from several homes.

Listeners argued that the burglary ring affected far more members of the community than did the out-of-town antics of a single police officer who was not acting under the police chief's direct supervision. Although the disgraced officer's story had merit as news and did reveal aspects of the management of the police department--a central issue in the mayor's desire to replace the chief--these listeners were correct in the underlying rationale that should always govern the choice and placement of news stories: the greater the impact on your listeners, the more significant coverage of the event should be. Bias is often perceived when listeners believe that significant stories are given diminished coverage in favour of sensational, salacious and scandalous news that has little real impact on their daily lives.

## Play it Straight

The popularity of sarcastic political talkers has infected some reporters who perhaps aspire to talk-show careers. I recently heard a story on a station in a midsized market about a downtown antidrug rally involving elementary-school students. The reporter affected a sarcastic tone in his voicer, which began

- NANCY REAGAN SAID, "JUST SAY NO TO DRUGS." WELL, WITH THE WAY THESE KIDS ARE RUNNING AROUND AT TODAY'S RALLY, THEY CLEARLY DIDN'T SAY NO TO SUGAR.....

Aside from being an ineffective lead that fails to provide listeners with basic information about the rally, this script seems merely a lame attempt by a smarmy reporter to make himself appear clever. It demeans the children who participated in the rally. Furthermore, the sarcasm implies that the rally was a waste of time. The reporter should not have been making social commentary on how children are being raised and on the efficacy of antidrug rallies. Listeners easily could have perceived bias on the part of the reporter, harming the credibility of station's news department as an accurate source of information.

Keep the tone of scripts informational, without partisanship or sarcasm. And give stories the proper amount of coverage, neither too little nor too much. These steps will help ensure that you become a trusted source of information in your community, and that your listeners will not ignore, or worse, turn off the radio during your newscasts.

## BE ENTERPRISING

Enterprise reporting is a term that has become unfamiliar to far too many radio journalists. Enterprise reporting refers to stories generated by a reporter on his or her own, as opposed both to stories assigned by the news director and to breaking news (such as police and fire department activity).

### *What Neighbours are Talking About*

Investigative journalism (of, say, the Watergate or Whitewater variety) is one type of enterprise reporting, and important political stories have been generated by reporters rather than news directors. Most enterprise reporting, however, is rarely that glamorous and involves bringing stories active within a small subset of the community out to a wider audience.

For example, residents of a working-class neighbourhood complain that an unoccupied house is the site of illegal drug sales and prostitution, and those neighbours want the house torn down. The owner, who lives in another part of the city, is an architect who says the building has historic value and that she eventually intends to restore the house. The neighbours blame the owner for leaving the property in disrepair, which they say invites criminals. The owner blames the neighbours for allowing criminal activity in their neighbourhood, activity that she says hinders her plans to restore the building.

This story does not belong at the top of a newscast, but it brings up a variety of important issues: public safety, preserving historic buildings, absentee owners, and disputes among differing groups about urban planning and city priorities. It may well be the most talked about story in the neighbourhood at that time, and because the issues it raises reverberate in neighbourhoods throughout the listening area, it is worth reporting on the air. But the story hasn't made the daily newspaper, nor has it appeared on television. How does the enterprise reporter find out about it?

### Paying Attention

Here's where young reporters have to learn to pay attention to what concerns ordinary listeners. When you're in line at the bank, the post office, the grocery store, you may hear about all sorts of events going on in various neighbourhoods. Some of these stories may deserve a wider audience. Barbers and hairdressers often have a wealth of information gleaned from their clientele. When you're getting your hair cut, think about whether that information might be of interest to your radio audience. Organization mailings and community newspapers often provide valuable leads to stories you might otherwise miss.

Cyberspace can also provide you with story ideas from farther away. E-mail lists and on-line forums contain postings that reveal the concerns of ordinary individuals. Sign up for a few of the lists or forums that cover your hobbies or interests (but be judicious; your e-mail box might get overloaded with junk). Although most of the postings will not generate stories, some will.

For example, on an e-mail list dealing with religion, a parent in Texas posted a message about a new book in the high-school library that the parent found inappropriate for his 14-year-old daughter. The novel was written for early teen readers and had been recommended by the school librarian. In learning about the novel from his daughter, the parent was offended by one particular scene in the book, and he sent an e-mail message to the list for advice on what to do. After reading this e-mail message, the enterprise reporter will want to investigate whether the book has generated any controversy at schools in the station's listening area.

Don't forget your own curiosity as you go about your daily life. I remember a former news director of mine a dozen or so years ago was furious with himself one day. On this particular day, the front page of the feature section of the daily newspaper had a large story about the sudden popularity of car air-fresheners shaped like little crowns. Not a major story, to be sure, but the news director said, "I must have seen these crowns inside a dozen or so cars, and I always wondered what they were. But I forgot that others might also be wondering, which made it a story worth investigating." Now that the newspaper had explained the mystery of the crowns, there was no longer a story to report.

### Gaining Respect as a News Source

This episode gets to an important aspect of enterprise stories: they distinguish your version of the news from that available on other radio stations, on television or in the newspaper. By reporting the stories no one else has...or has yet...you give your station added stature as a primary source for information. Listeners will perceive when TV stations and the newspaper are following your lead. (They also know when you are following them.)

Enterprise stories require a little more time than stories whose basic facts are already known to listeners. While it may be difficult to fit a wrap from such a story under 45 seconds, having an enterprise story should never be a license to go long (that is, more than 55 seconds). Condensing the story to its basic elements also forces the reporter to gauge how important the story really is and how interesting the station's listeners will find it.

You won't get any additional pay for enterprise stories--after all, most of the discovery will have to be done on your own time--but you will gain a satisfaction far greater than that from reporting assigned stories. You will also be developing news judgment and journalist's instincts, which will serve you well in your career ahead.

## DEALING WITH PROFANITIES

Language changes over time, and each generation understands words in a slightly different way. In addition, diverse ethnic, religious and social groups have distinct usages and interpretations of everyday speech. Language that is acceptable to some may be offensive to others, and often newsmakers will...both deliberately and inadvertently...use words that offend some listeners. Journalists need to take care when preparing reports that may contain a profanity.

### *Is it News?*

First and foremost is the issue of whether to report the profanity at all. As we all know, there are many causes for "cussing." Minor self-injury is one of them, and such a cause is generally not newsworthy.

For example, a local minister is hammering a ceremonial "first nail" as part of a volunteer project to renovate low-income housing. The minister sends the hammer down on his own thumb and then screams several choice words, to the great surprise of his congregants. While this is undoubtedly embarrassing to the minister and quite possibly amusing to the congregants, the episode is irrelevant to the story of the volunteer effort to fix up the housing.

Another example demonstrates that sometimes a profanity should be reported. At a public hearing concerning controversial behaviour by members of the police department, the mayor faces criticism from community activists and rival politicians concerning his administration. After listening to the angry...but not generally offensive...words of a city council member and potential mayoral candidate, the mayor becomes visibly irritated and utters a profanity-laced reply. Here we have a public official using a public forum to discuss public events. It is newsworthy that a mayor would utter a profanity in such a context because the utterance demonstrates how the mayor interacts with the public and with other city officials.

### Private Emotions in Public View

Another reason for profane speech is sudden, deep emotion, such as grief at the loss of a loved one. It has become fashionable for some stations to broadcast profanities spoken in these situations because the language reveals the strong emotions felt by the speakers.

In contrast, I believe that these sorts of actualities should not generally be aired. The people involved are usually private individuals thrust into the news because of the catastrophe that has just enveloped their lives. They are not prepared to make public statements, and they may well be embarrassed in the days to come concerning their words and behaviour at this moment of intense emotion. A good reporter should have enough sound to prepare pieces that adequately reveal the emotional state of a victim's relatives and friends without resorting to replaying their profanities.

### *To Bleep or not to Bleep*

If news judgment dictates playing an actuality containing a profanity, the further question arises whether to broadcast the cut unedited or whether to insert a tone to replace the offensive word. Altering an actuality should never be done without serious deliberation about the degree to which the meaning of and impression left by the cut will be changed. Some words are less profane than others and can be broadcast. Most profanities--including racial, ethnic and sexual slurs--are, however, best replaced in the actuality by a tone that extends from immediately after the offensive word's first phoneme to immediately before the word's last phoneme. This will allow listeners to figure out what the word is without actually having to be confronted by it.

To give one example, it's probably okay to broadcast the word "bastard," but not okay to broadcast "f*ck."

Finally, a warning on racial, ethnic and sexual slurs, though this warning also holds true for other types of profanity. When the utterance of such slurs by a newsmaker is worth reporting, care must be taken in the script to ensure that listeners are well prepared if an actuality...even (probably, preferably) a bleeped actuality...is played. Before the cart is played the anchor or reporter should say that

- THE FOLLOWING TAPE CONTAINS LANGUAGE THAT YOU MAY FIND OFFENSIVE to give listeners the opportunity to avoid listening to the profanity themselves or to prevent children from listening. Profanities...especially slurs...lend themselves all too easily to sensationalism, particularly when reporters in their eagerness to relate the story fail to provide adequate context for the utterance or adequate warning to listeners who may not wish to be confronted by offensive speech.

## POLLS, SURVEYS AND STUDIES

Polls, surveys and studies have increasingly become a newscast staple. Nearly every day we seem to be bombarded by a poll, survey or study indicating, or seeming to indicate, how everything from a disease to a politician (if the two are distinct) might be faring among the public. It's always a good idea to figure out beforehand the types of poll and study results you plan to tell your listeners and why.

### *Get an Expert*

Polling data are among the most misunderstood and misused information with which we deal. It helps to have an expert available to explain to our listeners...AND TO US...what a poll's results can mean. Usually there's an expert on polling at a nearby college or university.

Get in contact with that person and try to build a working relationship. Both you and your listeners will be grateful. Polls are conducted by various groups--polling organizations, news operations, colleges and universities, businesses and interest groups, as well as political consulting firms. These groups will generally provide some information on how any given survey was taken, such as how many people were interviewed, how those people were chosen, and how they were interviewed. There are advantages and disadvantages to various polling techniques, and your expert should enlighten you on how trustworthy the results may be.

### *The Numbers Game*

Care must be given when providing poll results to our listeners. On the one hand, a simplifying vagueness about the results can be deceptive. To say

- SENATOR ALISON WILLIAMS IS LEADING IN HER RE-ELECTION BID OVER CHALLENGER MARC ANTONY IN THE LATEST MIDDLEVILLE TIMES/ CHANNEL 8 POLL.

and to leave it like that gives listeners no impression on how close the race may be. Something must be said about the size of the lead, keeping in mind how the the method of sampling used affects the margin of error and other aspects of result reliability. Another presentation problem involves tossing ALL of the numbers from a poll to our listeners:

- SENATOR ALISON WILLIAMS HAS A 9-POINT LEAD...42 TO 33...IN HER RE-ELECTION BID OVER CHALLENGER MARC ANTONY IN THE LATEST MIDDLEVILLE TIMES/CHANNEL 8 POLL. 25 PERCENT OF THE 607 PEOPLE SURVEYED STILL HAVEN'T MADE UP THEIR MINDS, AND THE POLL HAS A MARGIN OF ERROR OF PLUS OR MINUS 4 POINTS, SO WILLIAMS COULD BE AHEAD AS MUCH AS 46 TO 29 OR ONLY 38 TO 37.

Aside from not being a particularly helpful interpretation of the polling data, this story throws so many numbers that listeners might think they're hearing sports scores or the lottery results. Numbers are, of course, necessary to this story, but they should be included judiciously, and hypothetical results created by manipulating the margin of error should not be included.

### *Whose Study is It?*

Reporters who take great care to reveal the source and accuracy of political polling data may be cavalier about surveys and studies that do not directly address political issues. This carelessness is especially apparent in the reporting of lifestyle surveys, medical studies, environmental-impact studies, and surveys of economic activity. As an example, the American Automobile Association released a study that said most pollution in the air came from factory smokestacks rather than from automobile exhausts. One major-market, clear-channel station told the story this way. First the anchor read the sentence,

- ARE CARS THE BIGGEST POLLUTERS OF OUR AIR?

Then followed a buzzing noise such as is heard when a wrong answer is given on "Family Feud" or some other TV gameshow. The anchor continued:

- WRONG! FACTORIES ARE THE NUMBER-ONE POLLUTERS ACCORDING TO TRIPLE-A....

Aside from the gimmicky (and credibility-destroying) presentation, this story gives undue credence to Triple-A's study. Triple-A is an interest-group for drivers of passenger vehicles, and the link between Triple-A and the study must be prominently reported. Stating the report's conclusions as fact at the beginning of the story provides too much bias and may prevent listeners from acquiring a critical understanding of the report.

### *It ain't over 'till it's Over*

Political polling provides a measure of how well a campaign is doing at a particular point in time. Surveys are useful in reporting on the progress (or lack thereof) of a campaign and on any changes that may take place in the campaign as a result of this feedback. But, as we all know, they are not official election returns, and while they may reflect upon the substantive issues in a campaign, poll results do not themselves represent a substantive issue worthy of extensive coverage. In other words, don't spend your time covering the polls instead of covering the election.

## Public Meetings

For many radio journalists, their first "beat" involves covering regular meetings of a governmental board such as a city council or school board. Properly reporting board meetings demands a significant investment of time and effort, but that effort will be richly rewarded through informing the public about their government and developing a sense of judgment about what makes news.

### *Know thy Board Members*

Make sure you know who the board members are. Study up on their backgrounds, careers, the neighbourhoods they represent, their political experience and political affiliation. You are coming to these meetings as an outsider, and only by demonstrating familiarity with the people and issues involved will you gain the respect and trust you need to do a proper job as a reporter. Being present at the meeting is only part of your job. While you should try to record all of the meeting's activities from the call to order to adjournment, rarely do the public deliberations provide compelling actualities. Your best opportunities for sound will come after the meeting has ended, through interviews with individual board members and members of the public. Ask them for reactions to the decisions taken, remembering to get reactions from both sides. Moreover, do not "play favourites" by interviewing the same board member meeting after meeting. Sometimes political caucuses designate one board member to speak on their behalf, but that's a decision for the caucus to make, not for you. By demonstrating knowledge and fairness, you'll readily be granted the interviews you need.

### *An Agenda for Reporting*

Board meetings follow an agenda that is usually available at least a day and perhaps even a week in advance. Some boards will oblige news organizations by mailing or faxing the agenda to them, though others may treat reporters like any other member of the public and require them to stop by the board's offices or city hall to pick up a copy. Get the agenda and study it before the meeting. Not only will you know what issues will be coming before the board, but you will also have the opportunity to do a preview piece ("Should skateboarding be banned from downtown? City council will take up the issue at tonight's meeting....") to air the day of the meeting.

### *Keep Your Focus*

Far too many news directors view board meetings as inherently dull, even though these meetings demonstrate the workings of government. Reporters only reinforce this view by failing to write interesting scripts. Perhaps this is because so many meetings go on...and on...and on for hours, and reporters lose focus on what the important issues were. Countless stories end up sounding like the following, slightly modified from what I heard on a small-market station:

- THE MIDDLEVILLE SCHOOL BOARD HEARD A REPORT AT LAST NIGHT'S MEETING. THE REPORT

WAS PREPARED BY ASSISTANT SUPERINTENDENT CHESTER ARTHUR. ARTHUR FOUND THAT STUDENTS COMMITTED 12 ACTS OF VIOLENCE LAST YEAR IN THE MIDDLEVILLE SCHOOLS, UP FROM FIVE THE YEAR BEFORE. ARTHUR TOLD THE BOARD THAT GREATER COOPERATION WAS NEEDED WITH POLICE BUT THAT THERE WAS NO NEED TO HAVE OFFICERS ASSIGNED TO THE SCHOOLS AT THIS TIME.

This 21-second reader misses the story. The lead should not be that the school board heard a report, but rather that violence was on the rise in city schools. There are a number of ways to bring the real story--violence in the schools--to the fore. Here's an example using a question lead:

- SHOULD POLICE OFFICERS PATROL MIDDLEVILLE SCHOOLS? ASSISTANT SUPERINTENDENT CHESTER ARTHUR DOESN'T THINK SO...AT LEAST NOT YET. DESPITE A DOUBLING LAST YEAR OF THE NUMBER OF VIOLENT ACTS COMMITTED BY STUDENTS ON SCHOOL PROPERTY, ARTHUR IS TELLING SCHOOL BOARD MEMBERS A DIRECT POLICE PRESENCE IN THE SCHOOLS IS NOT NECESSARY.

Remember that even though you may have sat through a meeting lasting 4 or 5 hours, you are condensing that meeting into a 20-, 30-or 40-second story. The issues facing the community provide you with your subject matter. With those issues forefront, you should be able to craft interesting stories that inform your listeners about their government and their community.

## IMPROVING NEWSROOM OPERATIONS

These pages address organization, preparation and performance. The goal of these lessons is to turn your newsroom into an efficient and credible source of information for your audience. The topics in this section deal with handling equipment failure, making your newscast distinct from your competitors, presenting a more professional sound and preparing for cyclical stories about schools and weather.

### *Improving On-Air Delivery*

Although the Newswriting for Radio website is devoted, as the name suggests, to improving the writing of radio news, many visitors have requested tips on speaking and vocalization. This page will address two of the most common faults in newsreading: monotonous delivery and slow reading.

### *Follow the Pattern*

The reading of news on the radio is expected to conform to a pattern of musical pitches or notes. If you were to speak to your friends using this exaggerated pitch pattern, your conversation would seem a bit too much like "sing-song." The pitch pattern--which is present in all speech--does not need to be as noticeable in direct conversation because the listener can pick up visual cues (such as facial expressions or hand gestures) that aid in interpreting the words spoken.

Radio--unlike television--must rely solely on vocal quality to convey this additional information, information that may include the length of a story, the story's seriousness and the credibility of sources. The pitch pattern is especially helpful in informing listeners when stories begin and when they end.

Pitch should be considered in relative terms as "high" or "low" based on the range used in normal conversation. Listeners hear the modulation between "high" and "low" pitch and interpret those changes, even though most listeners are unaware of the pattern. They become aware only when the pattern is not properly followed, at which point they become confused or bored by the story.

### *Change Pitches*

Stories begin on a "high" pitch and end on a "low" pitch. In between the pitch modulates from one clause or sentence to the next. Within a clause or sentence, the pitch falls slightly from beginning to end, except in questions, where the pitch rises at the end.

For example, in a standard, four-sentence script, the pitch begins "high," falling slightly at the end of the first sentence. The second sentence begins at a lower pitch than the end of the first sentence. The third sentence begins at a higher pitch than the beginning of the second sentence. The final sentence, like the second sentence, begins at a "low" pitch and gently falls towards the end of the script.

When news directors, program directors or general managers complain about monotonous delivery, they are referring to readers who remain on the same pitch throughout the script. The easiest way to gain an understanding of pitch is to listen to the pitch patterns of other anchors and reporters, and to practice, practice, practice. With time, the pattern will become automatic when you're on the air.

*Speed it Up*

The other common fault in newsreading concerns speed. Most beginning radio journalists read and speak too slowly. Perhaps we remember all too well when, in speech and debate class in junior high school, the teacher chastised us for being nervous and speaking too quickly.

Radio, however, cannot provide the additional, visual information that exists when speaking in public or on television. With only one mode of information-retrieval available, the radio listener prefers to process speech at a faster rate. Normal conversational speed is generally too slow for reading radio news.

Some reporters and anchors--notably those on public radio--seem to want to make an art form out of speaking VERY SLOWLY. Colleagues in public radio claim that their listeners prefer the news to be read slowly. I suspect this preference has more to do with aesthetics than with cognition, but in any case, choosing to read slowly because of the wishes of a public-radio news director may limit a reporter's subsequent career.

Many young journalists find their first jobs with public radio stations. Higher pay and greater opportunities may be found at commercial stations, but commercial-radio news directors often balk at hiring a reporter whose demo tape reveals slow reading. Even if your news director demands slow reading, use examples from the commercial network hourlies (e.g., ABC, AP, CBS, CNN) to set the speed for reading the news on your demo tape.

Monotonous delivery and slow reading are very common among beginning radio journalists. Understanding the causes of these faults can lead to their correction.

## R.I.P. "RIP 'N' READ"

A news director at a radio station in New England once complained to me that whenever he chats with folks at an area store or bank, he finds that these listeners often confuse his station's newscasts with those of his AM rival.

Much of his audience cannot seem to tell one station's news from another. While there are plenty of cosmetic changes that will make a newscast distinct--such as expensive sounders, employing announcers with unusual voices, or rearranging the clock to, say, stick traffic in the middle of the cast--often the most neglected aspect of the cast is the easiest and least expensive to correct: the actual words spoken by the anchor.

The primary reason the newscasts of so many stations sound the same is that these casts are using identical scripts, scripts written by wire news services. This is the practice known as "rip 'n' read." The name comes from the days when wire-service stories came into the newsroom on a bulky, teletype machine that spat out the stories onto a large roll of paper. An anchor would rip the story off the roll and read it on the air.

"Rip 'n' read" was a necessary evil in those days due to the lack of time that often existed between when the story finished printing and when the anchor had to go on the air. Even then, however, it was expected that anchors would rewrite wire copy if time was available.

The reasons for rewriting are manifold: to emphasize elements of the story that are particularly relevant to the station's audience; to create a newscast in which stories flow seamlessly one into another; to avoid repetition of the same wording in subsequent newscasts; and even to correct errors and faults of style in the wire copy itself.

These reasons are just as important today, when many newsrooms have the wires fed directly into personal computers on which stories can be edited before being sent to a printer.

## How to Destroy your Credibility

News directors should demand that wire copy be rewritten whenever time allows. This would, however, require leadership by example, and far too many news directors themselves partake of "rip 'n' read." I was reminded of this fact through a recent scan of the airwaves while I was in my car during morning drive, when many news directors have their anchor shifts.

I turned the dial to an AM news-talk station to hear the lead story, which concerned the decision of an area school district to require students at certain schools to wear uniforms. I knew the story quite well, for I had already heard the identical script read five minutes earlier during the news segment of an FM morning-zoo show. I heard the script again that morning on another AM station and another FM station.

The credibility of news operations in music-heavy formats is not particularly high to begin with, but credibility is fundamental to all-news and news-talk formats. Listeners quickly perceive when stories sound the same, not only between newscasts on one particular station, but also between the news reports on different stations as these listeners punch the buttons on their car radios. When listeners face the same words telling the same story over and over again, they come to believe that there's no news on the radio, and so there's no need to listen to news-based formats.

"Rip 'n' read" can be deadly to a radio news operation. Kill "rip 'n' read" at your station before "rip 'n' read" kills you.

## School and Weather Stories

Education and the weather may be the most important issues to your audience. This is especially true of AM stations with news-heavy formats, which regularly gain listeners in the fall and winter with the beginning of the school year and the arrival of unsettled weather. Reporters and news directors need to be prepared to cover school stories and weather emergencies that inevitably appear every year.

### *Be Prepared for the Start of School*

Keep a timetable in the newsroom of when school districts in your area come back into session. As schools open, you should have at least brief readers in your morning casts informing listeners that "It's the first day of classes in Middleville," or "Kids are heading back to school in Small town." If you have a separate traffic reporter, that person should also have a copy of the list of school openings and should remind drivers to watch out for children going to and from school. If you don't have a traffic reporter, make the reminder yourself in the final sentence of your readers on the start of school. Kids and traffic safety is an obvious story idea, and usually a state Triple-A official (who has probably sent you a press release) is available for interview.

### Keep Stories Interesting and Current

Other obvious story ideas may need careful attention to make sure they remain interesting. Back-to-school shopping is an example. Doing MOS of mothers buying notebook paper is dull, dull, dull. Examine store ads and look for the unusual. If you have school-age kids, you may already have been badgered to buy all sorts of nonsense--and if one of those requests strikes you as particularly wacky, it may strike your listeners as interesting, too! (If you don't have school-age kids, there's bound to be someone at the station who does.)

While there is a certain timelessness about the annual return of children to school, your stories should be firmly rooted in the present. For example, instead of a generic story about buying clothes for the kids, look at the more current topic of school uniforms (would uniforms end up being less expensive for parents? what do children think about having to wear the same clothes to school every day?). Another recent controversy involves "low-riding" pants, which some school districts have banned.

#### *Prep for School Closings*

Your station probably already has a procedure for receiving and announcing school closings. All reporters should be familiar with this procedure, regardless of whether or not the newsroom actually takes the phone calls from nervous superintendents cancelling school. Knowing how the lists of school closings are prepared and then make their way into the studio allows everyone to assist in ensuring that school closings are announced in a timely fashion. In addition, when listeners call the newsroom asking whether a particular school is closed, the reporter on the other end of the line will be able either to find the answer for the caller or to tell the caller when the school-closing list will next be aired.

The list of closed schools should be organized in logical fashion so that listeners may easily discover when their school should be announced. In small markets, alphabetical listings may be adequate. In medium-sized and larger markets, a combination of alphabetical and geographic organization (such as alphabetical listings within a list of counties) might be preferable.

### *On the Road*

Bad weather is often the cause of school closings, but when the schools are closed many worksites remain open. Listeners who have to make their way to work want to know about road conditions. Even if your station relies upon a commercial traffic-reporting service, there may well be several occasions during the year (such as the sudden arrival of storms) when you want to have a reporter on the roads. Reporters need little more than a cellular telephone, a tape recorder and a good timepiece. The reporter might drive along the major roads in the listening area, pulling onto exit ramps or into parking lots at set intervals to provide live reports. Reporters can also interview stranded motorists, or try to interview busy automobile towing and repair shop employees. It goes without saying that reporters should not become stories themselves by being stranded or involved in accidents, so use common sense when reporting from the road.

## Don't Shovel Tired Features

Weather-related stories can enlighten listeners, though care must be given to avoid the tired and trite. A few years ago we heard far too many stories about "El Nino"--the unusually strong warming of the waters of the Pacific off the coast of South America--that were sensational rather than informational. (I fear we are in for a similar barrage of bad journalism with the newly emerging El Nino.) Stories typically overdone during the winter include sales reports on shovels and snowblowers, features on the workday of a road-salting crew, and travel agents discussing where locals are heading to escape the weather.

A better approach for generating stories takes issues already of community concern and adds a seasonal aspect. For example, many communities have school buildings that are in poor condition. How are those buildings affected by winter weather? As another example, use of road salt is declining in some areas out of concern for the environment. What has been the effect on driver safety, and if safety has diminished, is the trade-off for a cleaner environment worth it?

### Coordinate your Efforts

In the news-talk format, cooperation with your talker can generate deeper discussion of the issues and help both of you in your separate tasks. For example, let's say your station has some midmorning or midday local talk, and the talker has scheduled a psychologist to discuss a child's first day at school. You can assume that the psychologist will talk about separation anxiety, so don't do that story in the morning. Instead, pick a different topic, such as school violence. Your talker now has a different subject to bounce off her guest, who will discuss separation anxiety and the psychological trauma violence inflicts on a young child.

Take a few cuts from the talk-show interview, and you now have a different story for afternoon drive. You will, of course, credit your talker ("...as psychologist Elizabeth Linden-Rahway told News-Talk 990 midday host Sarah Barnes..."), giving the sort of cross-promotion that warms the heart of any program director or general manager.

## TECHNICAL DIFFICULTIES

Two of the most dreaded words in broadcast news are "technical difficulties." Equipment problems can never be entirely eliminated. There will always be carts that malfunction, phone lines that go dead, and computer terminals that freeze up. With a little preparation and organization, you'll be able to handle those "technical difficulties" and get through your cast with minimal disruption.

### Prevention is the Best Medicine

Many on-air snafus are due to the carelessness that accompanies haste. Perhaps the most prevalent mistake involves playing the wrong cut. At stations that still use tape, this problem is easily prevented by properly labelling and stacking your carts. I was always amazed when visiting newsrooms at how often I saw carts lying around with only the tiniest of illegible scrawls to identify them. Carts should be marked with the name of the speaker (the newsmaker for an actuality, the reporter for a voicer or wrap), the number of seconds the cut runs, a slug (story title) that matches a story title on the script, and perhaps even the outcue and a further identifying number that matches a number written at the top of the script.

For example, you have a 10-second actuality of Middleville Mayor Jane Smith discussing plans for the city to build a downtown parking garage. The cut runs as follows:

- IT'S NOT WASTING TAX MONEY. IT'S SAVING DOWNTOWN. IT'S EXPENSIVE BUT IT'S MONEY WELL SPENT. THIS IS THE ONLY WAY TO KEEP BUSINESSES DOWNTOWN.

The label you put on the cart might read like this:

| #4 | PARKING | 0:10 |
|---|---|---|
| SMITH | OQ:"...DOWNTOWN." | |

Similar information should also appear on the hard copy of the script. The script should have a line break to indicate when a cart is to be played, and information on the speaker, the outcue and the duration should be given. Here's an example of what the script accompanying the previous cut might look like:

- .... CRITICS SAY THE PROPOSAL IS A WASTE OF TAX MONEY, BUT SMITH DISAGREES.

  #4 PARKING

  OQ: "...DOWNTOWN."

  CART RUNS 0:10

CITY COUNCIL WILL DISCUSS THE MAYOR'S PLAN AT TONIGHT'S MEETING.

Having this information on the cart label and in your script will help ensure you play the right cart at the right time.

## SOUND IDEAS FOR THE DIGITAL NEWSROOM

Many newsrooms are now tapeless, using digital sound files for actualities, voicers and wraps. Most computer audio-editing programs automatically assign a file number to each sound file, but the file still requires a slug for further identification. The slug should contain a word immediately followed by a number indicating which particular story uses that file.

For the story about the proposed parking garage, let's say this actuality is the second of three actualities taken from the interview with the mayor.

One of the actualities will be used by the reporter in a wrap, the other two in scripts to be read by an anchor. So there are three scripts to be created from this story, and this particular script and its accompanying actuality should be slugged parking02 to distinguish it from the other scripts and sound files (which would be slugged parking01 and parking03).

Computer programs may allow further identifying information, such as outcue and length of cut, to mark each sound file. The more information in your script, the better. This will help ensure that the sound file you select to accompany the story is the correct one.

## CART-ASTROPHIES AND OTHER GLITCHES

Another common snafu in newsrooms that still use tape involves not having the cart properly cued. This often happens during the second airing of a cut. The anchor during the first airing may have had to stop the cart immediately after the actuality or wrap finished (and before the cart could recue) because the cart machine was needed to play another cart during that cast.

It is the responsibility of the anchor about to go on the air, or the anchor's producer, that carts be properly cued prior to broadcast. Carts should be played in the newsroom before the next airing to ensure the carts are cued. (Anchors between broadcasts should be playing and listening to these carts anyway to aid in the rewriting of the accompanying scripts.)

If a cart is not properly cued, or if the cart machine malfunctions (such as playing the actuality very s l o w l y), stop the cart and say a sentence that summarizes to listeners what they would have heard without the "technical difficulties." Then return to your script and finish the story.

When I worked as a writer in Detroit, I was expected to type a few bare phrases summarizing a cart's contents, and that summary appeared at the bottom of the script, separated from the on-air story by a double line.

This summary was provided in case problems arose playing the cart. The anchors (who, in an all-news format, had 5-hour air shifts and may not have heard the tape before it was brought into the studio) needed that summary to ad lib when the cart failed.

In the tapeless newsroom, anchors often read their stories off computer screens. If the computers fail, neither the scripts nor the sound files will be available. It is crucial that a printout of all the scripts for the cast be taken into the studio. A frozen computer screen won't then lead to a frozen newscast.

## SNAP, CRACKLE, POP

Telephone connections also fail, or the quality of the connection may be too poor for broadcast. Poor quality connections are becoming more prevalent as more and more stations send reporters out with cellular telephones, whose quirks can at times be maddening.

If you in the studio have a hard time understanding the words of the speaker on the other end of the line (be it a newsmaker or a reporter in a live shot), your listeners...many of whom are in automobiles...won't fare any better. End the telephone interview or report immediately with a graceful apology to the listeners about sound quality and "technical difficulties," and move on to the next story. No matter how important the story may be, if the sound is incomprehensible, the value for radio news is worthless. The possibility of "technical difficulties" in a cast should remind anchors always to bring into the studio more stories than they would normally need.

If you're giving a cast that runs 3:30, bring in 5 minutes of copy and sound. If you have a 5-minute cast, bring in 8. A problem with a computer screen, cart machine or telephone line could easily cut a full minute or two from your cast.

You need to be prepared to get through the cast in a professional manner, and it is far more professional to complete with confidence a variety of different news stories than to try to return to a tape or a phone report that failed the first time around.

## PRINCIPLES OF WRITING RADIO DRAMA

First of all, the way you choose to present your script is really important if you want the reader to enjoy your play and to concentrate fully on it. Here are a few things which can make reading difficult:

- Plays presented on brightly coloured paper
- Plays printed with expiring cartridges so that the type is so faint you have to squint at it
- Plays printed on continuous listing paper with the content of each page dropping down on to the next one (one of our readers likened this to reading a toilet roll)
- Plays typed in unusual fonts which are really difficult to read, or typed in very large or very small fonts
- Plays typed in such a way that there's no differentiation between character names, sound effects and dialogue
- Plays hand written in pencil

A common mistake is to abbreviate characters' names down to a single initial so the reader has to keep stopping to think who's speaking. The best way to present a script is not so that it will stand out from the competition, but just the opposite- if it's neatly typed, double-spaced, with the characters' names in capitals down the left margin and sound effects or music described in italics, it'll be so easy to read, the reader will find it effortless. Then they can really concentrate on the content of the play. As for the content of the play-radio drama is very different from theatre and television. We often get scripts which say 'written for the stage but I thought it might do for radio' on the front cover. It usually doesn't. Stage directions like 'puts glasses on' or 'bends over and picks up a piece of paper' aren't going to be easy to get across to a radio audience. It has to be in the dialogue or sound effects, otherwise it will be lost. Stage plays can be adapted for radio, but not without a great deal of attention to detail.

There are no limits on the imaginative potential of the dramatist and there are no limits on how the radio dramatist can express that potential. The sound medium is free of all the physical and practical limitations of the stage and film set. A radio play can move through any dimension of time. It can move to any location. It can voice metaphysical, surrealist and subconscious feelings and images.

The radio dramatist needs a creative interaction with the listener, and the ability of the radio dramatist to create a unique world in the listener's imagination is a special quality generally denied to TV viewers or theatre-goers. Theatre, film and TV plays paint the colours for the audience, whereas the pictures in the mind of the radio listener are individual to that person alone. This gives radio a special intimacy.

Radio is very good at dramatising what people are thinking. The contrast between what people say and what they think can be shown very effectively on radio. 'Interior thought' is a convention which is special to the radio medium. In radio the listener can be instantly transported inside the head of a character and can hear those secret, private thoughts that are often better left unsaid. Radio drama has been described as 'The Theatre of the Mind'. The potential conflict between exterior dialogue and speech and interior thought creates a special ground of conflict which is a fertile area for the creative radio playwright.

The key to writing successful plays for radio is to realise that the listener can only understand what is going on by what he or she hears. The physical environment and the appearance of the characters depends on what they say and the images created in the listener's imagination by words and sounds and/or music. Radio drama has only one chance to be successful. A dissatisfied listener only has to twiddle the radio dial, or turn the switch off altogether and the playwright has lost the audience. It's important to bear in mind that a radio playwright can't afford to bore or confuse the listener.

All good writing requires a strong element of honesty and integrity from the writer. The great dramatists strive to express a truth about human experience or human nature. This means that superficiality, pretentiousness and ostentation are quickly recognised by the listener and will normally lead to failure when the listener switches off.

## SOME HORRIBLE TRUTHS

Most radio drama is very badly written. Radio drama is an endangered species. It has never taken a hold of mainstream programming on commercial radio in the UK. It used to be the mainstream in the States and Australia but lost out to TV in the middle to late fifties.

It is under threat within public radio services including the BBC because of the pressure of monetarist ideology and the fact that authors and radio drama directors have been too complacent. IRDP is a significant oasis and continues to support the principle of the original play.

## GROUND RULES

**The Beginning:** The beginning is everything. If this part of it does not work you are 'up shit creek without a paddle'. Your listeners will desert you. You have failed. You do not exist as a dramatist. Booo!

**The Moment of Arrival:** This is how you drop your listeners into the story. Don't give them a warm bed with comfortable pillows and a hot water bottle. The background and sub-text of previous histories is better explored through revelation in dramatic action. So parachute your listener into a top dramatic moment. Not the climax. That would be premature. Find the MOMENT to join the story. Avoid the slow snail's explicatory route. Kick 'em into a high energy trip and whoosh them through the rapids.

**Structure:** Set up...struggle...resolution. You can reverse this if the set-up is more dramatic and explosive than the resolution. Regard your play as a series of phases

**The Plot:** This is the story with lots of twists and turns. The more the merrier. Most listeners like good exciting plots. Without a good plot you're eating a souffle that has gone flat. You need plot, more plot and more plot. Run at least two story lines.

Two sub plots would be interesting. Keep the plots linked logically within the same play. The best system is a major and a minor story-line linked to one another. Get them to come together at the end.

**Surprise:** People are hungry ıor entertainment. If they wanted boredom they would be filling out their tax returns instead of listening to your radio play. Make people afraid, but also excited.

**Character:** Your main character must have the sympathy of the audience. Your audience has to identify with your main character. If this does not happen you have created a failure. Booo!

**Conflict:** Drama = conflict = audience. There has to be an emotional, financial, human, moral, physical struggle so your listeners can laugh or cry. Yes, you want your listeners to laugh or cry or laugh and cry. If you don't, give up.

**Polarities or Extremes:** The art of story telling is exploring the extreme limits of our psychological or physical existence. To pitch one polarity against another.

**The Climax:** I apologize for the sexual metaphor. But there is something in this. The better sex has foreplay, development, sustained excitement, surprise and affection, nay love followed by an explosion of ecstasy. Good radio drama is not all that different. If you don't use it, you lose it.

**Dialogue:** This is how we engage dramatically with the world. Characters inform, argue, amuse, outrage, argue through the ebb and flow of dialogue. When we do we talk and that is how great radio plays are made.....by talking in dramatic dialogue.

**Atmosphere / Ambience:** This sets the emotional spirit of the play. It determines whether your listeners believe in the world that you have created. Worlds are not created by dramatic dialogue alone. There is attitude and atmosphere. This is determined by detail and relevant detail. It could be in a sound effect. It could be in the writing. It could be in the music. It could be in everything. But the result is that the fifth dimension of radio writing-the imagination of the listener-is stimulated to become a picture palace of the mind.

**Emotion:** Got to be there. You have to generate an emotional response from the audience....preferably to the main character....also not so strongly in relation to the other characters. Emotion = love, hate, admiration. Never mind about the type of emotion.....concentrate on whether it is there or not. Emotional connection between the writing and the listener = good radio drama.

**Balance Character and Plot:** You have to have both. You cannot trade. One can predominate over the other. Where they are balanced equally....it can only work if characterisation relates to plot development. If your main plot is character intensive, make sure that your minor plot is plot intensive.

**Purpose:** Crook's golden rule is that every word, every line, every scene must serve a dramatic purpose in terms of characterisation and plot development. Drop anything that does not have a dramatic purpose.

**Tension and Humour:** To stop the listener dropping off or switching off, maintain the tension always and throw in the humour. Tension, humour, tension, humour, tension humour...like the foxtrot..Make the emotional rhythm of the play dance on the listener's heart and mind. Charm and alarm, charm and alarm. But they've got to be linked. Your character uses humour to react to the tension in the scene or play. Keep one character who uses humour to deal with difficult situations. Make sure the humour is verbal. Slapstick belongs to a different type of play or entertainment. Make sure you do not have characters taking it in turns to be funny. This is not stand up comedy or sitcom. Make sure that the character who uses humour has a consistent sense of humour.

Get your listener inside the world of your play. How?

a. Sympathy or empathy with the main character.
b. A bloody good set up.
c. A big, nasty antagonist or villain.
d. Great Plot...Great Story....twists and turns.
e. Crisis at the beginning is dramatic and a great start.
f. Emotional intensity. Hit some high points.
g. Escalating conflict so the structure climbs with tension and humour.
h. Strike the colours with detail so there's an atmosphere, mood...ambience.
I. Modulate charm with alarm...humour with tension...tension with humour...funny policeman nasty policeman.
j. Surprise, surprise...that's what you do to the listener, through the plot.

The principle of developing scenes

1. Introduction.
2. Character one...goal and objective.
3. Character two...goal and objective.
4. Purpose of scene in overall plot.
5. One of the characters achieves a goal.
6. Link to the next scene by introducing or pointing to location of next scene or presence of character in next scene.

Question marks in the mind of the listener. Always keep one, better two or three

THE PRINCIPLE OF CHARACTER

1. Believable and recognisable.
2. Purpose within the plot.
3. Characters have to have function. Character has to be consistent with function.
4. Characters have to be intentional.

5. Start with a stereotype to ensure rapid recognition, then twist the stereotype. Challenge the homily that there is nothing new under the sun by making it new under the moon.
6. Give each character a dominant physical or behavioural characteristic. Make the dominant characteristic purposeful. Make it extreme.
7. Your main character must be active.
8. Active character / urgent plot. The character's energy has to fight the urgency of the plot and the urgency of the plot makes the character more energetic.

## THE PRINCIPLE OF HERO / HEROINE

1. Listeners look up to main characters, want to admire them because we all want heroes and heroines in our lives. Life's eternal fantasy that transcendent people and transcendent moments conquer adversity.
2. If you are very clever you can transfer the hero from the obvious to the humble and make great the inferior or character who has greater potential for human dignity.
3. Charisma. Characters need intensity and conviction. They may not be perfect but they are attractive. You cannot identify with people who are unlike ourselves...too perfect, no beliefs...take themselves too seriously...lack a sense of humour..
4. Give your characters private moments when they drop their guards and allow us into their minds and hearts. Make the listener privileged. Use this moment for revelation.
5. The main character has to change and has to be changed by the plot.
6. You must have a main character and secondary characters. Your main character changes. Your secondary characters are probably more singular in their characteristics. Your secondary characters are already committed. Your main character is still weighing up the options.

7. You must have characters who are extreme in relation to each other...characters that are different make drama.

Where are we now?

Well, we should be here....

a. The main character is in the middle of the story.

b. You've used dominant characteristics.

c. The listener likes the main character.

d. The listener cares what happens to the main character.

e. The listener hates the antagonist.

f. The main character is developing.

## PRINCIPLES OF DIALOGUE

a. Dialogue must be a response to a situation, plot or action.

b. Dialogue must be a response to each character in the scene.

c. Dialogue must be comic relief.

d. Dialogue must connect to the next scene.

e. Avoid reflective, passive and neutral. Go for active, and direct and emotional.

f. Dialogue must be believable by being specific...by being specific to the character's background and emotional state.

g. If dialogue is reacting to action or situation then it must be dramatic and poised on polarities. The goals of the characters in each scene should be different.

h. Dialogue should be continuous. Tip...characters often take a tag by repeating the last word spoken by the first character.

i. Dialogue must relate to function.

j. You can mix direct with indirect between two characters because they have different goals.

k. Humorous dialogue is not a character telling a joke but a line or lines responding to the dramatic situation.

l. Heightened dialogue vs naturalistic dialogue. Heightened language is the language of the theatre...high octane communication...poetic, philosophical... charged..the expression of the playwright...It serves not only the development of the plot and character, but it also presents the view of the writer. Works well in radio. But there is now a tendency for more naturalism. Radio producers like to go out on location and explore realism. In these situations you must stick to natural dialogue.

## PRINCIPLES PECULIAR TO RADIO

1. The inner existence.
2. The tension and conflict between the interior and exterior.
3. More psychological.
4. Easier to explore the real and the surreal and to delineate the line between the two.
5. Have to work in the fifth dimension...the energy of the listener's imaginative participation.
6. The interior existence offers exploration of personal thoughts, fantasies, emotions and conflicts.
7. All levels of external conflict can be explored.
8. The precipitating event through plot has to threaten the inner life of the main character. This is the kick-off in radio drama.
9. The end or resolution in radio drama is more deeply rooted in the emotional equilibrium and insight of the main character. Changes are internal as well as external.
10. Time transposition and translocation are faster and more rapid and more complicated. Flashbacks.. flashforwards... different ages.
11. Radio requires less rather than more characters. Characterisation needs to be strong and fascinating.
12. Maintain the focus of the main character and plot.
13. Economy of words underlines subtextual surprise and engagement with the listener's imagination.

14. Wit is vital because language is so important... cleverness with words...energy with words..humour with words...Wit is advanced by surprising the listener...being aggressive with the listener..being fast, short and clever with the listener.
15. Irony is pathos and bathos. It's conflict between the inner life and outer action.

## WHAT MAKES RADIO DRAMA DIFFERENT?

So what makes a radio play different from one for theatre or television? What follows here are a few quick pointers to help you in the right direction. These points are explored further by Craig Warner, a successful radio drama writer.

Everyone knows the cliche about how radio "stretches the imagination". This suggests radio is hard work for the listener. You can't doze off in front of a radio play and expect to pick up the story again when you wake up. Good radio drama therefore, is not easy to write. To create the world of the play in the mind of the listener, you, the writer have to think as an impresario, sometimes acting as your own producer, director, set designer and dialogue coach.

In radio, there are no limits to the imaginative potential of the dramatist and to how the radio dramatist can express that potential. The sound medium is free of all the physical and practical limitations of the stage and film set. A radio play can move through any dimension of time and to any location. A radio play can voice metaphysical, surrealist and subconscious motivations and images.

The radio dramatist needs a creative intimacy with the listener to conjure a unique world in his or her imagination. Radio is very good at dramatising the contrast between what people say and what they think. Indeed, radio drama has been called the "theatre of the mind". "Interior thought" is a convention that is special to the radio medium; the listener is instantly transported inside the head of a character and can hear those secret, private thoughts that are often left unsaid. The medium liberates the scope of imaginative recall, providing a perfect opportunity to explore consciousness and dramatise all the voices that motivate different aspects of experience. Moving beyond the bounds of naturalism, radio drama can also give animals a voice, invest inanimate objects with character and give emotion to all aspects of nature.

**THE WRITER: CRAIG WARNER**

"I remember once when I was rehearsing a staged reading of a play in New York, I brought along a tape recorder so that I could tape the run-through of the play. When I got home I cued the tape up to a particular scene I wanted to hear, and played it. I was amazed. The whole scene seemed transformed. Suddenly there was not the three actors saying the lines in a dingy church hall-just the mystery of words and voices on their own, a kind of pure music from which there seemed torn away a thousand limitations that my sight had imposed. The dialogue seemed bigger, broader, more magical; this was my first experience of what radio drama might be like.

The first play I sent to the BBC was a stage play I wanted to adapt for the radio. The producer who read it liked it, but he said it was firmly rooted in the stage, and would not make a good radio play. He suggested I write something for the radio directly, something more 'radiophonic'. But what did this mean? I tried to conceive of the play by imagining someone in a room with nothing in it but a box with sounds and voices coming out of it. The producer was right: imagining the telling of a story in this way not only changed the conventions I wanted to use, but actually the story itself. I came up with the idea of a young man who could not speak. Everyone at his work and his home would treat him as though he was intellectually inferior; but the audience of this play would be able to hear his thoughts; they would be able to hear that he was extremely sensitive and highly intelligent, making it all the more moving that the other people in the play never took the time to discover this. This device was a successful one, and it made the play work in a way it could never have worked in any other medium.

It could almost be said that the medium's limitations are also it strengths. Spectacle is out of the question-but for this reason you can furnish a room with a word, clothe and equip and mount an army with a phrase. Vegetables and trees can speak. And the unimaginable and the contradictory can be used without difficulty-for instance, if one of your characters is a woman so beautiful that men instantly die when they set eyes on her, the role would be impossible to cast in any other medium but not on radio. Equally, in the radio world there can be round squares, objects that are all black and all white simultaneously, buildings so tall that their roofs hit the bottom of the earth. You cannot see the frown on an actress's face, but this is little payment to make in exchange for the freedom the medium allows.

Besides, a frown on an actress's face can always be embedded in the dialogue. Often people writing plays will provide emotional clues for the actors to help them interpret lines, like 'angrily' or 'happily'. But, although these may sometimes be helpful to the actor, it is unwise to expect them to say the lines 'angrily' in exactly the same way you hear it in your head. Their idea of anger might be different from yours. But they will be expected to say the lines as you wrote them, so for this reason it's always better to avoid emotional cues at first and to try to make the line an angry line instead. This is particularly true on radio, when the actor's facial expressions cannot be seen, nor can their postures or movements; emotions and all other clues about a character's inner life are portrayed entirely by the vocal delivery.

The other main instrument you have at your disposal in telling a story on radio is sound, and there are several different uses of sound on the radio. One is music. Music can be used as part of a story-for instance, when one character plays a song to another on his record player-or as a score, when the music is not 'heard' by the characters, only the audience, and is used to enhance a scene, for instance to make it more romantic or suspenseful. Many writers and producers use pre-recorded music to score a play-rock, jazz, classical, or any other kind of music that might be appropriate-or a composer can be asked to write original music.

Another use of sound in radio plays is the collection of sounds used to create an atmosphere. If a scene takes place in a crowded restaurant, on a beach, at a football game, or in an airport lounge, you will want the acoustic and the other background sounds associated with whatever location you've chosen. The BBC has almost every imaginable setting already recorded for use in radio plays, and occasionally plays are even recorded in actual locations rather in a studio.

A third use of sound is the use of sound effects. Sometimes these could be additions to the background sounds-for instance, if the scene takes place in a car driving through the city, and suddenly the car has to swerve to avoid hitting another car or there could be distinct sounds that carry the action of your story a bit further, like someone knocking on the door, a siren approaching, or sudden thunder. I find it more satisfying to limit the sounds I use as much as possible, so that each sound will stand out as a clear step in advancing the story, rather than as contributing to a confusion of sounds, which can make them less potent or ultimately meaningless. For this reason, each sound should be carefully considered so that it will be given the proper weight in your play-neither too much nor too little.

The most important thing when writing a radio play is to hear it in your head as you write it. But never let it become too perfect in your head. The drama is a collaborative art form, and the director and the actors, as well as the technicians, will all have creative ideas that will help to take the play out of your head and onto the airwaves."

## APPROACHES TO WRITING FOR RADIO DRAMA-KEY POINTS

The key, therefore, to writing successful plays for radio is to realise that the listener can only understand what is going on by what the listener hears. The physical environment and the appearance of the characters depend on what they say and the images they create in the listeners' imagination by words and sounds.

A radio drama play has only one chance to be successful. Dissatisfied listeners only have to twiddle their dial, or hit the off switch and the playwright has lost the audience. It is important to remember that a radio playwright cannot afford to bore or confuse the listener. Radio drama is capable of capturing the imaginations of the listener with very fine strokes of sound and much can be achieved with a subtle use of effects. Silence in radio drama can be as dramatic as the spoken word or a devastating sound effect. Entire plays have been constructed without a single word of dialogue. BBC Radio has transmitted a radio play which consisted solely of the sounds of a man being chased.

But of course speech will normally be the dominant element. It is in the dialogue that the writer will provide most of the essential information, but this should not sound explicit or it won't seem natural. It follows that the art of dialogue on radio is, at its best, extremely sophisticated. In order to convey information without sounding artificial or stilted the writer must consider the structure of scenes and of individual lines with great precision. It is not a matter of stringing together conversations. A radio play may predominantly consist of dialogue but a radio that was "all talk" in a static conversational sense would be very boring.

A variety of sound is essential for holding the listener's attention and engaging their imagination. This variety can be achieved by altering the lengths of sequence, number of people speaking, pace of dialogue, volume of sound, background acoustics and location of the action. On radio, one room sounds very like another if they're about the same size, but the difference between an interior and an exterior acoustic is considerable.

There are five technical features which make a good radio play stand out

1. Quality of characterisation. Can the listener imagine the experience of the character through the script? Is the character immediate to the listener and can they empathise with her or him? Do the characters undergo some significant change through the course of the drama and does that change encompass conflict?
2. Quality and Originality of Sound Design. Is your script uniquely suited to the radio medium? Have you created a sound atmosphere and 'sound set' that enhances and complements the mood of the writing, the characters

and the plot? Is sound used symbolically, ironically, surrealistically, or satirically and does it form part of the texture and artistic fabric of the play?

3. Quality and Originality of Dialogue. Are the characters created by the idiom and speech rhythms of their lines? Are characters developed by effective and revelatory dialogue? Is there a sense of reality in the speeches? If you are writing about real people do they sound like them?
4. Quality and Originality of the Plot. Are you able to keep the listener on tenterhooks? Do you leave the listener determined to hear the play to the very end? How logical and believable is the story? Is the listener sure of what is happening in each of the developing scenes?
5. Effectiveness of the beginning of the play in making the listener want to continue listening. Remember some drama producers insist that the writer has only a minute to engage the listener before they are liable to turn off!

## THE WRITER: ANGELA TURVEY

"Radio can take you anywhere-from the top of Mount Everest to a submarine at the bottom of the sea. You can crawl inside somebody's head and listen to their thoughts, cross continents or travel through time. The setting for radio drama is just as flexible-your imagination is free to go wherever it wants to without being held back by financial or practical limitations.

The lack of visuals is a powerful advantage in radio-it allows the audience to create their own mind pictures which are invariably more realistic than any special effects on screen or stage. Listening to a radio play is therefore, not a passive exercise: the listener's mind works with your words to create a dramatic experience. The intimacy of radio is also important in this, as your aim is ultimately to elicit a response in your audience.

A lot of my work is set in London and here, radio's unique ability to evoke mood and atmosphere come in to play. The desolation and eerie silence of London's Docklands inspired me to write 'Splendid Isolation', a story about a young woman establishing her independence for the first time. The location need not be exotic. My own rule is that wherever I set a play, I must make it real for the listener and entice them into hearing my story.

Obviously, radio also has it limitations. Everything you want to communicate to your audience must be done verbally or with sound effects whereas in a visual medium, one action may be enough to reveal character or show the audience something vital. Successfully conveying information without being clumsy or stilted is part of the skill of writing for radio and is something which will improve with practice and by listening to as many plays as possible.

Listening to radio drama, if you are familiar with it, is perhaps the first step in beginning to write for radio. Decide what you think works and what doesn't and bear these points in mind when coming up with ideas and writing dialogue. If you are unsure what to write about, my own advice would be to write the kind of play you would like to hear. When I first started to write for radio, I made the mistake of writing what I thought other people wanted to hear. Once I started to write about subjects and characters that genuinely interested me, I was more successful. Always remember the medium you're writing for and ideally, your play should rely on the strengths I have already mentioned.

Assuming you've got the most important elements in place and a director likes your idea, he or she will probably invite you for a chat about your script and perhaps suggest some rewriting. My first play was rewritten three times and each draft was a considerable improvement on the previous one. Eventually, I was offered a contract. I had to wait a few months for the studio recording which I found very exciting. I became more aware of the technical possibilities and kept this information in mind when writing subsequent plays.

Radio is sometimes well-known for producing a particular type of play which some sections of our society may well find interesting, but not particularly relevant to their own lives, experience or history. Barring certain radio-festivals, I had rarely heard a play on the radio with black actors in the leading roles or plays which reflected our multi-cultural society. So why don't I write one, I thought? If you listen to radio and likewise feel there is no voice to speak for you, why don't you become that voice?

I would say that directors are only too happy to receive scripts from all sections of the community, writing about subjects which concern them. What is important is that you wrap your theme in a good story with strong characters and exploit the advantages of radio. As a writer who is also black, I have had the pleasure of working with actors and directors from various cultural backgrounds to produce drama that is popular and accessible to everybody. Because of the number of original plays broadcast on radio every year, it is an excellent medium for allowing many different voices to have their say on air. So what are you waiting for? Pick up that pen and get writing"

## SCRIPT LAYOUT-A FORMAT FOR PRESENTATION

When submitting a script to a radio producer, it must be presented in a particular format. A list of recommendations follows and we advise wherever possible that you follow these.

1. Scripts must be typed or printed. Hand-written scripts will be returned unread. The script should be double spaced with a clear, 12 point font. Do not send scripts printed or photocopied so faintly that they are difficult to read.
2. Please use A4 sized white paper, and use one side of the paper only.
3. Names of characters should be clearly separated from the speech and should be given in full throughout. You know who Mrs B. is but the reader might not
4. Sound Effects, and other technical information should also be clearly differentiated from the speech.
5. Always attach a synopsis of the play, even with a completed script, together with a full cast list and brief notes on the main characters.
6. Always keep a copy of your script.
7. Make sure that all pages are firmly fastened and numbered consecutively. (Rehearsal scripts number each

speech, starting afresh at the top of each page, but this is not necessary when first submitting.)

8. If you want your manuscript returned, enclose a stamped addressed envelope.
9. Please remember, you may have to wait some time, often several months, before you get a response.

**SPECIMEN LAYOUT**

(INTERIOR. SMALL BEDROOM ACOUSTIC. CLOSE TO MIC MUFFLED BREATHING SUGGESTS THAT THE SLEEPER HAS HIS HEAD UNDER THE BLANKETS. WHICH HE HAS. HIS THOUGHTS ARE AWAKE HOWEVER. AND OCCUPY A LIMBO. INDICATED BY A SLIGHT ECHO.)

1. PREBBLE: (thoughts) I must say in concluding, Mr. Chairman-to conclude, that is, the preamble to my preliminary thoughts on this matter. Or, to put it more succinctly-the summation, as it were, of our serious thinking during our anticipatory study.....
2. CHAIRMAN: (thought acoustic) Get on with it, Prebble.
3. PREBBLE: I must seek the Board's indulgence if I go-briefly, I may add, briefly through the points which seem to me to lie-
4. CHAIRMAN: One minute, Prebble, I warn you. You know what'll happen.
5. PREBBLE: No, please, Mr. Chairman. I'm going as fast as I can-
6. CHAIRMAN: Ten seconds.
7. PREBBLE: No! You're counting too fast.
8. CHAIRMAN: Too late. Bring in the gong.
9. PREBBLE: No. (pleading) Not the gong. I tried. I tried. (A LOUD. DEEP-TONED GONG. SOUNDS RHYTHMICALLY. LIKE A GIANT CLOCK STRIKING.)
10. PREBBLE: (moaning) Oh, no. No. Stop. Please. I can't-I can't bear-

    (AT THE LAST TRIUMPHANT GONG. THE SOUND TURNS INTO A CHEAP ALARM CLOCK. RINGING IN THE BEDROOM.)

11. PREBBLE: (normal voice, waking up) Hmm? Oh-what time is it?
12. MRS HANDS: (approaching) Morning Mr. Prebble. I've brought you tea. But you'll have to be quick. It's the board meeting this morning and you never set you alarm right, did you?
    (CUT TO INTERIOR LARGE LIMOUSINE. TRAFFIC PASSING.)
13. CHAUFFEUR: Thought I'd come this way, Mr. Prebble. Can't get round Hyde Park Corner. Protest March.

## SKILLS FOR RADIO JOURNALISTS

This module covers the basics of radio journalism:

- Skills and responsibilities
- Writing for radio
- Presentation
- Interviews

**Module Objectives**: At the end of this module, you should be able to:

- Recognize techniques that are used by radio journalists
- Understand writing techniques used for radio
- Identify key practices for effective radio presentation
- Identify different techniques used for radio interviews
- Discuss how writing and presentation play a role in radio interviews

Throughout the module, examples and exercises will help you practice what you are learning. In order to master the skills presented, you should practice the techniques and ask for feedback from experienced radio journalists.

### SKILLS AND RESPONSIBILITIES FOR RADIO

Radio stations have many people with different skills and responsibilities. There are those who voices are heard on the air, like talk show hosts and reporters, and there are also people who work behind the scenes like sound engineers, producers, marketing managers, researchers and call-screeners.

Sometimes one person may take on several roles. In smaller radio stations, a talk show host may also do research or a news reader may file reports from the field. Even at larger stations, producers are often involved in research and booking guests. Whatever the structure or size of the station, remember that successful radio depends on teamwork and all roles are equally important.

This module focuses on the responsibilities and fundamental skills that a radio journalist needs to do her job.

**Responsibilities:** Professional journalists, whether they work in radio, television or print, are expected to adhere to basic principles. Journalists should be:

Accountable

Balanced

Independent

Journalism associations or unions in many countries have established codes of ethics for the practice of journalism. Many media companies have also established their own ethical standards. Find out more about codes of ethics from these websites:

- EthicNet-European Codes of Journalism Ethics
- International Journalists' Network
- Society of Professional Journalists
- Guiding Principles for the Journalist-Bob Steele, The Poynter Institute

**Skills:** This module explains three core skills of radio:

- Writing
- Presenting
- Conducting interviews

These skills can be used in different ways, depending to the kind of program being scripted or presented. For example, the style used to present a news bulletin is different from the style used in a late-night music show. Understanding the core principles of writing, presenting and interviewing for radio will help you adapt these principles for different programs.

## WHAT TO SAY: FINDING THE ANGLE

The first step in developing a news story is to find the angle, or the main point of the story. One way to find the angle is to clarify the facts and then ask the question, "So what?"

To answer the "so what?" question, you need to understand who the listeners are. What news interests them? What information is relevant to their daily lives? What are they worried about? What do they feel strongly about?

The answer to "so what?" will lead to the story angle.

**The Necessity of an Angle:** The angle is what makes listeners say, "Oh, that's important," or "That's interesting."

Identifying the angle helps to sharpen focus for the story and leads to clearer writing. A story without an angle that covers every aspect of an issue will be confusing and lose listeners.

**Finding the Angle:** While researching a story, ask:

- What is happening or what has been happening?
- Why is the story important?
- Why will listeners care about this story?
- What will listeners want to know?

Think about:

- Listeners
  - * Who are they?
  - * What will make them identify with the story and find it relevant and interesting?
  - * What do they already know or think about the issue?
  - * What other questions would they like to have answered?
- The story from all its perspectives
  - * Why did the event occur?
  - * What do people think about the event that occurred?
  - * Who is involved in the event and why?
  - * Will something happen in the future as a result of the news event?

## WHAT TO SAY: WRITING FOR LISTENERS

Writing for radio is different than writing for print media. Keep these differences in mind:

| Reading | Listening |
|---|---|
| • Readers usually focus only on what they are reading. They are usually not doing something else at the same time. | • Listeners are usually doing something else while listening to the radio, so their focus may be divided unless they are interested. |
| • Readers can go back to what was written before and re-read it to make sense or to clarify. | • Listeners hear words and sounds once and then they are gone. They only have one opportunity to understand and make sense of a story. |

## WRITING FOR THE EAR

Writing for radio means writing the way people speak. Keep the following tips in mind:

- Break the rules of grammar when necessary. Clarity is the goal.
- Say aloud what you've written to make sure it makes sense.
- Imagine that someone is listening while you are writing and pretend you are talking to that listener.
- Keep it simple by using just one idea per sentence and avoiding long words.

## WHAT TO SAY: TIPS FOR SCRIPTING

Like other kinds of writing, scripting involves several steps:

- Researching • Creating a structure • Writing

**Research:** Research is the foundation of any story. Consider these sources:

- News events related to the topic
- Stories previously written or aired about the topic
- People who can talk about the topic (interviews)
- Organizations involved in the story

Use a combination of research methods. Start with these basic research tools:

- The Internet. Use search engines to research a topic, find organizations or resources related to stories and locate archives of earlier stories. Some of the most popular search engines are AlltheWeb, Google and Yahoo.
- Publications. Newspapers, magazines and books can provide ideas and resources for stories.
- Contacts. Talk with colleagues and friends to find out what they think about a topic. They may be able to suggest people to interview.

**Script Structure:** The structure of a script depends on its purpose. Is it a news report? Is the purpose to entertain? To persuade? Or to share something important? Be clear about how the script will flow. What pieces of information will be included? In what order? While a news story requires a more formal style and approach, these tips can be useful for scripting:

- Imagine talking to a friend. What questions does the friend ask? Answering these questions one-by-one will help you write with the listener in mind.
- Draft a rough outline based on the "talking to a friend" exercise above. Decide whether to tell it chronologically, with the most important facts first or some other way.
- Start with an arresting sentence--called a "hook"--at the beginning to attract and hold the listener's interest.
- End the story by satisfying listeners that all important questions have been answered.

**Content:** Use the following tips to write for the ear. Remember that these general tips will need to be adapted accordingly when writing news stories.

- Write in short phrases. Keep it short, punchy and direct. Use only one idea per sentence.

Write in short, punchy and direct phrases. Use only one idea per sentence.

This version is grammatically correct, but it's not written for radio: We are going to hear a song by one of South Africa's best-known voices--Sibongile Khumalo--a woman who is equally skillful at performing opera, jazz and traditional music, and she will be singing a song called "Mountain Shade" which was composed by a young local composer called Moses Molelekwa.

Try rewriting it.

- Keep it short, punchy and direct.
- Make sure there is only one idea per sentence.

Take a look at one rewritten version. Do you see why it works better? Now here's a well-known voice. Sibongile Khumalo. Someone who's equally at home singing opera, jazz, traditional music, you name it. And the song? "Mountain Shade"--composed by another local talent. Moses Molelekwa.

Round off complicated numbers and write them in words.
Round off complicated numbers and write them in words.

For example, rather than:

- Authorities spent $3,589.50 on the system.

Try:

- Authorities spent about four thousand dollars on the system.
- Try to humanize statistics, facts and figures.
- Use verbal signposts such as "and," "but" and "so" to show structure in longer chunks of talk and to help listeners know where they are.
- Paint pictures with words. Remember, listeners have to use imagination to visualize what is happening.
- Write as if talking to only one person and create a connection with listeners by using personal words like "you" or "we."
- Use contractions like "can't," "won't" and "we'll." They will make the story sound more natural.

Here's an exercise to help you think about writing for radio.

Tone: Getting the content right is not enough. The tone, or voice, is equally important. Listeners should not be insulted or embarrassed by an inappropriate tone.

The tone for news writing should be:

- Unemotional.
- Direct and dynamic, but not sensational.

In other kinds of radio programs, such as talk shows or magazine programs:

- Be warm, friendly and enthusiastic.
- Treat listeners with respect. Don't patronize them.
- Talk to listeners but don't lecture them.

**Creativity:** All good writing springs from creativity, including news reporting even though it is more formal in style than other programs.

Creativity involves:

- Selecting specific details that paint pictures and allow the listener to imagine what is being described.
- Avoiding generalizations and adjectives such as beautiful, nice and lovely. Describe the scene in detail and let the listener decide whether it is truly beautiful.

### What to Say: What not to Say

Part of being a good radio host or presenter is knowing what not to say. If listeners are insulted or embarrassed, they won't want to listen any more. Being a good radio host requires cultural sensitivity and accurate knowledge about an audience, from what style of program listeners prefer to what topics interest them. Experienced radio professionals know what offends listeners.

Radio hosts should not:

- Make listeners feel like just part of a crowd.
- Use sexist or patronizing language.
- Talk unprofessionally or make amateurish requests.
- Send private messages to friends.
- Alert listeners to commercials so that they will want to turn off the radio.

These examples of actual phrases heard on the radio illustrate how listeners might respond.

| What was said: | Possible listener reaction: | Why this shouldn't be said: |
|---|---|---|
| Hello to all of you out there in listener land! | Well, I don't live in "listener land!" And I'm NOT "all of you!" | Makes listeners feel like part of a crowd |
| And thanks to our lovely newsreader, Angela. She's looking drop-dead gorgeous today! | Angela's a professional. Isn't that what you're supposed to be? Such comments are sexist and patronizing. | Sexist |
| Whoops! Finger trouble again -- we've just got a new computer in the studio--so do bear with me! | Why should I? I expect YOU to do your job. I've got problems of my own! | Unprofessional and amateurish |
| Well, I seem to have run out of time again. Join me again tomorrow. | WHY have you run out of time? Shouldn't you be watching the clock? | Amateurish |
| And here's a special song for my boyfriend, Sipho. He'll know why it's special. | Why should I be excluded just because you want to send a private message to what's-his-name? | Private message |
| Well, let's go off to the marketplace for a few messages from our sponsors. | Oh, commercials. I'll go and make a cup of coffee. Maybe I'll just switch off. | Commercial alert |

## REVIEW: WRITING FOR RADIO

Before moving on to the next section, let's review what's been covered so far. Choose the best answer for each of the questions below.

(1) What is the key to keep in mind when writing for radio?

a. Callers can ask a radio announcer to repeat messages.

b. Listeners often are paying full attention to the radio program.

c. The ear can process a picture of the words better than the eye can.

d. Listeners have only one chance to make sense of what they hear on radio.

(2) When writing for radio:

a. Always be careful to use correct grammar.

b. Use long words rather than simple ones.

c. Imagine talking to one listener.

d. Try to fit as many ideas into one sentence as possible.

## HOW TO SAY IT: TALKING TO ONE LISTENER

A good script is the beginning of a good radio show. Presentation--the sound or tone of the presenter--is next. Whether reading a script or speaking spontaneously, on radio how you say something is just as important as what you say.

Effective presentation depends on:

- Understanding the audience
- Understanding your own voice and body

### Audience: One Listener

In the section on writing scripts, you read about the idea of talking to only one listener. This principle is also the basis of all radio presentation, even news reporting. This practice will help you create intimacy and listeners will be drawn into the program. Because people listen to the radio almost everywhere (in their bedrooms, in their cars, while they are working) radio provides the opportunity to be close to the audience in a way that other media do not.

Respecting listeners-talking to them as equals, friends and colleague-is an important aspect to this relationship. Listeners should not feel preached to or patronized. By visualizing this closeness with listeners, the right tone will come naturally.

Choice of tone is also influenced by:

- *Type of Program:* The tone of a youth show announcer is different from that of a news reader. The presenter of a gender talk show will have a different tone than the host of a music program.

- *Time of Day:* Early morning programs require a lively, high-energy tone to get listeners going. News programs require announcers to use a formal tone. Talk show hosts try to come across as friendly and more casual.

**How to Say It: Body and Voice:** In addition to imagining one listener when talking, three other factors are key to effective radio presentation:

- Tension and stress
- Body positioning and gesturing
- Voice and speech

**Tension and Stress:** If a radio presenter is stressed, listeners will hear it in her voice, they won't focus on what she is actually saying. Tension ties the body's muscles in knots and can cause the voice to sound thin, strained, irritated or bored.

Before going on the air it is important to release the tension that stress, anxiety or other emotions can cause. Relaxation exercises, such as the ones listed to the right, can relieve stress by releasing tension from the body and calming emotions. Releasing tension opens the diaphragm, which promotes deeper breathing. This, in turn, helps the voice to sound more open and confident. During times of political turmoil or conflict, it is even more important for radio presenters and reporters to manage their personal tension.

"Radio should be a sane, comforting voice in times of tension or difficulty. Like a friend, your local station should tell you the truth in a calm, unemotional way--and help you to focus on solving the problem."

**Indonesian Radio Presenter:** Feeling anxious, angry, sad or depressed can make it difficult to sound sane, comforting or calm. But that is what radio presenters need to do for the sake of their listeners. Here's an example of how this all comes together in a tense reporting situation. Read how to keep your cool.

## POSTURE, GESTURING AND FACIAL EXPRESSIONS

**Posture:** Tension, as noted above, can cause the body to tie itself up in knots. Good body positioning, or posture, promotes confidence and allows for both a physical and psychological opening-up. Keep these tips in mind:

- Sit in a position that allows easy breathing and body movement.
- Never sit in a hunched or doubled-over position. Bad posture makes breathing more difficult and leads to a voice that sounds tense and uncomfortable.
- Good posture also involves
    * Allowing the back to open and lengthen
    * Allowing the neck and shoulders to be free
    * Sensing the support of the floor or chair

**Gesturing:** Gesturing is a natural part of conversation. A presenter who gestures naturally as she talks will communicate more clearly. Listeners will notice the difference even if they can't see the gestures.

**Facial Expression:** Facial expressions are critical to the sound of a voice. If this seems hard to believe, imagine talking to someone on a telephone. Often, a person's voice indicates whether she is frowning or smiling. Listen to the radio and decide by tone if the announcer is smiling or has a serious expression. On radio a smile is the equivalent of making eye contact. A smile, even if no one sees it, makes a person sound more inviting, confident and fresh. Of course, a smile is not always appropriate.

For example, news reports on serious subjects are seldom delivered with a smile, unless a lighter story is included at the end.

Also, think about the fact that there are many different kinds of smiles. In addition to smiles of happiness, there are smiles that indicate understanding, sympathy or comfort. Think about how and when a smile during the following programs might be used.

- Talk shows
- Shows that give advice or support to the community
- Human interest stories or interviews
- Music request shows

Practice what it feels like to read a script while smiling. Then read a news script with a more serious expression. Listen for the difference. Try listening to the radio to "hear" the expression on the presenter's face.

**Voice:** The best voice for radio is natural and relaxed. The more comfortable you are with yourself and your voice, the clearer your voice will be. Voice exercises can help build confidence and promote speaking clearly.

Listen to someone who mumbles or someone who lowers the volume of her voice at the end of her sentences and notice how hard it is to understand what she is saying. Since listeners can't interrupt the radio to ask what was said, radio presenters must take extra care to be clear. Here are some tips:

- Before you go on air, do some exercises (included in the link above) to free up your jaw and tongue.
- If you are planning to read from a script, practice aloud until you feel confident. Pay special attention to difficult words and foreign names.
- Practice your pace and rhythm. Are you speaking too fast or too slow? Remember to pause and breathe naturally. Ask someone to give you feedback.

## HOW TO SAY IT: PRESENTATION TIPS

Before going on the air:

- Avoid stressful situations.
  - * Get plenty of rest to feel free and alert.
  - * Allow plenty of time to prepare.
  - * Check for necessary items, such as script, reading glasses, water, etc.
  - * Wear loose, comfortable clothing.
  - * Use the relaxation exercises from the previous page.
- Prepare the voice.
  - * Avoid fizzy drinks and milky liquids. They can cause a film on the throat, which causes throat clearing.
  - * Don't eat sweets or chocolate. Sugar thickens saliva.

   * Allow time for voice warm-ups and breathing exercises, like those reviewed on the previous page.
- Prepare your body and posture.
   * Take a minute to relax your neck and shoulders. Do deep breathing to focus your mind and body. Breathe from the diaphragm.
   * Check your posture and make sure the microphone is in a good position.
   * Focus your thoughts and regulate your breathing.
   * Remember to gesture.
   * Finally, remind yourself that you are ready. Try saying to yourself:
- I'm going to talk to one listener, just beyond the microphone.
- I'm exactly where I want to be.
- I'm well-prepared.

On the air:

- Equipment and materials
   * Wear headphones over one ear so you can monitor how you sound and still be alert to what is happening in the studio.
   * Always have pen and paper ready.
- On-air discipline
   * Be prepared with cues. A cue is the introduction that a studio presenter gives to a pre-recorded story or a live interview. A good cue will lead the listener naturally into whatever follows.
   * Avoid giving long lists of what's coming up. Nobody will remember and lists are boring anyway.
   * Before announcing the time, make sure it's correct.
   * Give frequent station IDs and throw aheads.
- Professional discipline
   * Don't take personal phone calls.
   * Listeners are the first priority, even when visitors are in the studio.

- Scripts
  * Use these guidelines for reading scripts:
- Prepare. Unless there's a real emergency, never read anything on air that hasn't been practiced aloud. Tongue-twisters are not always apparent until they are spoken aloud.
- Understand. Never read anything that could be confusing to your listener. Your voice will reflect it. Take the time to re-write the script before reading.
- Mark the script. Underline key words, mark pauses (with "/" or another symbol), write phonetic pronunciations for foreign words.
- Choose the appropriate tone of voice. How much emotion/feeling should be conveyed? Should the tone be light-hearted or serious?
- Look ahead. Don't look at the script word by word. Train yourself to take in whole blocks of words.
- Handle mistakes professionally. If you make a mistake, don't panic. If it's a big error--one that could cause confusion or misunderstanding--apologize and correct it. Otherwise, take a breath and carry on. Don't draw attention to stumbles.

## REVIEW: PRESENTATION ON THE RADIO

Before moving on to the next section, let's review what was just covered. Choose the best answer for each of the questions below.

(1) Why should you smile when your audience can't see you?

  * Because presenting on the radio is always a happy occasion.
  * On radio (or on the telephone), a smile is the equivalent of making eye contact.
  * It helps with breathing.
  * Smiling lifts your voice and makes you sound more confident and fresh.
  * b and d

(2) Radio is about connecting at the human level, reaching the listener. What technique helps do this?

* Talking to all the listeners.
* Writing down what to say.
* Imagining that you are talking to one listener.
* Sounding energized and enthusiastic.

## RADIO INTERVIEWS

### Types of Interviews

It can take a lifetime to become a good radio interviewer. Every interview is different, with its own special challenges. In a program, an interview can run for several minutes or it it might end up as a brief, edited comment.

It's also helpful to keep in mind that people being interviewed might have different motivations for speaking to you. Sometimes people have a duty to speak because they are public officials. In other cases the interviewee does not have any obligation to talk, but chooses to do so because she has been persuaded that her experience is worth sharing.

This section explains two kinds of interviews: opening up and pinning down. Remember that the differences are not always clear cut and that interviews may have elements of both.

**Opening up Interviews:** An opening up interview encourages a person to share a story or experience. It is usually conducted in a relaxed and friendly way.

Opening up interviews include:

1. Human interest interviews
   * Examples
     - A chat with the leader of a youth choir who's just taken the group to perform at the International Choir Festival in Tokyo. How was the experience?
     - An interview with a former drug dealer who now runs a youth center for teenagers who have been involved in street gangs. What led to the change in his life?

2. Personal profiles
    * Examples
        - An interview with the first woman to be put in charge of the South African Prison Service. What kind of person is she?
        - An interview with a former Olympic swimmer who is now running for parliament. What prompted her interest in politics?
3. Highly sensitive interviews
    * Examples
        - An interview with a survivor of child abuse who now wants to tell her story for the sake of others who may be in the same position.
        - An interview with a Burmese woman who was abducted from her village and forced to become a sex worker in Thailand.

**Pinning Down Interviews:** A pinning down interview is used to get answers to questions in the news. Radio reporters use this type of interview when they need to ask tough questions of people who are accountable to listeners, for example, an elected official or a company spokesperson. Asking revealing or hard-hitting questions without sounding aggressive can be a challenge. Use these tips:

- Do not raise the tone of your voice
- Do not speak louder than the person you are interviewing
- If you need to interrupt, and you often do, wait until the person you are interviewing takes a breath and then slide in with your question.
- Make sure you have your facts straight!

Examples of pinning down interviews can include:

- Talking with the minister of health about a series of tainted vaccinations. What can she tell listeners about the vaccinations?
- Interviewing a company spokesperson about the sudden recall of a popular children's toy. What is he able to say about the safety of the product?

- Speaking with a company president about the embezzlement charges he is facing. What is his side of the story?

**Radio Interviews: Preparing to do an Interview:** Conducting an interview is a fascinating, complex and uncertain art. The interviewer never knows what might happen.

Preparation is key under such uncertain circumstances. Consider these important questions when preparing to do an interview.

**Questions to Think About**

| | |
|---|---|
| Who | • Who will be interviewed? |
| | • Who will be the interviewer? |
| Why | • Why is this person being interviewed? |
| | • Does this person have a story to tell? |
| | • Is the interview part of a bigger story or report? Or is the interview the story? |
| What | • What is the subject or focus of the interview? |
| | • What questions will be asked? |
| | • What needs to be done to convince the interview subject to participate? |
| | • What permission, if any, will be needed? |
| | • What, if any, ethical issues might the interview raise? How will you deal with them? |
| Where | • Will this interview be conducted on the street or in a studio or someplace else (e.g., a public cafe or private home)? |
| | • Is the situation likely to be dangerous? |
| | • Will there be an audience? |
| When | • When will the interview be conducted? Morning, afternoon, night? |
| | • When will the interview be aired? Morning, afternoon, night? |
| | • Will it be before, during or after an emotional or disturbing event, a happy, exciting event or neither? |
| How | • Will it be live or will it be taped and edited later? |
| | • How will the interview subject be prepared for the interview? |

- How much will the interview subject know about the focus of the interview beforehand?
- Will callers be allowed to ask questions?

The next section, Tips for Interviews, gives additional guidance for preparing for interviews.

## TIPS FOR INTERVIEWS

Use this checklist to thoroughly prepare for an interview.

**The Interviewer:** An interviewer:

- Is a great listener
- Knows when, and how, to ask follow-up questions
- Has good communications skills
- Has the ability to be flexible in the interview
- Understands that there is an order in which interview questions should be asked
- Knows how and when to ask "why?"

It's important to consider gender with respect to interviewing. For example, a woman who has survived rape may not feel comfortable being interviewed by a male journalist. On the other hand, women journalists have sometimes encountered difficulties when interviewing men, especially when the man is powerful. Sometimes this can take the form of sexual harassment. Like any kind of intimidation, sexual harassment must be taken seriously. It's not just a "women's issue" and should be openly discussed in newsrooms so support systems can be put in place.

What should you do if you encounter sexual harassment in the course of your work?

- Trust your instinct. If you are uncomfortable about a suggested venue or time for the interview, make an alternative arrangement. If this is not possible, take a colleague. At the very least make sure your news editor knows where you are going and what time you expect to be back. Take your mobile phone. Remember: no interview is worth putting yourself at risk. If it doesn't feel right, don't go at all.

- If the interviewee is making you uncomfortable with remarks or actions, make it clear that your station takes sexual harassment of its employees very seriously. If the interviewee does not heed this warning, leave. Make a note of what happened and inform your boss immediately so you can discuss what action to take.

**The Interview Subject:** Deciding who to interview also takes some consideration. When selecting interview subjects, these tips can help:

- Make sure the interview subject is confident and articulate. This is especially important if you are looking for more than a short clip or comment.
- Be gender-aware. Don't stereotype people according to their sex. Not all nurses are women and not all soldiers are men. Also, if a woman's husband or father does not "give permission" for her to be interviewed, how will you deal with this? Will you just give up or take time to discuss possible solutions with her?
- Think beyond the obvious. A person doesn't need to have a university degree to be an expert. For example, a market seller may give you a more interesting view on the economy than a university professor.
- Keep an eye and ear out for people who have a story to tell and an interesting way of telling it.

It is important to find out as much as possible about an interview subject.

- What are her credentials?
- Why is she the right person to interview?
- What is her background?
- What will she bring to the interview?
- Will she be lively?
- Will she offer a unique perspective?

Interviewing someone soon after she has experienced a traumatic or emotional event requires special skills. Here are some suggestions for these kinds of interviews.

**Asking for the Interview:** Use these tips to prepare before picking up the telephone to request an interview:

- First, decide:
  - Why you want to interview the person.
  - When you want to do the interview (time and date).
  - How to get in touch with the person (have a list of possible contacts).
- Before calling:
  - Rehearse the call. To keep from being nervous or forgetting something, write rough notes on what you want to say.
  - Be ready to suggest calling back later if the person isn't available now.
- During the call:
  - If it feels appropriate, smile to sound more assertive, confident and friendly.
  - Remember that this call is the only chance to get the person to say yes.
  - Be prepared to explain why the interview is important to listeners or to the story.
  - Be ready to counter comments like: "I'll need a list of your questions first." (See the information below for what to do when someone asks for questions in advance.)
- Remember to:
  - Be polite, positive, friendly and clear.

Once the person has agreed to the interview, she may want to see the questions up front. It is important to find out why she wants to see the questions and try to resolve those reasons without giving her the questions. Perhaps you can explain that you don't provide questions in advance but that you can go over the areas you plan to cover.

Providing a list of questions beforehand can create issues with:

- Follow up. If you agree only to ask approved questions, you will probably have difficulty asking any follow-up questions. If this happens, you won't be doing your job as an interviewer.

- Balance. The interview will be unbalanced if you are not able to follow up.
- Sounding rehearsed. If the interview subject knows exactly what you are going to ask, the interview will probably sound boring or rehearsed.

Use these preparation tips just before the interview.

**Interview Questions:** Brainstorming is a helpful process for coming up with an initial list of questions. This is often done with the program's producer or other colleagues.

Questions should:

- Explore the story or topic. What is the purpose of the story? What does the audience need to know? What will listeners be interested in knowing?
- Add dimension to the obvious. "Why" questions are important. They open up room for exploration and can delve into what is not obvious.
- Provide different perspectives. Coming up with the list of interview questions may uncover a need to interview more than one person. For some interviews and stories, more than one perspective is needed.
- Paint the picture. Questions that ask the interview subject for description are important. They help listeners "see" the story or message.
- Ensure the listeners are not left hanging. Wrap-up questions close loose ends and answer anything that is still unclear.
- Be simple and clear. Questions should be short, simple and clear. For guidance, review the writing tips covered in "What to Say." Multi-layered questions should never be part of an interview. They confuse the interview subject and the listeners.

Questions should follow a logical order. Consider these guidelines:

- The first question shouldn't be too deep, complex or broad because you run the risk of losing focus or control of the interview.
- Core questions do not necessarily have to follow the chronology of events. You won't have time to cover everything, so focus your questions according to the key issues you want to address.
- Follow-up questions are used when the interviewer wants the subject to elaborate.
  * Magic question:
- "Why?"
  * Opening up questions might start with:
- "Tell me more"
- "Take me back to the first time you..."
- "What was going through your mind when"
  * Pinning down questions might start with:
- "What do you mean when you say...?"
- "Let's be more specific. Are you saying?"
- "To recap...do you mean that?"
  * Closing questions wrap up the interview.
- "What's your message to..." (this works especially well for a profile or "soft" interview.)

### Interview Location

The type of program often dictates where the interview is conducted. For example, if the interview subject is a guest on a talk show, the interview will probably be in the studio. If the interview is part of a live news report, the interview is likely to be live from the scene.

At other times, where the interview is done depends on the topic of the interview and the interview subject. Think about:

- The interview subject's time schedule. If she's busy and her comments are needed for the story, the interview may have to take place at her location, possibly her office, home or some other place.

- Whether the interview subject can travel to the studio. If the distance is too great, the interview could be done by phone.
- What other factors may affect the interview location.
- Whether background noise will add to the interview. For instance, an interview with a fishing captain may benefit from the noise of the ocean in the background.

Doing an interview on location means that all the recording equipment has to be taken along. Make a list of what will be needed and check the items off the list before leaving.

Well-managed background sound is a great way to give context to the interview, but remember that it can also ruin your recording if you're not careful. These recording tips offer ideas to ensure good technical quality in the field.

## CONDUCTING AN INTERVIEW

Formal and informal interviews use the same skills:

- Listening
- Asking effective questions
- Sticking to the focus

These skills are part of everyday communication. This section will show how to polish these naturally learned skills and use them more consciously.

**During the Interview:** Remember the presentation tips that were presented in an earlier section. For example:

- Talk one-on-one.
- Smile appropriately.
- Relax and breathe naturally.
- Speak at a natural pace, not too fast, not too slow and pause appropriately.

Use written questions to help stay focused and on track:

- Ask open-ended questions--beginning with how, what, why--to encourage an interview subject to open up.
- Keep the questions short and simple. Never ask multi-layered questions that the interview subject struggles to understand.

- Ask questions to which there are only yes/no or one-word answers to pin down or focus the interview subject. (If she can't stop talking, for example!) A good follow up for many one-answer questions is "why?".
- Invite the interview subject to give specific examples, experiences and stories. For example, "Take us back to the first time you performed in public. What happened?".
- Keep thinking of the listeners. What would they want to ask?

During the interview:

- Show attention by using eye contact, body language and repeating key bits of information. ("You say you first started composing at the age of six. How did you start so young?") But be careful not to give too much audible feedback-like "mmm" or "OK." They sound irritating on radio and they'll cause you problems later if you have to edit the interview.
- Remember to help the interview subject come alive as a person and tell her story. An interviewer should be responsive but does not steal the spotlight or use the interview to show how clever she is.
- If it is necessary to interrupt the interviewee, do it with a smile as she takes a breath. Try not to raise the volume--or pitch--of your voice. Do not talk over what she is saying. It sounds aggressive.
- Listen carefully.
- Ask follow-up questions.

Track progress:

- Watch the clock and keep the interview paced to cover everything.
- Know when to start bringing the conversation to a close. Do it as naturally as possible. Don't say "Well, I'm afraid we have to stop there. We've run out of time." The interviewee and the listeners will feel cheated. And you'll sound unprofessional.

- Thank the person you interviewed simply. Don't go overboard.

- Remember that interviewing a guest or talking to callers by telephone requires distinct skills. Check out these tips for telephone interviews.

**Telephone Tips:** The telephone is an indispensable tool for radio. It's used for news sound bites, live interviews and phone-in contributions from listeners. But the telephone also offers special challenges. When using the telephone to conduct an interview or to talk with listeners, remember to:

- Speak more slowly than usual.
- Speak into the microphone/mouthpiece of the telephone.
- Make an extra effort to be clear.
- Let the caller know you're still at the other end by giving occasional verbal feedback: Mm-hmm, Right, I understand, Go ahead.
- Smile.
- Watch the voice levels on your equipment and be prepared to adjust them.
- Be extra alert about your control buttons. You don't want to accidentally cut someone off in mid-thought!

Problems will crop up on telephone chat shows. Use these suggestions to handle the most common ones.

| Problem | Suggestion |
|---|---|
| How do I handle the caller who won't shut up? | Smile and interrupt. For example, say, "Thanks for your point." Then move the discussion forward. |
| How do I handle a very upset or angry caller? | Show that you understand why she is upset by:<br>○ Using her name when you respond.<br>○ Not raising your voice. Be polite, friendly and professional.<br>○ Resisting the temptation to counsel her over the phone. You're not a psychotherapist. (Consider having the contact number of your local helpline at hand.) |
| What if the caller is making a great point, but the line is bad? | Apologize and cut the call. No matter how good the point is, if listeners can't understand or hear it, it's useless. If possible, ask the caller to call back and hope for a better line. |

## REVIEW: INTERVIEWING

Before we close out this module, let's review the material we just covered.

True/False:

(1) Always give the interview subject the questions up front.

T ❑ F ❑

(2) Use closed questions to get someone to answer yes or no.

T ❑ F ❑

(3) The interviewer should never deviate from the list of prepared questions.

T ❑ F ❑

(4) In a longer interview, invite the person you are interviewing to give specific examples, experiences, stories.

T ❑ F ❑

## MODULE SUMMARY

At the start of this module we indicated that you should be able to

Recognize techniques used by radio practitioners.

- The module described three techniques: writing, presenting and interviewing.

Understand writing techniques associated with the radio.

- The key is to write as you speak.
- Keep things simple and short.
- The module also covered story structure, sentence content, tone and word choice.

Identify key practices for effective radio presentation.

- The module covered two presentation principles.
  - * Talk as if addressing one listener.
- It also addressed the importance of body position and gesturing.
- Finally, the module described how voice and body are interconnected and gave tips for making the voice sound its best.

Identify different techniques used for radio interviews

- Interviewing is a primary way people interact on radio. This course covered two types of interviews:
  - * The opening up interview
  - * The pinning down interview
- The module covered some basic techniques for preparing and conducting interviews.

Discuss how writing and presentation play a role in radio interviews.

- Both writing and presentation skills are needed to successfully conduct an interview.

**Additional Resources:** To help you think about what you've learned about radio presentation, ask yourself:

- Who is your favourite radio presenter? What do you specifically like about this person? Is it her style, her presentation, her voice?
- As a listener, what do you find irritating in a radio presenter? Why?
- When you've listed what you like and what you don't like, write a description of the elements of a successful radio presentation.

# 9

# Writing for Radio: The Basics

## STRUCTURE OF A RADIO NEWS STORY

**Sound:** Generally, radio news stories split their time evenly between narration and sound bites. You want soundbites to be 30 seconds or less, but you want to use them often to break up your narration--if you read for much more than a minute uninterrupted, your listeners will start to get lost in the drone.

**Conflict:** Most stories, in fiction and news alike, build their narrative around a central conflict. Protesters versus police. Workers versus management. Community organizers versus government officials. Even more "human interest" stories have conflicts driving the narrative-a homeless person's struggle to stay warm, a poor mother's struggle to get healthy food for her kids. When you're conceptualizing your story, trying to figure out what the central conflict is--it will make it much easier to decide who you need to interview, and how you need to write it.

A typical three-minute radio story will be built around three 30-second soundbytes: one from each side of the immediate conflict, and one from an expert or analyst who's able to either arbitrate or put the conflict in a larger context. The lead is the most important part of your story. It needs to grab the listener's attention and make them want to listen to everything that follows. You can either: 1) do a quick summary of the who, what, when, where, and why of your story, 2) throw out a provocative piece of information that you'll then go on to explain, 3) pose a question the story will try to answer.

The lead must give the listener a sense of what the rest of the story will be about, and make them want to listen. Here's a tip: after you've finished writing your story, go back and rewrite your lead. You'll often find the story took you somewhere you didn't expect to be when you started it. The end is the best place to give your listeners information about what comes next-are there more demonstrations planned? Will there be an appeal? When does the new law take effect? Process for composing a radio story:

1. *Research Your Story*: Check out the web sites of the players involved. Look for recent news clippings on related issues. Make a note of who other reporters have spoken to---you may want to use the same sources. Make a list of the questions you need answered to do the story well, then try to figure out who has the answers and set up interviews.
2. *Gather Sound*: Record the interviews and other audio (e.g. ambient sound) you'll use. Take notes and mark times during the interviews-it will make it easier to go back and pull soundbytes later.
3. *Log Audio/pull Soundbytes*: Mark the cuts you think you'll use for your story. If you have time, transcribe them.
4. *Write*: Decide what cuts you'll us, put them in order, and then write your script around them.
5. *Check your Facts*: Go through the script and see if you can independently confirm the facts and figures your sources gave you.
6. *Re-write*: See if you can get someone with a fresh set of eyeballs to read your script and give you feedback. Then, do any structural changes you need to. Next, clean up your sentences. Finally, re-write your lead.
7. Record your narration and mix your audio.

## BROADCAST WRITING

Writing for radio is different from writing for print. First, you have less "space" for information, so you will have to prioritize and summarize carefully. Second, your listeners can't reread sentences they didn't understand the first time--you have to keep your writing simple and clear. Finally, the ultimate product is not what's on the page, but what comes out of your mouth--it's okay to break some writing rules, as long as the result is smooth and easily-understood. With that in mind, here are some tips.

**Write Short Sentences:** Take a close look at long, complex sentences: chances are you can break them up into two or three smaller ones. Don't try to pack in more than one idea per sentence. Grammarians take note: broadcast writing should minimize the use of dependent clauses, relative clauses, parenthetical remarks, and compound structures. You can almost always come out with a clean sentence by putting the subject first, and the verb second.

| Before | After |
|---|---|
| As a delegation of over 30 workers and community members stormed through the employee entrance of the 350-room Hilton hotel in downtown Glendale, hotel security could do little more than grasp their radios and call for backup. | 30 workers and community members stormed into the downtown Glendale Hilton. |
| Followed by a barrage of hotel managers, curious on-duty employees and about half a dozen security guards, the workers made their way through the winding corridors of the employee area and into the offices of the hotel's executive committee, where the concerned Hilton employees addressed their need for a union and insisted that management not interfere with their efforts to organize. | The hotel has 350 rooms. |
| | The delegation bypassed security by using the employee entrance. |
| | Security guards called for backup. |
| | The delegation made its way to the offices of the hotel's executive committee. |
| | Managers, guards, and curious employees followed. |
| | The workers said they need a union |
| | They also told management not to interfere with their organizing efforts. |

**Summarize and Prioritize:** There are less words in radio stories than print stories. Think carefully about what information is essential, and which details can be summarized. Here's how you might pare down the sentences we just broke out:

| Before | After |
|---|---|
| Thirty workers and community members stormed into the downtown Glendale Hilton.<br><br>The hotel has 350 rooms.<br><br>The delegation bypassed security by using the employee entrance.<br><br>Security guards called for backup.<br><br>The delegation made its way to the offices of the hotel's executive committee.<br><br>Managers, guards, and curious employees followed.<br><br>The workers said they need a union<br><br>They also told management not to interfere with their organizing efforts. | Thirty workers and community members stormed into the downtown Glendale Hilton.<br><br>The delegation evaded security and confronted the hotel's executives in their offices.<br><br>The workers said they need a union.<br><br>They also told management not to interfere with their organizing efforts. |

**Be Conversational:** It's okay to be less formal when you're writing for broadcast--do what it takes to make your copy easy to listen to. Here's how you might smooth out the flow of what we just summarized:

| Before | After |
|---|---|
| Thirty workers and community members stormed into the downtown Glendale Hilton.<br><br>The workers evaded security and confronted the hotel's executives in their offices.<br><br>The workers said they need a union.<br><br>They also told management not to interfere with their organizing efforts. | Workers at the downtown Glendale Hilton are organizing a union, and they say they don't want management to interfere. So today dozens of them stormed the building and confronted the hotel's executives in their offices. |

**Use Statistics Sparingly:** It is easy to lose your listeners when you put too many numbers in a story. If the precise number isn't that important to the story, use words like "most," "more," "relatively few," etc. When you do use numbers, round them-*i.e.*, substitute "about 5 million" for "4,850,326." When you're comparing numbers, try to use a plain-language fraction or multiple rather than giving two numbers:

| Before | After |
|---|---|
| Today, just 11% of americans get lung cancer—twenty years ago, that number was 22% | Lung cancer rates have dropped by half since smoking was outlawed |

**Put Attribution First:** You listeners need to know who they're hearing from.

| Before | After |
|---|---|
| "The attacks on Karl Rove are unjustified and immoral," said President Bush. | President Bush said, "The attacks on Karl Rove are unjustified and immoral." |

**Minimize Direct Quotations:** Paraphrase what people have said, unless the exact wording is important to your story.

| Before | After |
|---|---|
| President Bush said, "The attacks on Karl Rove are unjustified and immoral." | President Bush lashed out against the attacks on Karl Rove, calling them "immoral." |

**Read it Out Loud:** If what you've written doesn't feel natural coming out of your mouth, then there's something wrong with it.

Read it to someone else. This is the best way to find out if your story is missing information your listeners will need to understand it.

In general, the principles of clean writing apply the same as always-here are some time-tested guidelines:

- Kill adjectives and adverbs. They don't usually do any work.
- Use active phrasing-*i.e.* "management locked out the workers," NOT "the workers were locked out"
- Show, don't tell. "he pounded the table with his fist" NOT "he was very angry."

- Use non-judgmental language. Present the facts and let your listeners make up their own minds. For instance, don't tell them a policy is "racist"--show them how it impacts Latinos differently than Anglos.

## HOW WRITING A RADIO AD WILL IMPROVE YOUR COPYWRITING

Knowing how to write, and write well, is a skill that will come in handy in all sorts of situations. And if you combine good writing skills with the persuasive selling tactics found in, say, copywriting, you'll be that much more ahead of your competition.

Of all the different types of writing I've done in my life (and believe me, I've tried practically all of them) writing radio has made one of the bigger impacts on my writing style.

Below are three ways writing radio can help strengthen your writing style. (Oh, and these tips will also help you write better radio copy too.)

**1. Follow the rules.**

Sometimes rules are good. Especially rules that force you to write a certain way. (Think poetry--mastering those rules can have an amazing effect on your writing style.) Rules require you to slow down and think, to analyze your word, sentence, grammar, punctuation, etc., choices. And that can be very beneficial to your development as a writer.

Radio is short. You have to write something that fits into a 30-or 60-second slot. Not a lot of time or a lot of words. In that 30 or 60 seconds, you need to capture the listener's attention, explain why they should be interested in buying what you're selling, then let them know what you'd like their next step to be. Oh, and did I mention you need to have the business name in there at least twice and probably a tag line as well? And don't forget about music. Or sound effects.

Now the beauty of this is once you've mastered radio rules, you can apply it to all sorts of things. A 30-second pitch for your business you can tell people at networking events. A 15-second introduction before a speech. A quick product spiel for your voice mail. A 15-second pitch for your novel to spit out at agents and editors at writers' conferences. The possibilities are endless.

**2. Forces you to write tight.**

Remember, radio is short. Yet, there's still a lot you have to shove into it. So what's the solution? Absolutely no extra words allowed.

Be brutal. Cut out anything you don't need. In fact, radio is where I first learned to start cutting "that" out. Most "thats" you don't need, and nothing shows you this like radio.

Here's how I write radio. I start with a first draft. I read it over. I think it's pretty good--I have all the salient points in there. I read it out loud.

Now the fun begins.

Usually it's too long. You see, I time myself reading. So I have to start chopping words.

When you have to make a script fit into a certain time frame, it's amazing how many words you suddenly discover can be deleted. Or replaced with simpler, shorter words. Or how many sentences can be trimmed. Or phrases made more concise.

As you can imagine, writing radio has really honed my editing skills.

**3. Writing for the ear.**

Writing for the ear is different than writing for the eye. The eye is far more forgiving. Oh that sentence is a bit too long, but it's okay. Hmm, yes I do see that awkward phrase, but I'm fine with it.

Not the ear. The ear is brutal. It's like one of those headmasters from a Dickens' novel, standing in front of the classroom with a stick and banging it every time a student stutters on an answer.

The ear catches everything--sentences that are too long and don't allow you to take a breath; sentences that don't flow properly; long, complicated five-dollar words that twist the tongue in a knot and much, much more. Focus on writing shorter sentences. Simpler sentences. Vary your sentences. Use simple words. And that's just plain good old writing advice no matter what you happen to be writing. First, choose something you want the ad to be about. Maybe one of your products or services. But choose only one. More than one and you're just asking for trouble. (Rule of thumb--one message per ad No more. Otherwise you run the risk of losing your target market. Pick one message and make it very simple and very clear.)

Now do what I do. Write the ad. Start by keeping it under a general word count--100 words for a 30-second ad and 190 words for a 60-second spot.

Finished your first draft? Great. Now read it. And time yourself. (Those clocks on the computer desktop are great for this.)

What, you went over your limit? Better start cutting. See how many words you can take out and sentences you can tighten. Or replace words and phrases with something shorter.

Now read it again. Still too long? Or maybe now it's too awkward. See previous paragraph. Keep repeating until you end up with something that sounds smooth and fits in the allotted time.

Martin Esslin said, "The almost telepathic transference of images from mind to mind is the beauty and the glory of the radio play."

Also George Bernard Shaw once said about radio drama that "It provides the maximum of temptation with the maximum of opportunity." Well, he actually said it about marriage but let's not be pedantic. In radio almost anything is possible.

By far the most important piece of advice for anyone wanting to write for radio is to listen to as much as possible. Radio is a distinctive means of communication with its own limitations and possibilities and its own particular techniques and anyone who seriously wishes to sell their work to radio must make themself familiar with its existing output.

As with any other type of freelance writing, the writer must study the market. There is for instance, no single type of radio play, for the BBC's large output is broken down into distinctive series, each with their own characteristics. A play will have a far better chance of acceptance if the writer decides in the beginning if they are writing for a Radio 3 or Radio 4 audience such a Saturday night theatre or the Monday play.

The reality is the market is always right. You aren't writing for the general public, you're writing for a small handful of people whose sole opinion will decide whether your work gets produced. You don't have to know what the public wants but what a producer considers they want. But how can you find that out? One way is to buy the Radio Times, look at the radio drama listings, listen to the plays and keep a record. A record may have the following elements: date; slot; title; length; how many characters; producer; region; theme; category; plot. The purpose is to identify trends and identify producers who you feel will respond to your work favourably.

The BBC isn't afraid to tackle difficult issues these days, it's not as po-faced as it used to be. They're quite happy to broadcast difficult material. While you can get away with the odd non-sexual swearing in daytime, sexual swearwords are still referable though to the head of drama. Somebody somewhere along the line makes a decision about those words and how often and when they may be used. While the BBC isn't afraid of reflecting English as its spoken, they're not interested in gratuitously rubbing the audience up the wrong way.

These days the BBC are very concerned about people switching over. I learnt, in history at school, that people once had wirelesses and once you'd got a station you never dared moved that dial or you'd never get it back again. These days, with digital tuning, switching channels isn't a problem. There are now many more channels to switch to not just the Light, the Home and the Third as it used to be. Also radio drama is in competition with all other forms of drama including theatre and film but especially television. So when you write your plays the imperative is to keep the listener listening, capture the mood in the first minute. That doesn't mean there isn't the time for the slow-build but it should still have something that people can get a hook on from the start. As with all drama the story has to start early. Radio does some things much better than any other medium and they're always interested in plays that can be done in no other medium. Consider plays that not only can't be done in any other medium but are impossible to do the ironing to.

When were the forms of media created? When did advertising first show up? Who owns the media?

Creation of the various forms of media

* Newspapers & Magazines – 1880
* Movies – 1910
* Television – 1945
* Cable Television – 1980's
* Satellite Television, Internet, Digital Communication – End of the 20th century

  In 1920, radio was first developed, primarily for use by the military, strictly for sending History of the Media-Old Radios messages from one location to another. David Sternoff, the then-president of RCA, first had the idea to sell radio sets to consumers, or what were then called radio receivers. However, consumers needed a reason to buy radios, so RCA was the first to set up radio stations all over the country. Between 1920 and 1922, 400 radio stations were set up, starting with KBKA in Pittsburgh. Stations were also set up by universities, newspapers, police departments, hotels, and labour unions.
* By 1923, there were 600 radio stations across the United States, and $83 million worth of sets had been sold.

  The biggest difference in radio before and after 1923 was that the first advertising was not heard on the radio until 1923. RCA at the time was made up of four companies:
* AT&T
* General Electric
* United Fruit
* Westinghouse

United Fruit was one of the first global corporations, and one of the first to advertise on the radio. The AT&T division of RCA first thought about selling time on the air to companies, which marked the start of "toll broadcasting." WEAF was the first station to operate this way, causing widespread outrage, and accusation of "polluting the airwaves."

Because of this controversy, the practice of selling advertising time was called "trade name publicity." Sponsors linked their name with a program on the air, rather than advertising a specific product in a 30 second "commercial" as we know it today.

Why did AT&T decide to experiment with charging companies for air time?

AT&T was not making any money from broadcasting at the time since they only made transmitters, not receivers. They only made money when new radio stations bought the equipment required to broadcast. They did not make money from consumers buying radios.

AT&T also started the practice of paying performers for their time on the air, rather than only volunteers, which was standard practice for radio content up until that point.

10

# Audio Broadcasting

Radio broadcasting is an audio (sound) broadcasting service, traditionally broadcast through the air as radio waves (a form of electromagnetic radiation) from a transmitter to an antenna and a thus to a receiving device. Stations can be linked in radio networks to broadcast common programming, either in syndication or simulcast or both. Audio broadcasting also can be done via cable FM, local wire networks, satellite and the Internet.

The earliest radio stations were simply radio and audio telegraph systems and did not carry audio. The first claimed audio transmission that could be termed a broadcast occurred on Christmas Eve in 1906, and was made by Reginald Fessenden. While many early experimenters attempted to create systems similar to radiotelephone devices where only two parties were meant to communicate, there were others who intended to transmit to larger audiences. Charles Herrold started broadcasting in California in 1909 and was carrying audio by the next year.

For the next decade, radio tinkerers had to build their own radio receivers. KDKA AM of Pittsburgh, Pennsylvania (owned by Westinghouse) started broadcasting as the first licensed "commercial" radio station on November 2, 1920. The commercial designation came from the type of license-they didn't start airing advertisements until a few years later.

The first broadcast was the results of the U.S. presidential election, 1920. The Montreal station that became CFCF-AM began program broadcasts on May 2 1920, and the Detroit station that became WWJ began program broadcasts beginning on August 20, 1920, although neither held a license at the time.

Radio Argentina began regularly scheduled transmissions from the Teatro Coliseo in Buenos Aires on August 27, 1920, making its own priority claim. The station got its license on November 19, 1923. The delay was due to the lack of official Argentine licensing procedures before that date. This station continued regular broadcasting of entertainment and cultural fare for several decades.

When internet based radio became feasible in the mid '90s, the new medium required no licensing and the stations could broadcast from anywhere in the world without the need for "over the air" transmitters.

This greatly reduced the overhead for establishing a station, and in 1996, 'A' Net Station (A.N.E.T.) began broadcasting commercial free from Antarctica.

M.I.T. developed the "Radio Locator" List of Radio Stations. After stations started streaming audio on the internet, Radio-Locator added this to their search engine so anyone could locate a station's website and listen to a station offering a worldwide stream. This list also tracks "terrestrial" radio stations who may not have live audio on the net, or even a website, but are able to find station information by various other search queries.

## TYPES

Radio stations are of several types. The best known are the AM and FM stations; these include both commercial, public and nonprofit varieties as well as student-run campus radio stations and hospital radio stations can be found throughout the developed world.

Although now being eclipsed by internet-distributed radio, there are many stations that broadcast on shortwave bands using AM technology that can be received over thousands of miles (especially at night). For example, the BBC has a full schedule transmitted via shortwave. These broadcasts are very sensitive to atmospheric conditions and sunspots.

## AM STATIONS

AM stations were the earliest broadcasting stations to be developed. AM refers to amplitude modulation, a mode of broadcasting radio waves by varying the amplitude of the carrier signal in response to the amplitude of the signal to be transmitted. One of the advantages of AM is that its unsophisticated signal can be detected (turned into sound) with simple equipment. If a signal is strong enough, not even a power source is needed; building an unpowered crystal radio receiver was a common childhood project in the early years of radio.

AM broadcasts occur on North American airwaves in the mediumwave frequency range of 530 to 1700 kHz (known as the "standard broadcast band"). The band was expanded in the 1990s by adding nine channels from 1620 to 1700 kHz. Channels are spaced every 10 kHz in the Americas, and generally every 9 kHz everywhere else.

Many countries outside of the U.S. use a similar frequency band for AM transmissions. Europe also uses the longwave band. In response to the growing popularity of FM radio stations in the late 1980s and early 1990s, some North American stations began broadcasting in AM stereo, though this never really gained acceptance.

AM radio has some serious shortcomings.

- The signal is subject to interference from electrical storms (lightning) and other EMI.
- Fading of the signal can be severe at night.

AM signals exhibit diurnal variation, travelling much longer distances at night. In a crowded channel environment this means that the power of regional channels which share a frequency must be reduced at night or directionally beamed in order to avoid interference, which reduces the potential nighttime audience. Some stations have frequencies unshared with other stations in the U.S.; these are called clear channel stations. Many of them can be heard across much of the country at night. (This is not to be confused with Clear Channel Communications, which currently owns many U.S. radio stations.)

- AM radio transmitters can transmit audio frequencies up to 20 kHz (now limited to 10 kHz in the US due to FCC rules designed to reduce interference), but most receivers are only capable of reproducing frequencies up to 5 kHz or less. At the time that AM broadcasting began in the 1920s, this provided adequate fidelity for existing microphones, 78 rpm recordings, and loudspeakers. The fidelity of sound equipment subsequently improved considerably but the receivers did not. Reducing the bandwidth of the receivers reduces the cost of manufacturing and makes them less prone to interference. In the United States, AM stations are never assigned adjacent channels in the same service area. This prevents the sideband energy generated by two stations from interfering with each other. Bob Carver created an AM stereo tuner employing notch filtering that demonstrated an AM broadcast can meet or exceed the 15 kHz bandwidth of FM stations without objectionable interference. After a few years the tuner was discontinued; Bob Carver had left the company and Carver Corporation later cut the number of models produced before discontinuing production completely. AM stereo broadcasts declined with the advent of HD Radio.

## FM STATIONS

FM refers to frequency modulation, and occurs on VHF airwaves in the frequency range of 88 to 108 MHz everywhere (except Japan and Russia). Japan uses the 76 to 90 MHz band. FM stations are much more popular in economically developed regions, such as Europe and the United States, especially since higher sound fidelity and stereo broadcasting became common in this format.

FM radio was invented by Edwin H. Armstrong in the 1930s for the specific purpose of overcoming the interference (static) problem of AM radio, to which it is immune. At the same time, greater fidelity was made possible by spacing stations further apart. Instead of 10 kHz apart, they are 200 kHz apart-the difference between the lowest current FM frequency in the

U.S., 88.1 MHz and the next lowest, 88.3 MHz. This was far in advance of the audio equipment of the 1940s, but wide interchannel spacing was chosen to reduce interference problems that existed with AM.

In fact 200 kHz is not needed to accommodate an audio signal-20 kHz to 30 kHz is all that is necessary for a narrowband FM signal. The 200 kHz bandwidth allowed room for ±75 kHz signal deviation from the assigned frequency plus a 50 kHz guardband to eliminate adjacent channel interference. The larger bandwidth allows for broadcasting a 15 kHz bandwidth audio signal plus a 38 kHz stereo "subcarrier"-a piggyback signal that rides on the main signal. Additional unused capacity is used by some broadcasters to transmit utility functions such as background music for public areas, GPS auxiliary signals, or financial market data.

The AM radio problem of interference at night was addressed in a different way. At the time FM was set up, the only available frequencies were far higher in the spectrum than those used for AM radio. Using these frequencies meant that even at far higher power, the range of a given FM signal was much lower, thus its market was more local than for AM radio. Reception range at night was the same as daytime, and while the problem of interference between stations has not disappeared, it is far less.

The original FM radio service in the U.S. was the Yankee Network, located in New England. Broadcasting began in the early 1940s but did not pose a significant threat to the AM broadcasting industry. It required purchase of a special receiver. The frequencies used were not those used today: 42 to 50 megahertz. The change to the current frequencies, 88 to 108 megahertz, began at the end of World War II and was to some extent imposed by AM radio owners so as to cripple what was by now realized to be a potentially serious threat.

FM radio on the new band had to begin from step one. As a commercial venture it remained a little used audio enthusiast's medium until the 1960s. The more prosperous AM stations, or their owners, acquired FM licenses and often broadcast the same programming on the FM station as on the AM station (simulcasting). The FCC limited this practice in the 1970s. By the 1980s, since almost all new radios included both AM and FM tuners (without any government mandate), FM became the dominant medium, especially in cities. Because of its greater range, AM remained more common in rural environments.

## DIGITAL RADIO BROADCASTING

Digital radio broadcasting has emerged, first in Europe (the UK in 1995 and Germany in 1999), and later in the United States. The European system is named DAB, for Digital Audio Broadcasting, and uses the public domain EUREKA 147 system. In the United States, the IBOC system is named HD Radio and owned by a consortium of private companies called iBiquity. An international non-profit consortium Digital Radio Mondiale (DRM), has introduced the public domain DRM system.

It is expected that for the next 10 to 20 years, all these systems will co-exist, while by 2015 to 2020 digital radio may predominate, at least in the developed countries.

### Satellite

Satellite radiobroadcasters are slowly emerging, but the enormous entry costs of space-based satellite transmitters, and restrictions on available radio spectrum licenses has restricted growth of this market. In the USA and Canada, just two services, XM Satellite Radio and Sirius Satellite Radio exist.

### Other

Many other non-broadcast types of radio stations exist. These include:

- base stations for police, fire and ambulance networks
- military base stations
- dispatch base stations for taxis, trucks, and couriers
- emergency broadcast systems
- amateur radio stations

## PROGRAM FORMATS

Radio program formats differ by country, regulation and markets. For instance, the U.S. Federal Communications Commission designates the 88-92 megahertz band in the U.S.

for non-profit or educational programming, with advertising prohibited.

In addition, formats change in popularity as time passes and technology improves. Early radio equipment only allowed program material to be broadcast in real time, known as live broadcasting. As technology for sound recording improved, an increasing proportion of broadcast programming used pre-recorded material. A current trend is the automation of radio stations. Some stations now operate without direct human intervention by using entirely pre-recorded material sequenced by computer control.

## INTERNATIONAL BROADCASTING

International broadcasting is broadcasting deliberately aimed at a foreign, rather than a domestic, audience. It usually is broadcast by means of longwave, mediumwave, or shortwave radio, but in recent years has also used direct satellite broadcasting and the Internet as means of reaching audiences.

Although radio and television programs do travel outside national borders, in many cases reception by foreigners is accidental. However, for purposes of propaganda, transmitting religious beliefs, keeping in touch with colonies or expatriates, education, improving trade, or increasing national prestige, broadcasting services have operated external services since the 1920s.

### The early Years 1914-1939

The Dutch started regular international broadcasting on short-wave in 1927, following experiments in Eindhoven in 1925. This was followed by the BBC with the BBC Empire Service in 1932.

Other notable early international broadcasters included Vatican Radio (February 12, 1931), Radio Moscow, the official service of the Soviet Union which began broadcasting on long-wave in 1923 (this has since been renamed the Voice of Russia, following the collapse of the Soviet Union). Broadcasting in South Asia was launched in 1925 in Ceylon-Radio Ceylon, now the Sri Lanka Broadcasting Corporation is the oldest in the region.

In the 1930s, international broadcasting was a key means of promoting Nazi Germany foreign policy. German propaganda was organized under Joseph Goebbels, and played a key role in the German occupation of Austria and the Munich Crisis of 1938. During the Spanish Civil War, the Nationalist forces received a powerful Telefunken transmitter as a gift of Nazi Germany to aid their propaganda efforts, and until 1943 Radio Nacional de España collaborated with the Axis powers to retransmit in Spanish news from the official radio stations of Germany and Italy.

During the Second World War, Russian, German, British, and Italian international broadcasting services expanded and in 1942 the United States initiated its international broadcasting service, the Voice of America. In the Pacific theater, General Douglas MacArthur used shortwave radio to keep in touch with the citizens of the Japanese-occupied Philippine Islands.

### *World War II–modern International Broadcasting Begins*

Shortwave programming was a low priority in the Weimar Republic. Once Hitler assumed power in 1933, shortwave, under the Rundfunk Ausland (Foreign Radio Section), was regarded as a vital element of Nazi propaganda. German shortwave hours were increased from two hours a day to 18 per day, and eventually twelve languages were broadcast on a 24 hour basis, including English. A 100 kilowatt transmitter and antenna complex was built at Zeesen, near Berlin. Speciality target programming to the United States began in 1933, to South Africa, South America, and East Asia in 1934, and South Asia and Central America in 1938.

Mediumwave transmitters on the periphery of the Third Reich provided speciality programs to listeners in neighbouring countries. Nevertheless, the Germans always had a problem staffing their foreign services with announcers who were both technically competent and loyal to Nazi ideas.

Several announcers who became well-known in their countries included British Union of Fascists member William Joyce, who was one of the two "Lord Haw-Haw"s; Frenchmen Paul Ferdonnet and Andre Olbrecht, called "the traitors of [Radio] Stuttgart"; and Americans Frederick William

Kaltenbach, "Lord Hee-Haw", and Mildred Gillars, one of the two announcers called "Axis Sally". Listeners to German programs often tuned in for curiosity's sake--at one time, German radio had half a million listeners in the U.S.--but most of them soon lost interest.

The British launched Radio SEAC from Colombo, Ceylon (Sri Lanka) during World War II. The station broadcast radio programs to the allied armed forces across the region from their headquarters in Ceylon.

Following the war and German partition, each Germany developed its own international broadcasting station: Deutsche Welle, using studios in Cologne, West Germany, and Radio Berlin International (RBI) in East Germany. RBI's broadcasts ceased shortly before the reunification of Germany on October 3, 1990, and Deutsche Welle took over its transmitters and frequencies.

***The Cold War Era (1945-1991): Modern Practices, Modern Technology***

The Cold War led to increased international broadcasting, as Communist and non-Communist states attempted to influence each other's domestic population. Some of the most prominent Western broadcasters were the Voice of America, the BBC World Service, and the (covertly) CIA-backed Radio Free Europe/Radio Liberty. The Soviet Union's most prominent service was Radio Moscow (now the Voice of Russia) and China used Radio Peking (then Radio Beijing, now China Radio International). In addition to the U.S.-Soviet cold war, the Chinese-Russian border dispute led to an increase of the numbers of transmitters aimed at the two nations, and the development of new techniques such as playing tapes backwards for reel-to-reel recorders.

In addition to the superpower states, international broadcast services grew in Europe and the Middle East. Under the presidency of Gamal Nasser, Egyptian transmitters covered the Arab world; Israel's service, Kol Israel, served both to present the Israeli point of view to the world and to serve the Jewish diaspora, particularly behind the Iron Curtain. Ironically, the isolationist Albania under Enver Hoxha, virtually a hermit kingdom, became one of the most prolific international broadcasters during the latter decades of the Cold War, with Radio Tirana one of the top five broadcasters in terms of hours of programming produced (Although Radio Tirana's programming was almost universally regarded as insufferably dull).

At the end of the Cold War, many international broadcasters cut back on hours and foreign languages broadcast, or reemphasized other language services. For example, in 1984, Radio Canada International broadcast in English, French, German, Spanish, Czech/Slovak, Hungarian, Polish, Russian, and Ukrainian. In 2005, Canada broadcast in English, Chinese, Arabic, Russian, and Spanish There is a trend towards more TV (e.g. BBC World, NHK World, CCTV-9), and news websites. Some services, such as Swiss Radio International, left shortwave altogether and exist in Internet form. In addition, new standards, such as Digital Radio Mondiale, are being introduced, as well as sending programs over the Web to be played back later, as "podcasts."

Daily developments are followed in Radio Netherlands' Media Network blog.

Transmitter power increased during this period to guarantee better reception (and in some cases in an attempt to counteract jamming).

- 1950s: 100 kW
- 1960s: 200 kW, early 1960s (2 x 100 kW 'twinned')
- 1970s: 300 kW, but many 250 kW transmitters sold
- 1980s: 500 kW sometimes transmitters were "doubled up" to produce 1000 Kw output
- 1980s-Present: 600 kW single, 1200 kW from twinned transmitters.

## The move from Shortwave to other Technologies

In previous decades Shortwave (and sometimes high powered mediumwave) transmission was regarded as the main (and often the only) way in which broadcasters could reach an international audience. In recent years the proliferation of technologies such as satellite broadcasting, the internet and rebroadcasts of programming on AM and FM within target countries (Used mainly by Radio Free Europe following the end of the cold war) has meant that this is no longer necessairly the case.

Shortwave does possess a number of advantages over these newer technologies, including the following:

- The difficulty in censoring programming by authorities in target countries
- Low cost Shortwave radios are widely available in all but the most repressive countries in the world
- In many countries (particularly in most third world nations and in the Eastern bloc during the cold-war era) Ownership of Shortwave receivers is widespread (in many of these countries some domestic stations also used SW)
- Many newer SW receivers are portable and can be battery operated making them useful in difficult circumstances such as war-torn regions, disaster struck areas, refugee camps etc.
- Shortwave radios can be used in situations where internet or satellite technology is unavailable (or unaffordable)

But nowadays these benefits are widely regarded as being outweighed by the drawbacks such as these:

- Shortwave broadcasts often suffer from serious interference problems because of overcrowding on the wavebands, Atmospheric disturbances and Electrical interference problems (particularly in cities) from TV sets, computers, poorly designed domestic appliances and substandard electrical installations.
- Even under ideal reception conditions the audio quality of a shortwave broadcast is usually inferior to that of domestic stations (particularly FM stations)
- As more people around the world have access to television and the internet old technologies such as shortwave radio find it difficult to compete for peoples attention.

- In most Western countries ownership of shortwave radios is limited to interested enthusiasts. Therefore audiences are limited
- The dependence of shortwave radio on atmospheric conditions (The best frequency for hearing certain parts of the world varies by time of day and season) means that it can be difficult to use by non technically minded listeners.

Because of this many broadcasters are discovering they can reach a wider audience through other methods (particularly the internet and satellite television) and are cutting back on (or even entirely dropping) shortwave.

## Means

### *Mediumwave and Longwave*

Most radio receivers in the world receive the mediumwave band (535 kHz to 1700 kHz), which at night is capable of reliable reception from 150 to 2,500 km distance from a transmitter. Mediumwave is used heavily the world over for international broadcasting on a formal and informal basis.

In addition, many receivers used in Europe and Russia can receive the longwave broadcast band (150 to 280 kHz), which provides reliable long-distance communications over continental distances.

### *Shortwave*

Yet other receivers are capable of receiving shortwave transmissions (2,000 to 30,000 kHz or 2 to 30 MHz). Depending on time of day, season of year, solar weather and Earth's geomagnetic field, a signal might reach around the world.

An international broadcaster has several options for reaching a foreign audience:

- If the foreign audience is near the broadcaster, high-power longwave and mediumwave stations can provide reliable coverage.
- If the foreign audience is more than 1,000 kilometers away from the broadcaster, shortwave radio is reliable, but subject to interruption by adverse solar/geomagnetic conditions.

- An international broadcaster may use a local mediumwave or FM radio or television relay station in the target country or countries.
- An international broadcaster may use a local shortwave broadcaster as a relay station.
- Neighbouring states, such as Israel and Jordan, may broadcast television programs to each other's viewing public.

An international broadcaster such as the BBC, Radio France International or Germany's Deutsche Welle, may use all the above methods. Several international broadcasters, such as Swiss Radio International, have abandoned shortwave broadcasting altogether, relying on Internet transmissions only. Others, such as the BBC World Service, have abandoned shortwave transmissions to North America, relying on local relays, the Internet, and satellite transmissions.

## LISTENERS

An international broadcaster may have the technical means of reaching a foreign audience, but unless the foreign audience has a reason to listen, the effectiveness of the broadcaster is in question.

One of the most common foreign audiences consists of expatriates, who cannot listen to radio or watch television programs from home. Another common audience is radio hobbyists, who attempt to listen as many countries as possible and obtain verification cards or letters (QSLs). A third audience consists of journalists, government officials, and key business persons, who exert a disproportionate influence on a state's foreign or economic policy.

A fourth, but less publicized audience, consists of intelligence officers and agents who monitor broadcasts for both open-source intelligence clues to the broadcasting state's policies and for hidden messages to foreign agents operating in the receiving country. The BBC started its monitoring service in Caversham, Reading in 1936 (now BBC Monitoring). In the United States, the DNI Open Source Center (formerly the Central Intelligence Agency's Foreign Broadcast Information Service) provides the same service. Copies of OSC/FBIS reports can be found in many U.S. libraries that serve as government depositories. In addition, a number of hobbyists listen and report "spook" transmissions.

Without these four audiences, international broadcasters face difficulty in getting funding. In 2001, for example, the BBC World Service stopped transmitting shortwave broadcasts to North America, and other international broadcasters, such as YLE Radio Finland, stopped certain foreign-language programs.

However, international broadcasting has been successful when a country does not provide programming wanted by a wide segment of the population. In the 1960s, when there was no BBC service playing rock and roll, Radio Television Luxembourg (RTL) broadcast rock and roll, including bands such as the Beatles, into the United Kingdom. Similar programming came from an unlicensed, or "pirate" station, Radio Caroline, which broadcast from a ship in the international waters of the North Sea.

## RESTRICTING RECEPTION

In many cases, governments do not want their citizens listening to international broadcasters. In Nazi Germany, a major propaganda campaign, backed by law and prison sentences, attempted to discourage Germans from listening to such stations. In addition, the German government sold a cheap "People's Receiver" that could not pick up distant signals well. In North Korea, all receivers are sold with fixed frequencies, tuned to local stations.

The most common method of preventing reception is jamming, or broadcasting a signal on the same frequencies as the international broadcaster. Germany jammed the BBC European service during the Second World War. Russian and Eastern European jammers were aimed against Radio Free Europe, other Western broadcasters, and against Chinese broadcasters during the nadir of Sino-Soviet relations. In 2002, the Cuban government jammed the Voice of America's Radio Marti program and the Chinese government jammed broadcasts made by adherents of Falun Gong.

Yet another method of preventing reception involves moving a domestic station to the frequency used by the international broadcaster. During the Batista government of Cuba, and during the Castro years, Cuban medium-wave stations broadcast on the frequencies of popular South Florida stations. In October 2002 Iraq changed frequencies of two stations to block the Voice of America's Radio Sawa program.

Jamming can be defeated by using very powerful transmitting antennas, carefully choosing the transmitted frequency, changing transmitted frequency often, using Single Sideband, and properly aiming the receiving antenna.

## COSMIC RULES OF WRITING FOR TELEVISION

As a veteran writer and a licensed psychotherapist specializing in writers' issues, I know enough to know there aren't any rules when it comes to writing.

Except for the following, which I modestly call the Three Cosmic Rules of Writing. I'm serious. Learn these simple rules, then burn them into your hearts and minds. It couldn't hurt.

## YOU ARE ENOUGH

It's a growth industry: there are dozens of seminars, how-to books and audio tapes promising to teach you to write better, faster, more commercially. And there's nothing wrong with most of these. I know; I teach some myself.

Because, frankly, there ARE things a writer needs to learn about craft, the traditions of storytelling and the reality of the marketplace. But for the writer just starting out, there's a hidden danger: namely, the belief that if you just take the right seminars, read the right books or pick the right guru, then you'll be successful. That the person you are right now just isn't enough.

It's a classic belief system...writers who feel they have to be something more to succeed--smarter, better educated, funnier--with more interesting lives, more unique experiences.

As a therapist who works with writers, I see this everyday. Writers who feel they're somehow not enough. Who believe all the other writers are more talented, more confident, less burdened by doubt. It puts me in mind of that famous opening sequence of Woody Allen's 'Stardust Memories.' A glum Woody sits in a dark, dingy train car, with other lost souls. Looking out the window, he sees another train car--shining, brightly lit. Inside, beautiful men and women laugh and drink champagne, a festive vision of wit and privilege out of a Noel Coward play. Woody despairs. Why isn't he in the sparkling car, with the sparkling people?

Once, when a writer client of mine made reference to this scene to explain his feelings, what emerged was not only his sense of himself as inadequate, but something else, more insidious and undermining. Namely, the idea that he'd been dealt a bad hand--'I'm in the wrong car'--because of intrinsic defects in himself. If he were a better writer--smarter, more talented, whatever--he'd be in the right car. Those happy, glittering people were in the shining train car because they DESERVED to be there while he did not.

Thereafter, in our work together, his self-sabotaging behaviours could be understood as a natural result of his belief in himself as basically defective. When this painful self-concept was successfully illuminated and challenged, things began to shift in his view of himself.

What this anecdote illustrates is the real danger to your writing in seeing yourself as less than, not enough. Admittedly, a very common, self-limiting belief. To which I offer this thought, which will save you thousands of dollars in therapy bills and trim years off your spiritual journey: everybody thinks the party's happening somewhere else.

But it isn't. It's happening right here, right now. With you.

You--with all your doubts and fears, joys and sorrows--are enough. You--the one reading these words at this very moment-have everything you need to become the writer you want to be.

'Me?' you may be asking. 'Just as I am?'

Yes, you, who may, at this moment, be feeling scared, frustrated, blocked, discouraged. If so, join the club. Because so does every other writer in the world, even the most successful ones, who, after all, were once struggling writers themselves.

And now that they're successful, guess what? They still struggle. They have the same doubts, fears, longings, worries. They just don't give these feelings the same negative meanings you do. Smart writers recognize their feelings as important information about their inner lives, as the raw material of their writing craft. Just grist for the mill.

Which brings me to the Second Cosmic Rule of Writing: 'Work With What You're Given'

## WORK WITH WHAT YOU'RE GIVEN

One of my favourite New Yorker cartoons by George Booth depicts a tormented, obviously 'blocked' writer sitting at his typewriter, crumpled paper strewn about, surrounded by literally dozens of dogs--napping, barking, hanging from the window sills, etc. The writer's wife stands in the doorway, glaring at him in weary disdain. 'Write about dogs,' she says.

Aside from its dark humour, the cartoon's truth is that the frustrated writer often doesn't see that a subject for his writing is right in front of him--the dogs; i.e., the obvious elements that actually inhabit his life.

In other words, work with what you're given. Writers have to practice SEEING, really seeing the world around them. As a writer, your job is to do this consciously and artfully, using craft and imagination as well as memory and reflection. You have to pay attention.

Tolstoy said, 'Love those whom God has put before You'; the Tao says, 'Love the Ten Thousand Things.' In short, love, that is--see--everything.

What do I mean by this? To 'love' the totality of what we experience is to accept all our responses to it, to be enlivened by the variety of ways we experience events, good or bad, painful or joyful. The artist's task is to see every moment--and our reaction to it--as potentially interesting, challenging and worthy of our creative participation.

Viewed from this perspective, a writer is never bored, never longs for things in his or her life to be more exciting, more interesting, more something else than they actually are. Except, of course, when you DO feel that way, in which case you should write about that boredom or that longing. That's your grist for that particular day. It's working with what you're given.

- Which brings me to the Third (and, thankfully, last) Cosmic Rule of Writing...namely, 'Writing Begets Writing.'

If you're stuck on a difficult scene, write it anyway.

Write it badly. Write it in verse. Write it as a journal entry, a Dennis Miller rant. If you're frustrated at being stuck, write about that. I don't care. But write.

If you have angry, self-critical feelings, give them to a character in your story. If there isn't a likely candidate, invent one. There IS one, anyway: you. Your anguish, doubt, fears and frustrations are as vital and elemental to what you're writing as any character or plot point. Might as well make use of this fact.

## WRITING BEGETS WRITING

Writing begets writing. Just as worrying begets worrying. Obsessing begets more obsessing. Pacing back and forth begets--well, you get the idea.

When you risk writing from where you're at, you set in motion a whole set of internal processes. The first rotten sentence you write has a life you can inhabit, evaluate, cross out. This first attempt can be replaced by a second, hopefully less rotten sentence--maybe a good piece of description or a sharp line of dialogue.

Then again, maybe not. But it doesn't matter. Just keep going. As William Goldman reminds us, some scenes you write are just going to be sludge, but they're important connective tissue. They keep things moving; they're links in a chain. Weak links, perhaps, but you can always go back and strengthen them later.

With what? The knowledge that you've written, for one thing, because writing doesn't just beget writing, it also begets--and reinforces--the reality that you can write; that pages will accumulate.

Look at it this way: Every hour you spend writing is an hour NOT spent fretting about your writing. Every day you produce pages is a day you DIDN'T spend sitting at a coffee shop, bitching about not producing any pages.

Writing begets writing. Not writing begets...well...not - writing. You do the math.

There you have it: the Three Cosmic Rules of Writing.

(1) 'You Are Enough.'

(2) 'Work With What You're Given.'

(3) 'Writing Begets Writing.'

## THE INS AND OUTS OF TV SERIES WRITER DEALS

The television business has undergone a dramatic change in recent years. In the past, studios would lavishly spend millions of dollars on long-term development deals with TV writers referred to as 'overall deals' in the hope that during the two to four year term of such arrangements (during which the studio is paying the writer's overhead plus a salary), the writer will create a hit show for the studio. Those days are now gone--unless of course you're Dick Wolf or David Kelley!

Nowadays, a writer is typically engaged to perform the initial step of writing a pilot script, and the studio is granted a number of options to engage the writer to render additional services on the pilot episode and/or series (both writing and producing). The benefit of this arrangement to the studio is clear: if the studio is not happy with the script, it can cut its losses relatively early, having committed only to payment of the initial script fee. Such deals, referred to as 'one-off's,' used to represent only a fraction of the deals that studios would enter into when developing television pilots and series, but are now the dominant form of television series writing deals. To give you an idea of what we're talking about and a heads-up for important things to consider when you're negotiating a deal, below is the basic outline of a television 'one-off' pilot/ series writing agreement.

**Pilot Writing Fee:** The first item you would negotiate in connection with these types of agreements is invariably the pilot script-writing fee. Under the WGA Agreement (which governs most television projects, as all of the major networks are guild signatories), union minimum (or 'scale') for such services is approximately $30,000 for a half hour script and $43,000 for a sixty-minute script. For scale, the studio will be entitled to a story, first draft and final draft of the script (also called a teleplay).

In most instances, the studio will bargain for a story, first draft, two sets of a revision and a polish. Usually, the writer/ creator will receive more than scale and pilot writing fees can range from $50,000 (for a relatively inexperienced writer) to $250,000 or higher for an A-level television writer (i.e., one who has already created at least one successful series, such as David Milch). As we mentioned above, this is the only money that the writer is guaranteed to receive under the 'one-off' deal.

**Pilot Producing Services:** The next issue of negotiation you would need to concern yourself with is the nature of the writer's services (if any) in the event that your script is well received and the pilot episode is ordered to production. In many cases, the studio will guarantee the writer employment as an 'executive producer' of the pilot episode at a negotiated fee. Other times (for example, if the pilot writer is not an established television writer or 'show-runner'), the studio might agree to attach the writer to the project at a lower level, such as a consulting or supervising producer. The writer's role in connection with the pilot is ultimately a result of negotiation, taking into account the writer's clout and prior experience. The WGA does not govern producing fees, as such services are not deemed to constitute writing. The fees for such producing services can range anywhere from $15,000 to $100,000.

**Series Services/Compensation:** If the pilot is 'picked up' by the network (i.e., series episodes are ordered to production), the studio can choose to exercise its option (negotiated up front, as part of the 'one-off' deal) to engage the writer as some type of producer on the series. A writer's series episodic producer fee will generally be lower than the pilot-producing fee, as there is less work to do once the first episode (i.e., the pilot) is completed.

Another point that is negotiated as part of the pilot/series deal is the length of time that the pilot writer (or 'series creator') will be 'locked' or attached to the series, thereby continuing to receive screen credit and a fee. A studio will usually agree to lock the writer/creator to the series for at least one year, and in many cases two years. Again, this depends largely on the writer's status in the television industry. Top writer/producers, such as Steven Bochco, might be guaranteed an executive producer fee and credit for the 'life' (i.e., duration) of the series. A writer/creator might also be guaranteed the opportunity to write (and be paid for) a specified number of episodic scripts during each year of the series.

In addition to series producing fees, you may negotiate for a 'series sales bonus' (i.e., a sum of money payable as a bonus if and when the network orders series episodes based on the pilot). While the dollar amount of a series sales bonus will vary and is subject to negotiation, it is fairly standard today for a series sales bonus of $25,000 to be granted in the event the writer receives sole 'written by' credit on the pilot and sole 'created by' credit on the series. This bonus may be reduced if the writer receives shared credit and/or if fewer than a set number of episodes (usually 12) are actually produced.

Finally, the WGA Agreement requires that the writer or writers accorded 'created by' credit on a series receive a royalty (or payment) for each episode of the series that is produced beyond the pilot. The current WGA required royalty for network prime-time programming is approximately $1,000 per episode. Subject to this minimum, the actual amount of the royalty payable to the series creator is negotiable and may be as high as $6,000 per episode for top guns.

**Profit Participation:** A writer's profit participation in a television project is typically more significant than with respect to a feature film, and is more likely to generate payment to the writer for two reasons. First, as television writer, you can normally negotiate for a percentage of the profits in excess of five percent (which is the standard participation for motion picture writers with limited exceptions). In addition, television writers are generally more successful than their feature film counterparts in extracting favourable terms from the studios relating to the calculation of such profits. Second, an enormously successful series may generate so much cash relative to its costs, that regardless of the precise definition of the project's 'net proceeds,' it is likely to generate some payment in many cases.

We think it is therefore imperative for a writer's representative to take great care in negotiating the definition of 'project proceeds' in the writer's contract. A top-level showrunner/creator will often be able to negotiate for 15 percent or more of the 'adjusted gross receipts' (gross revenues less certain defined deductions and a reduced distribution fee), or for up to 50 percent of the 'net proceeds,' reducible by net participations granted to third parties. If a project survives the uphill battle toward syndication, these profits may indeed materialize.

**Credit:** Assuming that the production falls within the WGA's jurisdiction, the Writer's Guild Agreement will determine the form of most writing credits. Typically, the writer or writers receiving 'written by' or 'story by' credit on the pilot will be accorded a 'created by' credit on the series. The WGA does not, however, govern producing credits. The terms and conditions relating to the writer's 'executive producer' or 'supervising producer' or even 'consultant' credit need to be specifically addressed by contract. In recent years, a number of established writers have requested 'logo' credits (which will typically appear in the end titles) in addition to their producer credits. For example, a 'Chase Films' logo appears at the end of every episode of The Sopranos at the request of that series' creator, David Chase.

**Perks:** As is the case with most talent agreements, writers can usually negotiate for some basic 'perks' (which may or may not be granted, depending upon their status), such as: (i) first-class travel if the studio or network requires the writer to travel; (ii) first class accommodations; (iii) a per-diem; and (iv) ground transportation to and from airports, hotels, and sets. In addition, some writers request that the studio provide an exclusive office and assistant during all periods in which they are expected to render exclusive services. Finally, a reserved parking space is considered a bit of status symbol in Hollywood and is requested by most series creators. This is merely a brief overview of television pilot/series writer agreements. There are several other terms and conditions that vary from deal to deal, which writers should be aware of when entering into such agreements. Before signing any contract, we strongly recommended that writers consult with an experienced entertainment attorney who can review the agreement in detail.

## THE ESSENCE OF STORY

What is the essence, or heart and soul, of a great story? There are seven critical elements: the change of fortune, the problem of the story, the complications, crisis, climax and resolution of the classical structure, and the threat, which is by far the most important. In this article, we will examine the threat and its relationship to the other six critical elements that constitute the very essence of story--that without which there would be no story. The first element is the change of fortune. There is an entity (i.e. an individual, a family, a town, a country, the world, etc.) and that entity goes from a desirable to an undesirable state or condition or the reverse. Or as Aristotle put it: 'The proper magnitude (of a story) is comprised within such limits that the sequence of events, according to the laws of probability and necessity, will admit of a change from bad fortune to good or from good fortune to bad.'

In 'The Exorcist,' a little girl is possessed by the Devil and a state of misfortune exists. Then, the principal action, casting out the Devil, brings about a state of good fortune. In stories that end unhappily, it's the reverse. In 'Othello,' a state of good fortune exists at the beginning. The principal action, perpetrated by Iago, destroys the Moor with jealousy and a state of tragic misfortune is the result.

The second element, the problem, brings about these changes of fortune. This problem is a prerequisite in all stories. You have a problem and that problem is resolved. No matter how big or small the story, it will be focusing on, or related to, a problem. And everyone in that story will somehow be involved in that incident. And everything everyone does in that story will in some way affect the outcome of that incident. And revealing how that problem was created and how it can be resolved is at the very heart of a story. In 'Kiss The Girls' and 'The Silence Of The Lambs,' a serial killer is on the loose. That is the problem that brings about the change of fortune and that is the problem that has to be resolved. The solution to those problems will be the principal actions that give a unity of action to these stories.

In 'Gladiator,' a tyrant has usurped the Roman Empire, preventing the restoration of the Republic.

In 'The Sixth Sense,' there are two problems: a murdered child psychologist is stuck in limbo, and the spirits of dead people are haunting a little boy's mind.

In 'Independence Day,' aliens have invaded the Earth. In 'Star Wars,' the Evil Empire has taken possession of the galaxy. In 'The Iliad,' the Greek army is being decimated because their best warrior has dropped out of the fight.

In the legend of King Arthur, the kingdom is in a state of anarchy and has to be reunified. In 'Jaws,' it's a shark problem. In 'The Mummy,' it's a mummy problem. In 'The Perfect Storm,' it's a weather problem. In 'Traffic,' it's a drug problem. In 'Armageddon,' it's an asteroid problem. In 'Indecent Proposal,' it's a temptation problem. In 'Erin Brockovich,' it's an environmental problem. Each of these stories, and hundreds of others I could name, revolve around a problem that has to be resolved. Can any problem be a story? Technically, any problem can be a story if its solution contains a classical story structure--i.e. complications, a crisis, a climax and a resolution. Generally speaking, however, an audience wouldn't be interested in a story about some minor problem, like finding your lost keys, unless something truly funny or horrendous like the end of the world would happen if you didn't find them.

Story is especially interested in problem-solving actions that involve crises--critical events that threaten life, health, wealth, freedom, love, security, happiness, etc. while testing the limits of human endurance and ingenuity.

Story focuses on problems for the same reason the news only reports the bad things that are happening in the world-and not the good--because problems are where it's at. If everything is in perfect harmony, and there are no problems to worry about--we're in Paradise.

And that's one of the functions of story: to help guide us to higher, more desirable, less problematic states of being. One of the ways that a story does this is by revealing the truth and nature of problems and their solutions. Next, there's the super important element called the threat. The threat is the agent or perpetrator that creates the problem that brings about the negative state. In 'Kiss the Girls,' the serial killer is the threat, and the act of murder is the inciting action that creates the problem that brings about the change to a state of misfortune.

Equally significant in a great story is the fact that this threat will become the source of resistance that opposes the action when someone tries to solve this problem and restore a state of good fortune. This resistance will create the classical structure that occurs when a problem-solving action encounters resistance. In 'Harry Potter,' Voldemort is the threat. His efforts in the seven books to take possession of the wizard world create the problem that brings about an undesirable state. And he will be the source of the resistance that creates the classical structure whenever Harry tries to solve these problems and restore a state of good fortune.

In 'The Exorcist,' the Devil is the threat. He takes possession of a young girl and that is the inciting action that creates the problem and brings about the change of fortune. He is also the source of resistance that creates the complications, crisis, climax and resolution when the priest tries to solve that problem.

In 'Ordinary People,' the mother is the cause of the problem that has brought about the negative state, and she will be the source of resistance when the psychiatrist, played by Judd Hirsch, and the boy's father, played by Donald Sutherland, attempt to solve the mystery of the boy's suicidal tendencies.

In 'Jaws,' the shark is the threat that causes the problem. In 'Dracula,' it's the Count. In 'On the Waterfront,' it's Johnny Friendly. In 'Gladiator,' it's Commodus. In 'Braveheart,' it's the British. In 'The Iliad,' it is the Trojan, Paris. In the Egyptian myth of Osiris, it's Osiris' brother Set.

In all of these cases, the threat performs the action that creates the problem that brings about the change of fortune. It also is the source of resistance that creates the classical structure when someone tries to solve the problem and reverse the state of misfortune. You can see this same pattern at work in real life as well. In World War II, Hitler was the threat, and his 'taking possession of Europe' created the problem and the state of misfortune. He was also the source of the resistance that created the complications, crisis, climaxes and resolutions of the classical structure when the Allies tried to solve this problem. In our latest war, this is also very evident. Osama Bin Laden, his Al Qaeda terrorist network and the Taliban are the threat. Their attack on the World Trade Center and Pentagon is the inciting action that created the problem that brought a very undesirable state of fear to the United States. And they will be the source of resistance that creates the classical structure as we try to solve this problem.

In all of these examples, the threat is the cause of the problem that brings about a change of fortune and is the source of the resistance that creates the classical structure when the good guys try to solve the problem. The problem, change of fortune and components of the classical structure constitute the very essence of story--that without which there would be no story. If you think about it, this is easy to see. Without a problem and change of fortune, there is no story. If the story ends in the same place it began, without some significant progress up or down, the audience will wonder what the point of it was. It will be a very unsatisfactory experience.

Without complications and a crisis, there is no story. If Cinderella goes to the ball, falls in love with the prince and marries him without a single hitch, or if Indiana Jones goes after the Holy Grail and finds it without running into any difficulty whatsoever, there is no story. The audience is left muttering: So what? If there are complications and a crisis, but no climax and no resolution, you will have the same problem. You will leave your audience feeling completely unfulfilled. They will have the distinct feeling that the story was left unfinished. The threat, then, is not only the heart of the high concept great idea, (see our eZine article on the high concept dated July 21, 2001), it creates the problem that brings about the change of fortune and provides the resistance that creates the classical structure, all of which make up the very essence of story. An element that does all of that is an element worth thinking about and understanding.

# 11

# Television Writing

Chad currently works as a Creative Executive at the Littlefield Company/Paramount Studios. He has previously worked in television development and production at 20th Century Fox, CBS Productions, NBC Studios, and Regency Television.

If you think writing for film and television is essentially the same, here's a helpful hint: Think differently.

Although teachers often lump feature and television writing into one category, they're actually separate, rarely overlapping worlds. This article focuses on the industry and craft of television. We'll explore the industry's structure, how shows work and how writers break in.

The television industry consists of three main entities: networks, studios and production companies. They may look similar on the surface, but each works in a unique way.

Networks program and broadcast material. The non-cable networks are NBC, CBS, ABC, FBC (Fox), the WB, and UPN. Although they suggest shows to studios and production companies, networks don't always produce their own programming.

Studios hire writers to develop material for networks. While most studios are owned by networks, they may sell product anywhere. Twentieth Century Fox is owned by FBC, but ABC airs Twentieth's The Practice.

Production companies, like studios, produce material for networks. Production companies are independent entities that make deals with studios wishing to partner with valuable producers. Imagines' Ron Howard is an acclaimed director/ producer with a Twentieth deal. Warren Littlefield ran NBC for nine years before partnering the Littlefield Co. with Paramount. By joining forces, studios and production companies can access each other's stables of talent (writers, directors, producers).

Studios and production companies make two kinds of deals with writers:

*A development deal employs a writer to develop a single idea (paying from $30,000 to $500,000, depending on the writer). Because development deals focus on one project, writers can have simultaneous deals at different companies.*

Overall deals pay more than development deals (usually in the low millions) and bind the artist to a particular entity. Overalls are the holy grails of TV development. Jason Katims (Roswell) has an overall at Twentieth. Although Katims develops only for that studio, Twentieth may sell his shows to any network (Roswell aired on WB and UPN).

Thus is the basic structure of Hollywood's TV machine. But how does this machine work? Let's follow a show from conception to airdate. A show begins in...

Development season. From July through November, writers pitch shows to studios and production companies. Executives rarely meet first-time writers. Most developing writers have sold features or worked on staff. Had Kevin Williamson never written Scream, he wouldn't have sold Dawson's Creek to Columbia-TriStar (which sold the series to WB).

Studios also hire writers to write ideas conceived in-house. Warner Brothers Television owned the rights to Superman before hiring Miles Millar and Alfred Gough to write Smallville.

Studios then work with writers to perfect network pitches. Networks rarely buy scripts; they buy concepts. This allows input in shows' development and spares writers from finishing scripts that don't sell.

After hearing approximately 1000 pitches, networks buy 50 to 75 ideas, or script commitments. Writers then develop scripts and networks receive about 75 pilot scripts. Thus we enter... Pilot season (January-April). From these scripts, networks shoot 15-20 pilots. Scripts that don't get picked up may be sold to other networks. Ed was developed and axed at CBS before being picked up at NBC.

Networks view finished pilots in April and May. Mid-May brings the upfronts, enormous affairs where networks announce season lineups to advertisers. Each network debuts two to six new shows each fall and a handful more at midseason (January-March). When a show goes, we enter...

Staffing Season. Between April and June series hire writers for the upcoming season. Agents submit clients' materials, and creators and executives meet with writers they like. Of the hundreds of submissions received, most shows staff 4-10 writers. Staffs begin writing immediately. Because most new shows premiere in fall, they commence shooting in early August.

### HOW THE STAFF WORK

A staff is the hierarchy of writers that writes a TV Show. At the top of this hierarchy is the showrunner, often the program's creator. Running a show isn't simply visualizing a series; it's hiring, inspiring, and organizing an entire writing team and production staff. Most showrunners have spent years writing television and receive an Executive Producer credit on the series. Before running 8 Simple Rules To Dating My Teenage Daughter, Tracy Gamble paid dues on Home Improvement, My Two Dads and others.

While staffs arrange their hierarchy differently, here's the basic ladder (from top to bottom): executive producer, co-executive producer, supervising producer, producer, co-producer, executive story editor, story editor, staff writer.

Most writers begin as staff writers, or "baby writers."

Each level comes with its own perks and payscale. TV writers are salaried (except for those with overalls), and baby writers make between $60,000 and $80,000 a year. Showrunners-depending on their cache and the show's success-make closer to a million. As writers ascend the ladder, they eventually get offered development deals and-hopefully-overalls. All shows use staffs, although different staffs work differently. On half-hours (sitcoms), writers write as a group. They sit in "The Room" and discuss jokes, stories, characters, etc. While individuals may write first drafts, scripts are always revised by committee. On hours (dramas) the staff structures the season together before assigning individual episodes. Writers then write alone, often under the showrunner's supervision.

How to break in:

Unless you sell a movie that earns a development deal, there are two basic ways to get staffed:

Have a great agent. As any agent will say, "breaking a baby" (getting a job for a first-time writer) is nearly impossible. Many shows don't hire low-level writers. Those that do want specific voices, and-in an ever-diversifying world-shows strive to find ethnically diverse babies. Even with a great agent, it may take three years to break a baby.

Get promoted from being a writers assistant. Writers assistants do everything from taking notes in the Room to making copies and offering story feedback. Naturally, showrunners like hiring people who know office dynamics and the voice of the show.

Writers assistants begin at the bottom. Jobs as production assistants (grunt work) abound. After a year. P.A.'s graduate to "writers P.A.," slaving away for writers themselves. That leads to a writers assistant gig, which-hopefully-becomes the coveted staff job.

Aspiring writers need two weapons: strong original material, and strong specs.

Original material consists of plays, screenplays or sketch material. Showrunners want writers who have unique voices and can fashion characters and stories. But they also need writers who can mimic others' tones and characters, so it's important to have....

Specs, or sample episodes of shows currently airing. Showrunners use specs to evaluate one's grasp of character voices, the ability to tell stories within a particular structure, and knowledge of a series present state of affairs. To write a spec, watch and outline several episodes of the show. How are the stories structured? Are there B Stories and runners (subplots and continuing gags or themes)? Write down lines for each character.

Does one character always have the sassy comeback? Does another speak in one-syllable words? Scrutinize the show till you know it in your sleep; if you can't think the characters' thoughts, you're not ready to write.

Outline your spec based on original ideas. Continue watching and revising as you write. With each episode, update the script. The more current your spec, the stronger a showrunner's response.

Also pick a series that's frequented by showrunners and executives (The West Wing, Sopranos, etc.) You may love Yes, Dear, but few people watch it. If readers don't know the show, your spec won't get rave reviews.

Get your material to as many people as possible. In an industry based on networking, you can't shy from peddling your work. If everyone's six degrees away from an agent or executive, you must find those paths.

Don't send specs to their own shows. Showrunners feel they know their show better than anyone, and-regardless of what they actually produce, and regardless of what you may have written-your two visions probably won't connect.

Rather, send your specs to similar shows. CSI specs go to Law & Order, Malcolm in the Middle to Bernie Mac.

Of course, most shows won't accept cold submissions. They take scripts only from agents and mangers and, even then, mostly from agents or managers they know well. Your job, then, is to make friends. Once you know a story editor, an agent's assistant, or even a camera operator, ask them to read your stuff. Or pass it to their boss.

I recommend finding a job in the industry. Even P.A. jobs or studio receptionist gigs provide industry knowledge and access to contacts. This not only helps you move forward, it impresses agents who want clients in positions of upward mobility. Now that you understand the fundamentals of the industry, there's only one thing left to do. Keep writing. Television, first and foremost, is a medium of storytelling. If you have the chops, you'll get there. It just helps to know the ropes.

## SEVEN STEPS TO A SUCCESSFUL SPEC SCRIPT

It's easy to learn the format of writing for television from a book or writing class. It's a much harder thing to capture the voice and the tone of a particular series,Use this exercise to learn what makes your favourite TV series work, then craft a spec script that showcases your writing talent.

And to make your script fit flawlessly into the run of the show. Television is the one medium where you don't want your own unique voice to shine through. The characters' voices and thoughts and ideas need to stay true to the ones already established by the series' creators. Here's an exercise to help you capture the established voice of the show you wish to write.

Videotape a new episode of a show you love and that you watch often. Watch the first half, then shut off the television You are going to write the ending yourself.

Start by brainstorming all the possible ways the episode could end. For example, on the show I work on Sex and the City, in the first half of the episode "Ghost Town," Carrie and Miranda learn that Steve and Aidan are opening a bar together. At the halfway point, Carrie has just run out of the bar after hearing Aidan's voice because she is afraid to face him again. Think up as many ideas as you can for ways to resolve this story. Carrie could see Aidan and discover that he's married to someone else.

She could realize she never loved him. Or maybe she realizes that she loves him still. Maybe she never sees him at all-she goes back to the bar only to discover he's left New York for good. There are dozens of possible resolutions-let your imagination run wild.

Pick the ending you think best suits the characters and the show, then write it out, keeping in mind the way the characters act and talk and behave. You know these characters; how do you think they would solve their problems? You have about 12 pages to resolve the main story line, plus tie up any subplots or "B" stories.

When you finish, put your pages down and turn the television back on. Watch the broadcast ending straight through. Compare the ending you wrote to the one your just watched. As you go through your script, ask yourself these questions.

1. Why did the writers pick the ending they did?

   This particular episode of Sex and the City ends with Carrie discovering she has been in love with Aidan all along and decided to try to get him back. Think about why this particular ending works best for the show. If you ended your script with Aidan having left town, there are fewer possibilities for future stories between the two characters. Carrie scheming to get Aidan back, however, gives the writer plenty of material for many more episodes to come. Does the ending you wrote help move the series forward?

2. Is your ending believable? However you chose to resolve the episode, make sure that your story episode, makes sense in the world set up by the series' creators. You should never have a major character die, move to a different city, or do anything which would have permanent repercussions on the character and the show. A spec script needs to show that you understand the constraints of the series and are able to work within them.

   You might write a hilarious scene where Charlotte and Mr. Big get drunk and get married. Funny though it may be, it would never happen in the world of Sex and the City, and writing a story line like that would hinder your script form being taken seriously by anyone familiar with the show.

3. Did you leave any loose threads in your ending? Contemporary sitcoms are often intricately plotted, with four or five story lines all intertwining and building upon one another, leading to a resolution which affects all the characters. A show like Seinfeld will throw half

a dozen plot elements into the mix, and all need to be resolved by the show's end. Make sure the ending you wrote satisfies all the questions raised in the beginning of the script.

If you have trouble resolving each story line thoroughly and appropriately, try doing this exercise on an older series like Mary Tyler Moore or The Odd Couple. These shows tend to have simpler, more linear story lines and fewer subplots. They are great practice for building up to writing a more complicated script for a contemporary show.

4. Does the language you write fit the character? A joke that would be hilarious on Malcolm in the Middle would fall flat on Fraiser. The character in your script should talk the way you expect them to. If you have Malcom's brother Reese using 25-cent words or Fraiser's brother Niles using poor grammar, viewers will instantly recognize the inconsistency in the characters, and you will lose your audience.

5. Have you taken care of business? All shows have recurring elements they always feature. Each episode of Sex and the City shows Carrie typing a question for her column on her laptop computer. Just Shoot Me begins scenes by showing words from the cover of Blush Magazine. Frasier always included a scene at the radio station, with Fraiser giving humorous advice to the caller.

   Including these elements in your script can ground your story in the world of the series, and establish that you thoroughly understand the parameters of the series for which you want to write.

   Many shows also often have recurring "bits'-themes or character which appear frequently but are not mandatory parts of each episode. "Itchy and Scratchy" cartoons are certainly an important part of The Simpsons, but they do not occur every episode. The same goes for Jacks' cabaret act on Will & Grace, and Ross' line "We were on a break!" on Friends. Using some of these elements in your writing can add specificity to your episodes and are a good way to show your understanding of the series' history.

Similar to business that always appears is business that never appears in a show. No one would believe a Sex and the City script which referred to Mr. Big by his real name or a Fraiser episode where we actually see Niles' wife Maris. Make sure you don't break any of the rules of the show by revealing something the staff writers intentionally keep secret.

6. Have you covered the basics? Shows vary in terms of length and number of scenes. The second half of a Fraiser episode might take place in three long scene, one each at the radio station, Fraiser's apartment and café.

   A show like Sex and the City, however, will use 10 or 12 shorter scenes, cutting quickly from the girls' apartments to bars to stores and back again. Only a few lines are said at each location before moving on to the next scene.

   The ending you write should have roughly the same number of scenes as the ending that was broadcast. Also be aware of the number of exterior scene in your show. While there are numerous scenes in Sex and the City of the women walking down the street or sitting in the park, we rarely see the Friends characters outdoors. Make sure the number of exterior shots in your ending is comparable to the broadcast ending.

7. What's the tone of your ending? "Sitcom" is short for situation comedy, and comedies need to be funny. Even sad or moving story lines are invariably lightened with a joke. When Miranda's mother died on Sex and the City, the writers contrasted her sorrow with Charlotte's outrage at the giant, glitter-covered flower arrangement the florist mistakenly sent. And Monica and Chandler's wedding on Friends was all the more touching for Joey not being able to remember all the parts of the ceremony he was officiating.

# Bibliography


Anthony, R. and John Williams Tebbel: *American Media History*, Belmont, Thomson/Wadsworth, 2005.

Bagdikian, Ben: *The Media Monopoly*, Boston, Beacon Press, 1997.

Berry, David: *Ethics and Media Culture*, Woburn, Focal Press, 2000.

Bertrand, Jean: *An Arsenal for Democracy: Media Accountability Systems*, Cresskill, Hampton Press, 2003.

Charles, Ramirez: *Latin Looks: Images of Latinos and Latinas in U.S. Media*, Boulder, CO: Westview, 1996.

Chermak, Steven M.: *Victims in the News: Crime and the American News Media*, Boulder, Westview Press, 1995.

Daniel, Webster: *The Media in America*, Santa Barbara, ABC-CLIO, 1995.

Darrell, M.: *The Rise and Fall of the Media Establishment*, Boston MA: Bedford/St. Martin's, 2001.

Day, A: *Ethics in Media Communications*, Belmont, Wadsworth, 2003.

Downing, John: *Ethnic Minority Media: An International Perspective*, Thousand Oaks, CA: Sage, 1992.

Earl, R.: *Writing for Mass Communication*, White Plains, NY: Longman, 1996.

Emery, Michael: *The Press and America: An Interpretive History of the Mass Media*, Boston, Allyn and Bacon, 1999.

Ericson, Richard: *Crime and the Media*, Brookfield, Dartmouth Publishing, 1995.

Finberg, Howard, and Bruce D. Itule: *Visual Editing: A Graphic Guide for Journalists*, Belmont, CA: Wadsworth, 1990.

Fiske, John: *Media Matters: Everyday Culture and Political Change*, Minneapolis MN: U. Minnesota Pr., 1996.

Gillmor, Dan: *We the Media: Grassroots Journalism by the People, for the People,* Sebastopol, CA: O'Reilly Media, 2004.

Good, Howard : *Media Ethics Goes to the Movies*, Westport, Praeger, 2002.

Gordon, A. David: *Controversies in Media Ethics,* White Plains, Longman Publishers, 1999.

Hudson, Robert V.: *Mass Media,* New York, Garland Publishing, 1987.

Hutchison, Earl R.: *Writing for Mass Communication,* White Plains, NY: Longman, 1996.

John Williams Tebbel: *American Media History,* Belmont, Thomson/Wadsworth, 2005.

Kelly, A.: *Police and the Media,* Springfield, Thomas Books, 1987.

Langman, Larry: *The Media in the Movies,* Jefferson, NC: McFarland & Company, 1997.

Merrill, C.: *Journalism Ethics: Philosophical Foundations for News Media,* New York, St. Martin's Press, 1997.

Nacos, Brigitte L.: *Terrorism & the Media,* NY, Columbia University Press, 1994.

Patterson, Philip : *Media Ethics: Issues and Cases,* Boston, McGraw Hill, 2002.

Ripley, Jr. Casey: *The Media and the Public,* New York, H.W. Wilson, 1994.

Robert, V.: *Mass Media,* New York, Garland Publishing, 1987.

Seiter, Ellen: *Gender, Race and Class in Media,* Thousand Oaks, CA: Sage, 1995.

Sohn, Ardyth: *Media Management: A Casebook Approach,* Mahwah, Lawrence Erlbaum Associates, 2003.

Surette, Ray: *Justice and the Media,* Springfield, Thomas Books, 1984.

Teeter, Jr.: *Voices of a Nation: A History of Mass Media in the United States,* Needham Heights, Allyn & Bacon, 1997.

Warner, Charles: *Media Management Review,* Mahwah, Lawrence Erlbaum Associates, 1997.

West, Darrell M.: *The Rise and Fall of the Media Establishment,* Boston MA: Bedford/St. Martin's, 2001.

# Index

◆◆◆